D

THE COURTIER AND THE KING

Ruy Gómez de Silva (provenance unknown).

THE COURTIER
AND THE KING

RUY GÓMEZ DE SILVA, PHILIP II,
AND THE COURT OF SPAIN

JAMES M. BOYDEN

University of California Press

Berkeley · Los Angeles · London

The publisher gratefully acknowledges a grant from the Program for Cultural
Cooperation between Spain's Ministry of Culture and United States Universities.

University of California Press
Berkeley and Los Angeles, California

University of California Press, Ltd.
London, England

Library of Congress Cataloging-in-Publication Data

Boyden, James M., 1954–
    The courtier and the King : Ruy Gómez de Silva, Philip II, and the court of
Spain / James M. Boyden.
    p. cm.
    Includes bibliographical references and index.
    ISBN 0-520-08622-8 (alk. paper)
    1. Gómez de Silva, Ruy, príncipe de Eboli, 1516–1573. 2. Spain—History—
Philip II, 1556–1598. 3. Spain—Court and courtiers. 4. Philip, II, King of Spain,
1527–1598. 5. Nobility—Spain—Biography. I. Title.
DP181.G65B6 1995
946'.043'092—dc20
[B]   93-41011

Printed in the United States of America
9 8 7 6 5 4 3 2 1

The paper used in this publication meets the minimum requirements of American
National Standard for Information Sciences—Permanence of Paper for Printed Library Materials, ANSI Z39.48-1984.

For Sally, the bravest soul I know

Contents

Acknowledgments

Without the gracious aid of several institutions and many individuals, I could never have completed this book. The University of Texas at Austin and Tulane University both provided financial support for research and writing. In Spain I was afforded generous access to the holdings of the Archivo Histórico Nacional (AHN) and the Archivo General de Simancas. I am grateful to the professional staff of both archives, and especially to Don José Antonio Esteban at the AHN and Doña Isabel Aguirre Landa at Simancas. Eileen McWilliam has been a shrewd editor and staunch advocate for this book at the University of California Press, and I thank her for all of her efforts. I am indebted as well to Laura Driussi for her skill and patience in overseeing the production of the book, and to Sarah K. Myers for adept copyediting.

Carolyn P. Boyd directed the dissertation that was the basis for this work. She is an exemplary mentor and friend, and I can never repay her for the concern, kindness and patience that she invested in this work and its author. My other teachers, among them José Ferrer, Myron Gutmann, Nancy N. Barker and Standish Meacham, are also due a large measure of gratitude.

In graduate school and since, I have been lucky in my colleagues. I particularly wish to thank my fellow members of the Tulane University Department of History for their warm personal and scholarly support during some difficult times. My sincere thanks for a wide range of assistance, encouragement, criticism and advice go to Paul Bushkovitch, Paul Charney, Valerie Hansen, Bruce Hunt, Maija Jansson, William Jordan, Richard Kagan, David Lagomarsino, Colin MacLachlan, William Maltby, Edward Muir, Helen Nader, Geoffrey Parker, Charles Royster, Peter Sahlins, the late Adrian Van Oss, and Lee Palmer Wandel and to the readers for the University of California Press. I extend a special *abrazo* to Paul Hiltpold for fifteen years of friendship and unquestioning aid. Such errors of fact and interpretation as remain in this book are, of course, my sole responsibility.

My remaining debts are personal and immeasurable. To Charles and Marie Boyden, to Sally Hunter Graham, and to James Wieferman, I offer this book in scant recompense for their love, understanding and sacrifice.

Prologue

In his house near the palace, in the dusty heat of Madrid's summer, the king's favorite lay dying. "I should not like to be in the state he is in," wrote one of his enemies, "for today they have mourned him here."[1] Although his face had been swollen for some time, the final illness had come upon him quickly. On 26 July he took to his bed. He was given the last sacraments that afternoon, and by eleven at night it was thought that he was dead.[2]

But the old courtier rallied. He lingered three days more, lucid most of the time, while powerful men passed through the sickroom and the court awaited news of his condition. Even Philip II came to visit him, thus granting a final signal honor to his old friend.[3] On 28 July the dying man made his will before witnesses, including two of the king's secretaries, Juan de Escobedo and Juan de Losilla.[4] The contingent of priests—a friar of Alcántara, a canon of Barcelona, two Franciscans from Pastrana—and the imminence of death combined to turn his thoughts to the fate of his soul. The will provided for perpetual prayer vigils in three religious houses and for the dowering of three orphaned girls. Later on the 28th the powerful secretary Antonio Pérez and the son of the duke of Gandía joined with Losilla to witness a codicil to the will.[5] Pérez later wrote to the king that their friend had "done very completely all that a Christian knight must and [understood] everything pertaining to his salvation" with his accustomed lucidity.[6]

On 29 July 1573 the fading nobleman added a final codicil to his will, in which he freed three of his slaves. He could not sign the final document, "due to the gravity of his illness," so it bears instead the signatures of the witnesses, again including Escobedo and Losilla.[7] The Venetian ambassadors wrote home that

> he is utterly given up by the doctors; he takes no food, and they are watching over him, while praying to our Lord God for his soul. . . . It

is held for certain that this death will greatly upset His Majesty, because he loved him a great deal.[8]

Death came for the favorite at eight on the evening of the same day.[9]

The news of his death sparked a variety of reactions. That very night his young widow left Madrid, bound for a convent she and her husband had founded.[10] Meanwhile, the king wrote that the death had caused him great sorrow.[11] Philip II had lost a friend and counselor, and his grief had an effect on the affairs of the monarchy. Two weeks later an observer of the court claimed that "His Majesty is as alone as Your Grace imagines, and reduced to a state where he does not trust even his own hands and doesn't confide in nor make decisions with anyone."[12] Ormaneto, the papal nuncio, wrote that the deceased "is going to a better life; we must all lament greatly the loss of a good, loyal and competent minister."[13] The *beata* Catalina de Cardona, who had served the dead man as an almoner for many years, was even more certain of his happy destiny in the afterlife, reporting that after his death he had appeared to her cloaked in the robes of glory and giving thanks for the salvational benefits of the alms she had distributed on his behalf.[14]

The dead man also had many enemies, and they too noted his passing. Some of them expressed hope, less confident than Ormaneto's and Cardona's, that God might forgive their fallen adversary.[15] One, at least, was less charitable: "His Excellency [the duke of Alba] and his affairs have lost, in he who died the other day, an enemy as mischievous and as ill-intentioned as any man ever had. . . . Your Grace may well believe that Hell contains no disposition so damned."[16]

The dead man, so variously mourned, was Ruy Gómez de Silva. He had begun life as the second son of a minor Portuguese nobleman. When he died, at age fifty-seven, he was the prince of Eboli, the duke of Pastrana, a grandee of Spain, the *sumiller de corps* of the Catholic King, *contador mayor de Castilla,* and a member of the Councils of State, War and Finance. Although his influence in the state had waned in the last years of his life, he remained the king's oldest friend and had once been his chief minister.

Ruy Gómez de Silva rose to great influence at the court of Spain in the era when that court became the center of power in Europe. His gifts were those of the politician and the courtier. Unlike his great rival, Alba, he was not born to power and authority, but instead owed his position entirely to the favor of the king he served. Ambition, favored by fortune and furthered by courtly talent, was the motor of Ruy Gómez's rise. This ambition did not abate when he had become the king's favorite and a major force in the management of government and of the royal household. Rather, it was transformed into a concern that his name and his power should not die with him. In the final decade of his life he set out to convert the ephemeral status conferred by fortune and favor into the unquestionable, permanent prestige of a birthright. In this too he succeeded.

Ruy Gómez built the ducal house of Pastrana, which from its inception stood in the first rank of the noble houses of Spain. This was an extraordinary accomplishment; the Spanish Habsburgs created many titles but few lasting noble dynasties. The founding of the house was the crowning achievement of the life of Ruy Gómez de Silva, the end result of his rise to prominence and of his skillful manipulation of the perquisites of public power, based on personal favor, to forge a transmissible private power founded on high birth and landed wealth.

Ortega y Gasset wrote that

> The privileges of nobility are not originally concessions or favors, but on the contrary conquests. . . . Private rights or *privi-legios* are not, then, passive possession and simple enjoyment, but rather represent the elevation reached by the person's endeavor.[17]

For Ruy Gómez de Silva the attainment of the pinnacle of aristocracy, the *grandeza*, was indeed a conquest, first of favor and then of fortune itself. His life history affords a case study in personal advancement and social mobility by means of courtiership, through the suave exercise of the grace and wiles so celebrated in the courtly manuals of the sixteenth century. The crucial achievement that ultimately allowed Ruy Gómez to reach the heights of nobility was the establishment of a special relationship with his prince and master, Philip II. Given his origins, this was a lofty and unlikely accomplishment, and the first portion of this treatment of his life will attempt to explain his success in achieving it. In the course of this explanation the accoutrements of favor—power, and a marriage that provided wealth, status and influential connections—will be examined. Finally, we will see how Ruy Gómez utilized these advantages to escape an adverse conjuncture and create the aristocratic house that secured his fortune and that of his lineage.

PART ONE

THE RISE OF RUY GÓMEZ DE SILVA

La Fortuna es la que differencia las
mas vezes a los Grandes de los Chicos.

Antonio Pérez (*Las obras y relaciones,* 1654)

1

From La Chamusca to the Court of Spain

The biography of Ruy Gómez de Silva has not been written, nor will it ever be, at least not as a full-scale life. His role in affairs of state was usually that of a fixer at the court, operating from behind the arras. Many of his activities required no written report, and if he was a great correspondent, the bulk of his letters have not survived. "Ruy Gómez," William Maltby has justly observed, "remains as elusive in death as he was in life."[1]

It is possible, however, to trace his career in considerable detail, and this is a worthwhile task: as well as being one of the most important political men of the third quarter of the sixteenth century, he was perhaps the most polished and successful courtier of his time. For years he was the intimate friend and counselor of Philip, prince and then king of Spain. Study of this relationship between favorite and monarch, central to the destiny of the former, reveals a great deal about the latter as a youth and young man. Ruy Gómez's rise also illustrates, perhaps better than any other example, the possibilities of social mobility open to a man whom fortune blessed and who knew how to maneuver, intrigue and exert influence in the treacherous corridors of power near the king. "The Court," wrote Luis Cabrera de Córdoba, "is so dangerous a gulf that few pass through it without adversity. . . . Rui Gomez was the first pilot who, in such huge undertakings, lived and died secure, always choosing the best port."[2]

Nothing in the circumstances of his birth indicated that Ruy Gómez de Silva[3] would one day earn such a lofty eulogy. He was born in La Chamusca, on the Tagus River near Santarém in Portugal, probably in 1516.[4] He was the second son of Francisco de Silva, the lord of the town, and his wife, Doña María de Noronha. The Silvas were an old family in the region. The historian Salazar y Castro says of Francisco de Silva, with some exaggeration, that he was "one of the most eminent Fidalgos of his time in Portugal, and [among those] who had the most genteel and splendid Houses."[5] He was the great-grandson of Diego Gómez de Silva, one of the *ricos-hombres* of Portugal, who was related by birth and marriage to the powerful families of Coutinho and Sousa. Diego Gómez was a second son (his father was Gonzalo Gómez de Silva, lord of Vagos, Tentugal and Boarceos) and made his name in the military service of John I of Portugal and his successors. He fought against the Castilians at Aljubarrota (1385) and thirty years later commanded a ship in the invasion of Ceuta. In 1416 he was rewarded with the title of *alferez mayor* (chief standard-bearer) of Portugal.[6]

The eldest son of the *alferez mayor*, the first Ruy Gómez de Silva, was also a soldier. He fought in the conquest of Tangiers in 1437, and in 1445 he was with the Portuguese column that aided John II of Castile against the *infantes* of Aragon. He was rewarded for his services to the Crown by the grant in 1449 of the village of Ulme near Santarém, which had been confiscated following the rebellion of its previous lord. Possession of Ulme was granted to Ruy Gómez and his heirs in perpetuity, and it comprised the first entailed property of the house. Ruy Gómez lived until 1487 and received several other *mercedes* from the Crown. The most important of these was the grant for two generations of the *reguengos* of the villages of Nes Pereyra, Riba de Bouga, Monçon and Villanueva de Fascoa. Among these, only the *reguengo* of Nes Pereyra was of substantial value. Ruy Gómez's marriage to Blanca de Almeida may have contributed to his success in obtaining *mercedes,* since her father was a surveyor of the royal treasury. Royal favor extended to the couple's children as well: their eldest daughter was given a prominent position in the household of the Infanta Isabel of Castile, daughter of the Catholic Kings and wife of the Portuguese Prince Afonso.[7] Their son, Juan de Silva, inherited his father's holdings in 1487. He had maintained the family tradition of military service, fighting for Afonso V in Africa and in the Castilian campaign of 1475–1476 on the side of Juana *la Beltraneja.* During this campaign, at Zamora in 1475, the king extended the grant of the *reguengos* for another generation; Juan de Silva's son would enjoy these revenues too. This extension was confirmed by John II in 1487.[8]

Juan de Silva was a member of the Royal Council under John II and Manuel. He was a man of considerable prominence in the kingdom, and his house, in his newly acquired town of La Chamusca, was fine enough to serve as a stop on the honeymoon sojourn of Manuel and his bride, Leonor of Castile, in 1518. All five of the children of Juan de Silva were borne by his third wife, Doña Juana Enríquez. A lady of high birth but small dowry, Juana Enríquez was the daughter of the *aposentador mayor* (chief quartermaster) of Portugal and the great-granddaughter of Henry II of Castile. She and Juan de Silva drew up a joint will in 1520, in which they created a *mayorazgo* for their eldest son Francisco, comprising the town of La Chamusca and their estates and principal house there. Juan de Silva died shortly thereafter, in February 1520.[9]

Francisco de Silva was not a soldier like his forebears, but instead seems to have lived a quiet life as a country gentleman.[10] In or around 1512 he married María de Noronha in Lisbon, under a dispensation of consanguinity granted by Pope Julius II. The groom was both a second cousin and a third cousin of the bride's father, Ruy Tellez de Meneses, who was the lord of Uñao and *comendador* of Orique and a prominent member of the powerful Meneses family. Francisco de Silva was also distantly related to María de Noronha's mother, Guiomar, whose marriage to Ruy Tellez had formed a link between the powerful clans of Meneses and Noronha.[11] The couple's large family was already well started when Francisco de Silva succeeded his father in 1520. Their marriage produced eight children— three sons and five daughters—who survived into adulthood.[12] Of these, at least the two oldest boys, Juan and Ruy Gómez, were born in the first five years of the marriage.

Ruy Gómez de Silva was the second son, and the date of his birth remains somewhat mysterious. Modern historians have accepted 1516,[13] evidently on the basis of Salazar y Castro's unsupported statement that he was born "around" that year. Salazar's work is, for the most part, quite accurate, and he may have had access to information, such as a baptismal record, that has since been lost.[14] His estimate is at least roughly corroborated by an independent source, the Venetian ambassador Federico Badoero, who described Ruy Gómez de Silva as approximately thirty-nine years old in 1556, which would place his birth in 1516 or 1517.[15]

Nothing is known of Ruy Gómez de Silva's early childhood. In addition to the principal house at La Chamusca, his father owned another mansion nearby in Ulme, which may have been used primarily as a hunting lodge. La Chamusca, the larger of the two villages, was celebrated for its fruits and wines. It lies in a fertile plain near the Tagus about thirteen miles upriver from Santarém and fifty-five miles from Lisbon. A century and a half later, La Chamusca and Ulme together had 400 householders.[16] Both villages were under the jurisdiction of Santarém until 1561, when, as a favor to Francisco de Silva, they were granted the status of *villas* and their jurisdiction was transferred to their lord.[17]

Ruy Gómez's early childhood was spent in these towns dominated by his father, where the boy's ancestors had "always been seen to live as gentlemen and to subsist from their *mayorazgos* and their *encomiendas* and holdings and patrimonies," without resort to any "base occupation."[18] The marks of his family's status were visible all around him: his forebears "having resided there, they built sumptuous palaces in La Chamusca and ennobled it with public buildings."[19] The elegance of these rural mansions is open to question, but the predominance of the Silvas in their provincial domain is not. A seventeenth-century observer noted that the arms of the house of Silva ("un león leonardo en campo blanco coronado") were emblazoned on a great marble tomb in the parish church of La Chamusca and "on the hall of the Audiencia of this town and on the rest of the public buildings."[20]

These symbols of his family's station may have thrilled the young Ruy Gómez, but they were destined to comprise the inheritance of his older brother. Francisco de Silva's estate was entailed in primogeniture, and since he seems to have added very little to it during his lifetime, there was no possibility of establishing another *mayorazgo* for a cadet line. Moreover, Francisco's daughters would require dowries. Thus some arrangement had to be made for his second son. Like his father, Francisco de Silva was a member of the Council of State and spent some time at court in Lisbon.[21] He may have sought patronage for his son Ruy Gómez there or when the court visited Almeirim, near La Chamusca, in 1523.[22] As it turned out, his connections through marriage with the house of Meneses proved decisive in the placement of his second son.

Ruy Tellez de Meneses and Guiomar de Noronha—the maternal grandparents of Ruy Gómez de Silva—were, as a contemporary reminisced, "among the most Illustrious [persons] of this kingdom [of Portugal]."[23] Confirmation of this high status is provided by the fact that, in the mid-1520s, Ruy Tellez was named *mayordomo mayor* of the household of the Portuguese Infanta Isabel. The daughter of King Manuel and the sister of John III, Isabel had been promised in marriage to the Emperor Charles V.[24] Ruy Tellez's position provided an opportunity for placing his grandson, the young *segundón* Ruy Gómez. In 1526 the Infanta Isabel was conducted to Castile for her marriage to the emperor. Isabel's entourage was led by two of her brothers, who delivered her in February 1526 to Charles's representative, the duke of Calabria, at the frontier between Elvas and Badajoz. The *infanta*'s household, headed by Ruy Tellez, accompanied her; among its members was Ruy Gómez de Silva. The boy's grandfather had secured a post for him as one of the Infanta's *meninos* (pages, serving boys). Once in Castile, Isabel and her party were escorted to Seville, where she married Charles V.[25]

Thus, at the age of nine or thereabouts, Ruy Gómez de Silva left his native land and began his career of service at the Castilian court. This was a crucial turning point for his fortunes and for those of the house of Silva, which henceforth would look for favor and advancement to the kings of Spain rather than to those of Portugal.

Nothing concrete is known of the next few years in the life of Ruy Gómez de Silva. Presumably he and the other Portuguese servants of the empress moved with Charles V's peripatetic court. Years later Ruy Gómez recalled that he had been raised in the empress's household by a black woman, Nativa d'Almeyda.[26] Salazar asserts, on uncertain authority, that the boy advanced rapidly as a result of his grandfather's patronage and his own talents and that he was the first person to be assigned to the service of Prince Philip, who was born in Valladolid on 21 May 1527.[27] Cabrera states that Ruy Gómez "was reared with the king Don Felipe II," and Badoero makes a similar claim, so perhaps the young page did serve the prince in his infancy.[28] Neither Ruy Gómez nor anyone else held a formal position in service to Philip, however, until the latter was nearly eight years old. The care of the infant prince was entrusted to the empress's household during Charles V's absence from Spain in 1529–1533, and this arrangement remained unaltered until the eve of Charles's departure for the Tunis expedition in the spring of 1535. On the first of March in that year, the court residing at Madrid, Charles named Juan de Zúñiga governor and tutor of Prince Philip. Zúñiga was charged "to look after, to wait upon, and to govern [the prince], and to instruct him in good and praiseworthy habits."[29] The prince was not to have a formal household, and thus no *mayordomo* was appointed, but he was assigned three *maestresalas* (waiters) and three *trinchantes* to serve him at table. These functionaries were all young nobles and "*criados* of the Emperor"; among the *trinchantes* was Ruy Gómez de Silva. Payment of the salaries of this proto-household remained the responsibility of the empress's establishment, and her own pages, including Zúñiga's son, Luis de Requesens, were to serve the prince in rotation. Presumably the six table servants also retained duties in Isabel's household.[30]

A few months after his appointment as a *trinchante* Ruy Gómez de Silva was involved in an incident that might have cost him his career at court, or worse. Late one night, probably in early December 1535, in the presence of Prince Philip, Ruy Gómez came to blows with another young nobleman, Juan de Avellaneda. Zúñiga was absent when the incident occurred, but the young men, who had unsheathed their daggers, were restrained by the duke of Sessa and two other gentlemen. In the melee the prince received a scratch beneath his eye. He was evidently untouched by the drawn weapons but instead brushed his face against a sharp brooch on someone's clothing or wounded himself with a baton he was carrying.[31] The president of the Royal Council (Juan de Tavera, cardinal-archbishop of Toledo)[32] was notified of the incident and ordered Zúñiga to investigate. The latter conferred with the empress, who ordered Ruy Gómez and Avellaneda confined to their lodgings but was not unduly upset over the affair. "Since they are boys," wrote Zúñiga, "Her Majesty says that she will punish them as such."[33]

Cardinal Tavera was less sanguine. The next morning he presented the facts of the incident to the council and the *alcaldes* of the court. Then he led a delegation of counselors to meet with the empress. They argued that the affair was serious, since "a great mistake might have happened." Because of the gravity of the circumstances, the two young men should be tried and punished by the council. Isabel demurred, replying that "it was not necessary for any other magistrate to take cognizance of it." She dismissed the counselors, saying that she would make the necessary inquiries and assess punishment herself.[34]

The empress was as good as her word. She decided that the two combatants should be confined in fortresses outside Madrid; she assured the president that she would order that "they should be thoroughly punished." Two days after the incident the council learned that Ruy Gómez and Avellaneda had been taken to their respective prisons by constables.[35] Tavera continued to believe that the empress had made light of a serious matter. He wrote to the emperor that, although the prince had not been badly injured, "the effrontery was great, and [so was] the laxity and paucity of fear and respect of those young men, particularly in drawing weapons; . . . [This was] a dangerous and brutish affair."[36] Charles V assured the president that he had behaved properly, but he supported his wife's handling of the affair. At the same time Zúñiga was ordered to ensure that there could be no repetition of this incident.[37]

No further information has come to light regarding the punishment of Ruy Gómez and Avellaneda. It seems, however, that it was neither severe nor lengthy, since the empress, on Christmas Eve 1535, granted Ruy Gómez a formal title as *trinchante* to the prince, with an annual salary and allowance of 50,000 *maravedís* (133⅓ ducats).[38]

From later events it is clear that in his teenage years, if not earlier, Prince Philip developed a close attachment to his Portuguese table servant. Had the president of the Royal Council had his way in 1535, though, this attachment would have been nipped in the bud, since it is evident that the punishment Tavera deemed appropriate would not have ended with Ruy Gómez returning to Philip's household. The incident of his altercation with Avellaneda, in itself trivial, provides some insight into the precarious nature of Ruy Gómez's position at court as an adolescent in the 1530s. The empress's rather surprising intervention was all that preserved him from an ignominious obscurity; Isabel's motives in interceding for the young page thus bear examination. She asserted that she did not want to deal too sternly with such young men, and mercy surely had some part in her actions. But a perceptive court observer found another reason for her behavior:

> The Empress has taken it very well. . . . [A]ll the members of the Council and those of the court perceived it as very grave. Her Majesty wished to calm them, since one [of those involved in the altercation] is a Portuguese, and she commanded the *alcaldes* and members of the Council that none of them should take notice of it.[39]

Isabel's motive thus appears to have been based less on a willingness to forgive boyish behavior than on a desire to protect a young countryman who had come with her to Castile. That she so quickly reinstated him to her son's service suggests that she must have been personally fond of Ruy Gómez. It may also have indicated a wish to maintain a Portuguese presence in Philip's immediate household, which was dominated by her husband's adviser, the stern Castilian Zúñiga.[40]

The career at court of Ruy Gómez de Silva was preserved at this critical juncture by the empress's mercy and patronage. Neither for the first time nor for the last, Ruy Gómez enjoyed fortune's favor at a decisive point in his life. Evidently he made good use of his second chance; in 1539, after the empress's death, his continuance at court was assured when his salary as *trinchante* was doubled by order of Charles V.[41]

The historical record yields little information about Ruy Gómez de Silva during the next several years. The favor of the empress had kept him in close proximity to the prince, but there is no reason to suppose that Ruy Gómez enjoyed Philip's particular favor in the decade after his altercation with Avellaneda. For example, the transport manifest for a journey of Philip's household from Valladolid to Madrid in the early 1540s reveals that Ruy Gómez was assigned one cart. This was a paltry allotment, considering that even his co-*trinchante*, Juan de Benavides, was granted two carts and the major figures of the household, ten times that many.[42] Perhaps attempting to eke out his meager wages, Ruy Gómez in 1543 solicited the prince, through Francisco de los Cobos, to grant him the confiscated goods of two convicted murderers from the town of Alcaraz.[43]

Ruy Gómez de Silva took part in the festivities surrounding the wedding of Philip to María of Portugal in 1543, but again there is no mention of special favor. He did, however, demonstrate his facility at some of the courtly arts. He was one of the principal dancers at the gala in Salamanca on the night after the formal betrothal of the prince and princess.[44] A tournament held soon after in Valladolid to celebrate the wedding was the scene of a more splendid display. Ruy Gómez and the prince of Asculi (Don Luis de Leiva) entered the arena together, twenty-third and twenty-fourth among the thirty-one knights who participated. They were resplendent in black velvet and cloth of gold and came onto the field accompanied

by a number of pages attired in matching velvet livery and sere-
naded by six minstrels riding a decorated chariot pulled by white
horses.[45] The prizes in the tournament were monopolized by the
highest-born—Philip himself, the admiral of Castile, the duke of
Alba—but Ruy Gómez had at least made a dazzling entrance before
the very select crowd on hand.[46]

By 1547 Ruy Gómez had risen in the prince's estimation. In May
of that year Philip, governing in the emperor's absence, granted him
one-eighth of the royal revenues from the mines of Xerez de Badajoz
(Jerez de los Caballeros). This grant, of uncertain value, was pre-
dated to 1 January 1546 and was to run for a period of ten years.[47]
Later that year Ruy Gómez was entrusted with a diplomatic mission. Philip sent him to Charles V to congratulate the emperor on
his victory at Mühlberg and to wish him a speedy recovery from a
serious illness. Ruy Gómez traveled by post-relay and found the
emperor at Augsburg. Charles sent him back to Spain with orders
for Philip to proceed to the Low Countries as soon as possible. There
father and son would be reunited, and the prince could tour his
future northern states. After a "very swift" return journey Ruy Gómez rejoined Philip's court at Monzón, where the *cortes* of Aragon
were being celebrated.[48] Evidently Philip was pleased with his performance. Back in Valladolid the next spring, he rewarded Ruy Gómez for "his many and constant services" by increasing his share of
the revenues from the Xerez mines.[49]

Also in 1548 Ruy Gómez was named to a prestigious post for the
first time. In August of that year the Castilian court was reorganized
in the Burgundian style, with its more elaborate ceremonial. This
innovation was likely intended to prepare Philip for the usages of
the northern courts that he would soon visit. Charles V put the duke
of Alba in charge of the reorganization, naming him *mayordomo
mayor* of Philip's household. Among the new posts created in the
changeover was that of *sumiller de corps*. Ruy Gómez de Silva was
one of the five initial *sumilleres*. His colleagues were prominent Castilian noblemen, including Alba's eldest son and the count of
Cifuentes, and another former *trinchante*, Juan de Benavides, later
marquis of Cortes.[50]

The post of *sumiller* conferred little formal authority but provided
something even more valuable at court: constant access to the
prince. According to the historian Ballesteros y Beretta,

> The service incumbent upon the *sumiller de corps* was that most imme-
> diate to the person of the sovereign. . . . He slept in the same chamber,
> on a low pallet that the valets set in place and removed at the appro-
> priate times. He followed His Majesty everywhere, even if the king
> was entering the queen's rooms, and they [the *sumilleres*] could never
> lose sight of him, except at a direct signal from the monarch; in this
> case they would bow and retire to the next room.[51]

Presumably the five *sumilleres* observed a rotation in these duties.
An order of precedence existed among the five named in 1548, with
Ruy Gómez holding the second position, behind Don Antonio de
Rojas.[52]

Within a few years the system was altered so that there was but
a single *sumiller de corps*, while the other gentlemen of the bedchamber had to be content with a lesser title. Ruy Gómez de Silva became
first *sumiller* late in 1551 and was the sole holder of this title until
his death in 1573.[53] This ceremonial post, which kept Ruy Gómez
in close proximity to Philip, was perhaps the principal key to his
influence at court.

No documents or contemporary histories indicate directly why
Ruy Gómez de Silva rose to comparative prominence by the late
1540s. Garibay and Cabrera simply observed that the prince grew
up in the company of Ruy Gómez and that the two became very
close.[54] Relying on these authorities, Prescott drafted the clearest
statement of the prevailing wisdom:

> He [Ruy Gómez] had been early received as a page in the imperial
> household, where, though he was several years older than Philip, his
> amiable temper, his engaging manners, and, above all, that tact which
> made his fortune in later life, soon rendered him the prince's fa-
> vorite.[55]

Years later the apologist of William of Orange alleged a less flat-
tering basis for the favor enjoyed by Ruy Gómez. According to this
scurrilous source Philip was, at the time of his marriage to María of
Portugal, already married to "the Ladie Isabella Osorius," by whom
the precocious sixteen-year-old prince had fathered two or three
children. Orange's defender further asserted that Ruy Gómez would
attest to the reality of this marriage, "for he was the procurer
thereof, whereby also he obtayned that great credite, and so much
goodes in Spaine."[56]

This tale is likely an invention,[57] but it points indirectly to a more plausible reason for the prince's liking for Ruy Gómez de Silva. Consider the situation of Prince Philip in his early adolescence. His mother had recently died, and his father was usually absent; his governance and instruction were in the hands of much older, dour men, like Zúñiga and the tutor Juan Martínez Siliceo. It is not far-fetched to assume that, under these circumstances, the prince was lonely and felt the need of more youthful and lighthearted companionship. Ruy Gómez de Silva was one of the youngest men in his household and had been a favorite of the prince's mother. He was an accomplished horseman and dancer, a handsome young man of medium height and slender frame, "graceful and full of elegance in all his movements."[58]

Philip may have come to regard Ruy Gómez rather like an older brother, a somewhat worldly confidant, playmate and model. There is no way to know for sure, but it is interesting to note that Lerma and Olivares owed much of their ascendancy with Philip's son and grandson to similar sets of circumstances. Each of the great seventeenth-century *validos* initiated his conquest of power by playing the worldly indulgent uncle to a sheltered and introverted young prince.[59] Perhaps there was even a faint glimmer of truth in the charge made in Orange's *Apology*. In the next century Olivares would be charged with having corrupted the prince in order to enhance his own favor, and the rumors, however blatantly fueled by jealousy of the *valido*'s influence, cannot be entirely dispelled.[60] By the same token, it is neither demonstrable nor inherently implausible that Ruy Gómez may have taken charge of his prince's initiation into worldly pleasures and debaucheries; certainly, decades later he implied some knowledge of the king's "past amours" to the French ambassador Saint-Sulpice.[61]

It is also worth noting that Ruy Gómez's favored position became cemented in the long period of Philip's political apprenticeship, while he acted as a semi-autonomous ruler under the surveillance of Charles V and his ministers. In 1543 Charles for the first time left the young prince as regent in Spain. The emperor made it clear that Philip was to leave his childhood behind:

> Moreover, son, you must alter your life and intercourse with people. Until now all your retinue have been boys, and your pleasures those which are enjoyed among such. From now on, you are not to gather them near you, except to tell them how they are to serve. Your princi-

pal retinue is to be comprised of old men and others of reasonable age, who have virtues and good practices and examples, and the pleasures that you take shall be with such men and moderate.[62]

Philip was to rely on Francisco de los Cobos, the churchmen Tavera and Valdés and the duke of Alba for political and military counsel and on Zúñiga and Siliceo in his private affairs. While he recommended these men to his son, Charles also pointed out their faults and told Philip to be on guard against their self-serving ways.[63] Left alone in this situation, it is not surprising that Philip turned for friendship and advice to a man more nearly his own age, a man who, moreover, did not share the awesome authority and daunting experience of the advisers left him by his father.

Ruy Gómez de Silva was no longer a boy, and thus association with him did not contradict Charles V's instructions, but his lack of independent stature and fortune may have enhanced his appeal in the eyes of the insecure Philip. His counselors, even Alba, who was much younger than the rest, were all men of high status and long experience of government and war in the emperor's service. Philip doubtless felt intimidated by them, and he may have resented the fact that, while they showed him deference, these men still reported his decisions and actions to his absent father. He must have welcomed a companion who, as Cabrera wrote of Ruy Gómez, "attended upon him without harassing him or obstructing him when he desired solitude . . . [and] held him in uniform respect in all his actions."[64]

Ruy Gómez de Silva, then, owed much of his success to being the right man in the right place at the right time. He was raised from obscurity because Philip needed a man of his own in the midst of a retinue selected by, and primarily loyal to, his father. Ruy Gómez's case provides a classic illustration of the principle later enunciated by his protégé, Antonio Pérez: "The condition of being the favorite is dependent upon Fortune and the will of another."[65]

Ruy Gómez enjoyed another stroke of good fortune in that he had won the prince's support at a juncture when the field of opportunity for a man on the rise was considerable. His open emergence into favor coincided with the disappearance of the grand old men of Philip's household. Cardinal Tavera died in 1545; Zúñiga and García de Loaysa, in 1546; and Francisco de los Cobos, in 1547.[66] Moreover, Don Alvaro de Córdoba, identified by López de Gómara as Philip's favorite, died in 1545 as well.[67] Once the old advisers were gone, Alba, the youngest of the emperor's men, emerged by default and by dint of his imperious personality as the leading figure in the reorganized household of 1548. In the words of his biographer, he had become by 1550 "a true caudillo, a soldier with a large political following . . . [at] the nexus of three key institutions, the court, the army, and the Church."[68] Within a few years, though, Philip's favor would transform Ruy Gómez de Silva into a figure capable of standing up to Alba, and the court became polarized around these two men after Philip became king.[69]

Philip, coming into his majority and already a widower,[70] had dealt with affairs of government in his father's absence for five years and was now in a position to assert himself more forcefully. In elevating a man of his own to counterbalance Alba, Philip, the everdutiful son, was in part implementing his father's advice to guard against becoming too dependent on great nobles and to use Alba's talents without succumbing to his pretensions.[71] At the same time this may be seen as an expression of submerged resentment toward the absent, dominant and omnicompetent father and as an arrangement of a test of wills through surrogates.

Even when he had emerged as a man of some importance, though, Ruy Gómez was still far from being the social equal of the court's principal figures. He had no private wealth or prospects, and his noble status itself was disparaged by the Castilians. Throughout his life, even when he had become a grandee of Spain, Ruy Gómez de Silva was denied the courtesy title of "don," which was accorded to humble *hidalgos* of Castilian birth.[72]

The title of *sumiller* was a first step in imparting stature to the prince's man. Others soon followed. Also in 1548, Philip arranged a match for Ruy Gómez with Doña Teresa de Toledo, the sister of Gómez Dávila, the second marquis of Velada. The prince granted Ruy Gómez 10,000 *escudos* to provide him with some substance in the eyes of the bride's family. Nevertheless, Doña Teresa chose to enter a convent rather than marry him.[73] She may have had a genuine religious bent—there were several nuns in the family—or the convent may have been the only graceful escape from a marriage, arranged by the prince, that was considered demeaning. Either way, this jilting must have been a blow to Ruy Gómez's ego and to his and Philip's hopes for his social advancement.

After this disappointment Ruy Gómez left Spain as a member of Philip's retinue on his journey to be sworn as heir in his father's northern realms.[74] In November 1548 the royal party was carried from Catalonia to Italy on Andrea Doria's fleet. Most of the fifty-eight galleys of this flotilla were assigned for the transport of the dignitaries in Philip's entourage, their gear and households; one was designated solely for Ruy Gómez's use, which provides some measure of his stature.[75] Moreover, while his baggage traveled in this private ship, Ruy Gómez himself was among a handful of luminaries who sailed with Philip in the royal galley.[76] In January 1549, the prince's party left Milan on the overland journey to the north and reached Brussels at the beginning of April, having crossed Austria and southern Germany. Ruy Gómez was an active participant in the round of tourneys and balls that accompanied the royal tour, revealing himself along the way as a partisan of fancy dress. In Milan he rode in the cane-play (*juego de cañas*) outfitted as a Moor in the squadron of the count of Luna, while at Ghent on 18 July 1549 he danced in the guise of a German alongside ten companions cross-dressing as "*damas tudescas.*"[77] The following spring Ruy Gómez was himself the organizer of a tournament in Brussels to commemorate the completion of Philip's circuit of the Low Countries.[78] At the end of Philip's sojourn in northern Europe, Ruy Gómez received a commission as captain of horse from Charles V as a reward for his services to the emperor and his son. He retained this honorary command of a company of cavalry until his death.[79]

The prince and his entourage returned to Spain in the summer of 1551. Soon afterward Philip, with his father's approval, granted Ruy Gómez de Silva the *encomienda* of Argamasilla in the military order of Calatrava.[80] There is no reliable record of the value of this Manchegan *encomienda*, which, like all those of the three orders, was a territorial lordship held essentially in fee from the king as grand master of the orders. It is likely that the *encomienda* was worth 1,000–2,000 ducats per year to Ruy Gómez, after the payment of various mandatory imposts and the salaries of parish priests and estate agents.[81]

Ruy Gómez's career as a knight and *encomendero* in the military orders was long and rather confusing, so a synopsis is in order. When he entered the order of Calatrava in 1540, Ruy Gómez had already been, for an unspecified time, a *caballero* of Alcántara.[82] Entrance in Calatrava necessitated that he put aside his habit of Alcántara. Perhaps he had been nominated for an *encomienda* or presented with some other inducement to switch orders. Evidently he reversed his course and returned to Alcántara sometime in the 1540s, since he had to resign that order's *encomienda* of Esparragal in order to accept Argamasilla around 1551.[83] This pattern continued throughout his life: he was subsequently to hold the Alcántara *encomienda* of Herrera, which he resigned to his young second son in 1571 in order to take up the post of *clavero* in the order of Calatrava. This is an exceptional example of mobility within the orders. It can be assumed that each successive *encomienda* brought greater status and more income, culminating in the very lucrative *clavería*, worth 9,600 ducats per year in 1573.[84]

The income of Argamasilla must have been quite welcome to Ruy Gómez in the early 1550s. His increasingly prominent position at court imposed considerable expenses. In 1552, for example, he was the organizer and sponsor of a great joust at Toro, where the court was assembled for the wedding of Philip's sister to a Portuguese prince.[85] More important than the income, however, was the status of knight and *encomendero* of a military order, which certified Ruy Gómez as a man of ancient noble and Old Christian lineage. The great families of Castile might resent him as a foreign upstart, but they could not cast aspersions on his ancestry without calling into doubt the *hábitos* that were the tangible badges of their own purity of blood.[86] The *encomienda* of Argamasilla also imparted considerable additional status, since its holder was ex officio president of the general chapter of the order of Calatrava, and Ruy Gómez indeed presided over this assembly when it convened in 1552.[87] Even so, Philip desired still greater distinction for his favorite, so he asked his father to grant Ruy Gómez a wealthier *encomienda*, a request Charles V ignored, at least in the short term.[88]

Ruy Gómez de Silva was still unmarried, and thus, despite his position at court and in the order of Calatrava, he was a man without substance independent of the prince's favor and without useful family ties in Castile. He had no title, nor a personal fortune nor prospects of one. The position that was his primary asset on the marriage market was personal and not hereditary. Even Philip's intervention had not been sufficient to secure a match for him in 1548. Ruy Gómez continued to press for a marriage for himself while he was with Philip in the north. He enlisted the aid of Diego Hurtado de Mendoza, the Spanish ambassador in Siena, in negotiations that were proceeding in 1550;[89] in all likelihood he urged his case with Philip at every opportunity.

When Ruy Gómez returned to Spain in 1551 he was more clearly than before the favorite of a prince who was now grown and almost undoubtedly would be king. His heightened status enhanced his marriageability, and, with Philip's assistance, he soon arranged a very satisfactory match, with Doña Ana de Mendoza y de la Cerda. She was the daughter of the second count of Mélito, (another) Diego Hurtado de Mendoza, and the Countess Doña Catalina de Silva, the sister of the fifth count of Cifuentes. Born in 1540, Doña Ana was a most desirable bride, "because of her blood, her beauty, and the inheritance of so noble a House, one of the most-sought-after marriages of that time."[90] She was the only child of the count and countess of Mélito, and in the early 1550s it was already very probable that there would be no more heirs.[91] Thus she stood to inherit a great entailed fortune and could make her husband and their heirs the masters of a major noble house.

It is not known who first proposed that she should be married to Ruy Gómez de Silva. There is, however, no evidence to support Maltby's contention that "the house of Mendoza" arranged the marriage as a political stratagem to increase the family's influence at court: "[I]n the virtually landless favorite [Ruy Gómez] they saw the kind of opportunity that comes but once in a generation, and courted him with almost indecent haste."[92] The Mendozas were an immense and widely ramified family, and no indication exists that they acted as a concerted group on this marriage or, for that matter, on any other issue. Doña Ana's father was ambitious for himself, however, and his daughter's hand was a useful bargaining chip for the attainment of his personal goals.

In all likelihood the initial suggestion for the match came from Prince Philip, who was eager to see Ruy Gómez well and wealthily married. In any event, the prince entrusted the negotiations for the marriage to the prospective bride's maternal uncle, Juan de Silva, count of Cifuentes. The count was a lifelong friend of Ruy Gómez, with whom he had served at court since childhood.[93]

Cifuentes successfully concluded the match—by one account, the count and countess of Mélito accepted the offer "joyfully"[94]—and the capitulations were signed in Madrid on 18 April 1553.[95] From the terms of the contract it may be judged that, overjoyed or not, the count of Mélito drove a hard bargain. Ruy Gómez could hardly complain, though, since the prince met each of Mélito's demands and presented his favorite with a marriage that was designed to confer private stature in Castile commensurate with his public position at the court.

Ruy Gómez de Silva's marriage marked the culmination of his rise from obscurity and set the stage for the next phase of his life. In the following decade he would attain the stature of a true *privado* and the king's chief minister and would take the first steps toward becoming a landed magnate in his own right. His marital connection with the house of Mélito and, through it, with the high Castilian aristocracy, was to be crucial to the future course of his career and especially to the establishment of his own house of Pastrana. It would be well, before turning to the specific terms of the marriage, to examine Doña Ana's pedigree and prospects in some detail in order to appreciate fully the value of this match.

2

A Marriage Contract

Doña Ana de Mendoza y de la Cerda was a great match in the marriage market of the court of Castile. She stood to inherit the house of Mélito, a cadet line of the Mendoza family that traced its ancestry to the great Cardinal Pedro González de Mendoza (1428–1495). The fifth of seven sons of the first marquis of Santillana, the cardinal was renowned less for his spirituality than for his grandeur and political acumen. As cardinal-archbishop of Seville he served as captain-general of the Isabelline forces in the war of succession of 1474–1476 and won great influence with the victorious Catholic Kings. He was rewarded in 1483 with the primate see of Toledo, acted as grand chancellor of Castile and was instrumental in the establishment of the Inquisition. The cardinal was so prominent in politics and government that Pedro Martir dubbed him "the third king of Spain."[1]

In addition to his public accomplishments, Pedro González de Mendoza fathered three sons. The first two, Rodrigo and Diego, were borne by Doña Mencia de Lemus, a Portuguese lady-in-waiting to Henry IV's queen.[2] These sons, and a third by another noblewoman, were legitimized by the pope and by Ferdinand the Catholic in 1489.[3] Rodrigo served with valor in the Granadine war and was created first marquis of Cenete and count of Cid in 1491. His father had previously established a *mayorazgo* for him, comprised for the most part of properties situated in the Kingdom of Valencia. The marquis died in Valencia in 1523, leaving three minor daughters as his heirs.[4]

The second son, Diego, was to become the founder of the house of Mélito. He was raised in the cardinal's castle of Manzanares, and in 1489 his father established a *mayorazgo* for him, comprising the town of La Puebla de Almenara (southeast of Tarancón) and a third of the royal *tercias* of the city of Guadalajara.[5] Like his brother Rodrigo, Diego fought in the campaign of Granada. In 1500 he went to Naples as first captain of infantry in the army of the "Great Captain" Gonzalo Fernández de Córdoba. He fought with great distinction throughout the campaign and, especially at Rubo and Cerignola, "performed notable deeds." In 1503 the Great Captain rewarded Diego with the County of Mélito (Mileto), which had been confiscated to punish its rebellious previous owner, Jacopo Sanseverino. Ferdinand the Catholic confirmed this grant later in the same year and again in 1507, after the Treaty of Granada had restored the estates of most of the Neapolitan rebels.[6]

Diego returned to Spain as count of Mélito and of Aliano and grand justiciar of the Kingdom of Naples.[7] Subsequently he served Charles V as Lieutenant for the Crown of Aragon. Most of his efforts in this post were devoted to the affairs of Valencia, where, despite some initial bungling, he put down the revolt of the *Germanías*. Later he was a counselor of State.[8] The count of Mélito married Doña Ana de la Cerda y Castro, his second cousin (she was a great-granddaughter of the marquis of Santillana) and the niece of the first duke of Medinaceli. Her father, Don Iñigo de la Cerda, had attempted and failed in 1501 to seize his elder brother's duchy by force. After the death of their parents Doña Ana and her brother made an agreement on the partition of their lordships (*señoríos*) of Miedes and Mandayona that left her with the lion's share, presumably as a marriage portion.[9] A lord and military hero of the stature of Diego de Mendoza was, despite his illegitimate origins, an extremely good match for the daughter of a rather disreputable younger son.

This marriage produced eight children, of whom three sons and two daughters survived into adulthood.[10] In 1529 Don Diego and Doña Ana founded a *mayorazgo* for their eldest son. The couple had been contemplating such a move for fifteen years at least; they were first granted royal permission to form an entail in 1514.[11] The new *mayorazgo* of Mélito combined into a single inalienable entity Diego's patrimonial estate, his Italian county and other acquisitions, and the properties that Ana had brought to the marriage. This was a substantial set of holdings. The Italian component of the *mayorazgo* comprised complete judicial and economic control over an area of Calabria equivalent to the jurisdictions of eight modern communes. In Castile Diego had acquired perpetual *juros* secured on the *alcabalas* of many New Castilian towns and villages, which, at least on paper, were worth about 3,000 ducats a year. These *juros* were in-

cluded in the *mayorazgo,* along with the town of La Puebla de Almenara and the Guadalajaran *tercias* bequeathed by the cardinal.
The *mayorazgo* was further enhanced by the de la Cerda properties,
Miedes and Mandayona, with their hinterlands and taxes, in the
diocese of Sigüenza, and by the "cassas prinzipales" that the couple
had built in Toledo's Santa Leocadia parish.[12] In 1553 this *mayorazgo*
was thought to generate yearly revenues of more than 22,000
ducats.[13]

The first count of Mélito died in 1536, and his titles descended to
his son Diego Hurtado de Mendoza.[14] In 1538 the second count married Doña Catalina de Silva y Andrade, the daughter of Fernando
de Silva, fourth count of Cifuentes and a prominent figure at court.[15]
Cifuentes had only two surviving children, Catalina and a son, Juan.
For reasons that are unclear—perhaps Juan was frail?—Catalina
was for many years considered the probable heiress of the substantial house of Cifuentes.[16] She bore her husband one child, a daughter, in June, 1540, at Cifuentes.[17] This daughter, Ana, was baptized
with the surname of Silva, in honor of her maternal ancestors. The
count and countess of Mélito doubtless expected to have sons to
carry the patrilineal names. No siblings were ever born, though, and
their daughter passed into history as Doña Ana de Mendoza y de
la Cerda; she came to use the *apellidos* that had been mandated by
the founders of the *mayorazgo* of Mélito for its holders.[18]

Little is known of Ana's childhood. The traditional authorities
state that she was raised in the household of her maternal grandparents in Cifuentes and Alcalá de Henares. This story is called in question, however, by the fact that her grandfather was a widower at the
time of Ana's birth, died when she was five, and in the interim was
occupied at the peripatetic court as the governor of Charles V's
young daughters. All writers on the subject agree that Ana was a
spoiled only child, but they cite no evidence for this except her willful character as a mature woman.[19]

Ana first appears in the sources as, in effect, a commodity, the
object of the marriage negotiations completed in 1553. She was two
months short of her thirteenth birthday when the agreement was
made to marry her to a man as old as her father.[20] There is no indication that she was consulted at all about the match, although she was
doubtless at least shown her future husband. Nothing is known of

the course of the negotiations, which were conducted by her uncle the count of Cifuentes. In view of Ana's status and desirability as a probable heiress, it is likely that she was the object of other suits beforehand or concurrently. Her youth was no impediment; marriages could be, and regularly were, arranged for children seven years old and even younger.[21] She was, moreover, said to be "very pretty although she is small."[22] There is every reason to believe that Ana could have been matched with a man of much higher station than Ruy Gómez de Silva. Her paternal aunts, whose expectations had been humble in comparison, had been married to titled noblemen, the counts of Concentaina and of Chinchón.[23]

The formal marriage contract itself points to the principal reason why the count of Mélito chose to marry his daughter to a relatively obscure Portuguese courtier. The document bears, in addition to the signatures of Mélito, his wife and Ruy Gómez, those of Prince Philip and his secretary. Significantly, its title is "What is agreed and capitulated between our lord the Prince and [the] Count and Countess of Melito regarding the marriage that has been negotiated between Ruy Gómez de Silva . . . and Dª Ana de Mendoza, daughter of the said Counts."[24] The principal parties to this agreement were not, as one would expect, the prospective groom and father-in-law, but instead the latter and the prince. "In order to effect this illustrious marriage," Salazar noted, "Philip interposed all of his authority."[25] The marriage may have been Philip's idea to begin with, and in essence the prince acted in loco parentis for the much older Ruy Gómez when it came to striking the final bargain. It was usual for the royal head of the household to approve and intervene in the marriages of officials of the court, but in this case, as we shall see, the prince went to great lengths and considerable expense to forge an advantageous match for his favorite.

The terms of the compact as written were quite simple. For the time being the couple was to be betrothed "por palabras de presente," which would place a rigid impediment against either of them marrying anyone else. This form of betrothal was widely regarded in pre-Tridentine Europe as constituting a valid marriage without the necessity of a subsequent ecclesiastical ceremony to bind the alliance.[26] Nevertheless, it was agreed that Ruy Gómez and Ana would be wed "en [h]az de la santa Madre Yglesia" and the marriage consummated within two years of the date of the contract (18 April 1553).[27] Presumably the delay was in deference to the bride's tender age.

The economic agreement was also quite straightforward. Prince Philip agreed to endow the couple with income of 6,000 ducats per year in perpetuity. This income was to commence within two years. It was assumed that Ana would inherit the estate of Mélito and that when she did the royal grant would be added to its *mayorazgo* and passed on to the couple's heirs. If there were no children and Ruy Gómez predeceased Ana, she was to collect the 6,000 ducats for the remainder of her life and could bequeath it to her offspring by a subsequent marriage; only if she died childless would the income cease upon her death. Ruy Gómez was to have the 6,000 ducats if the marriage was dissolved. The door was not closed on the possibility that a male heir would forestall Ana's claim to the Mélito inheritance. In this case her father would be obliged to provide her with a *dote* of 100,000 gold ducats, which, along with the royal grant of income, would form the basis of a new *mayorazgo* for the couple and their descendants.[28] For his part Ruy Gómez agreed to give Ana an *arras*[29] of 10,000 ducats. He also pledged that, should his mother-in-law be widowed, he and Ana would see to the repayment of her *dote* and *arras*[30] and would provide her with an income of one million *maravedís* (2,666 ducats) a year, situated on the most reliable revenues of the *mayorazgo* of Mélito.[31]

In addition to signing the capitulations and pledging the gift of the 6,000-ducat *juro*, Philip made the extraordinary gesture a few days later of riding from the Pardo hunting lodge to Alcalá to attend the betrothal ceremony, where he served as best man.[32] Beyond the pleasure of bestowing great favor on his friend, it is difficult to see what advantage the prince secured from his very prominent role in arranging this marriage. Experienced observers seem to have regarded his generosity as excessive. Juan de Samano informed Eraso, who was with the emperor, of the marriage and the revenue bestowed on the couple, but he asked that this information remain confidential, since "I would not want to be the source" through which Charles V learned of the affair. "This is a favor such as His Majesty [the emperor] has not made in his time to any *privado* of his own. I would dearly like to know how it shall seem to His Majesty."[33]

On the other hand, the match seems to have afforded several distinct advantages to the count of Mélito. For acceding to what the prince so obviously wanted, hardly an impolitic move in itself, Mélito received in return an advantageous modification of the financial arrangements usual in a marriage of this importance. He did not have to pay a *dote* in cash to his daughter's husband. Instead, Ruy Gómez would have to be content with Ana's claim to inherit the Mélito title and estates and with the cash provided by Philip, which must be seen both as a marriage portion paid by a surrogate and as the provision of a respectable fortune for the landless favorite.

Although precise figures are not available, there is reason to believe that the count was in no position to pay a large marriage portion in the early 1550s, and thus he probably welcomed this arrangement. In those years Mélito faced a battery of challenges, initiated by family members, to his possession of his estates. The most serious of these was a suit brought in the Collateral Council of the Kingdom of Naples by his mother, alleging that, after his father's death, Mélito had unjustly taken possession of the Italian properties. She argued that they were hers by right for her lifetime, by virtue of the provisions of the will of the first count of Mélito. This suit led, in September 1551, to a court order blocking formal assent to Diego's investiture as count of Mélito. This injunction was soon overthrown, but it was succeeded by another and by the presentation of evidence that Diego had previously acknowledged his mother's claims. By the end of 1551 the suit was bogged down in a legal duel that threatened to drag on for years, as "many writs, provisions, decrees, objections with considered opinions, and proofs were submitted by first one and then the other party." More important, as long as this skirmish lasted the dowager countess was able to collect a portion of the revenues of the estate. Diego's collections were further constricted by embargoes ordered by the court pending resolution of the suit.[34]

This was not the only legal challenge facing Mélito. His second cousins, the grandchildren of his de la Cerda uncle, were in this period conducting a suit against Mélito and his mother over the possession of Miedes and Mandayona.[35] The count was also entangled in a web of litigation over the Italian towns of Rapolla, La Amendolea and San Lorenzo. This dispute had a complicated history, beginning in 1518, when Charles V had promised the first count of Mélito compensation in money and land for the Lucanian County of Aliano. The reversion of this county and title had been awarded to Mélito but was subsequently granted to Antonio Caraffa for political reasons.[36] The promised recompense was not forthcoming until 1532, when Charles granted Mélito the aforementioned towns, which had been confiscated from disgraced rebels of the Caracciolo and Abenavalo families. The revenue of these properties fell far short of the 3,000 Neapolitan ducats per year pledged in compensation, largely because the emperor stipulated that Lucrecia Caracciolo, the wife of the outlawed lord of San Lorenzo, must be repaid her marriage portion from the proceeds of that estate. It was estimated that her claim would be satisfied by 1540; thereafter the full yield of San Lorenzo would go to the house of Mélito, thus reducing the initial shortfall of about 1,900 ducats per year. The Crown was obligated to make good this and any subsequent deficits.[37]

The matter did not turn out as planned. After the death of the first count his widow, Ana de la Cerda, claimed these properties as hers, under the terms of her husband's will. In 1539 she founded a *mayorazgo* for her second son, Gaspar Gastón de la Cerda, that included the towns of Rapolla and Amendolea, reserving their usufruct to herself for life and disqualifying her eldest son from inheriting them.[38] Next she appears to have sold San Lorenzo to Lucrecia Caracciolo for 14,000 ducats, including the unpaid balance of her marriage portion.[39] Not surprisingly the second count, Diego Hurtado de Mendoza, raised strenuous objections to these proceedings. He claimed the three towns as his own and initiated formal proceedings to take possession of them. Subsequently they became an issue in the suit with his mother.[40] Then his brother, Gaspar Gastón, brought suit over Rapolla and Amendolea in the Chancillería of Valladolid. Diego succeeded in having this transferred to the Neapolitan courts in 1551 but not in having the suit dismissed.[41] Meanwhile Mélito sued his mother in Naples to block her sale of San Lorenzo. With the outcome of this litigation still pending, he gave San Lorenzo to his third brother, Baltasar de la Cerda, who in turn sold it to Caracciolo for 17,000 ducats. This maneuver short-circuited their mother's sale of the town, which had been judicially postponed for the duration of the suit.[42]

The count of Mélito may have hoped—and indeed may have

been encouraged to hope—that his marriage alliance with the prince's favorite could help to procure a favorable disposition of the litigation that encumbered his estate. The resolution of the suit with his mother gives some reason to suspect that such hopes were not entirely in vain. In early 1552 the suit had taken a turn for the worse, from Mélito's point of view, when the emperor ordered an extension of the time period allowed for registration in Naples of various renunciations of his rights made by Mélito years earlier in favor of his mother and brother. In the meantime Mélito had repudiated these renunciations, and the time allotted for their registration had expired, but the royal intervention reopened the possibility that they might be validated.[43] This must have been interpreted by Mélito, and more importantly by the judges in Naples, as a sign of the quarter where lay royal favor in the matter.

Nevertheless, the judgment rendered on 8 October 1553 by the Collateral Council was wholly in favor of the count of Mélito. The regents of the council ordered that he could proceed to take full possession "of the whole estate of Mélito and [the] city of Rapolla and territory of Mendolia [*sic*]," as rightful firstborn heir and successor of the first count. The claims of his mother and brother were quashed, and the former was ordered to repay to Mélito the estate revenues she had collected since the suit began.[44] There is no evidence beyond the timing of the judgment to indicate that Mélito's new relationship with Prince Philip had any bearing on the outcome of this suit. It is, however, suggestive that this reversal of the apparent trend of the litigation coincided so closely with the conclusion of the marriage pact.

Although monetary considerations and the strong possibility of benefit from the influence of Philip and Ruy Gómez doubtless swayed Mélito,[45] further evidence indicates that he received greater proofs of favor in return for his daughter's hand. This is not surprising, since it is clear that Ana's parents regarded the match as a mésalliance. The contract stipulated that the heirs of Ruy Gómez and Ana must bear the *apellidos* Mendoza y Silva and carry the arms of Mendoza at the right-hand place of honor on their shields.[46] Such a reversal of names and arms could scarcely have been demanded of a suitor of rank equivalent to Ana's. Furthermore, contrary to the usual custom in such matters, Ana was to live with her parents and not in the house of her new in-laws in the interim between the betrothal and the final solemnification of the marriage. As Erika Spiva-kovsky remarks, "the proud Mendozas would not allow their daughter to go to a more modest house in Portugal."[47] Nor, what was perhaps more likely, did they want Ana to reside at the prince's court in the absence of a princess and her female household.[48] There was simply no comparison in wealth and status between the count and countess of Melito and their future son-in-law. In order to pledge 10,000 ducats in *arras*, a rather ordinary sum by the stan-dards of the great houses of Castile, Ruy Gómez de Silva had to obtain royal permission, which Philip granted, "so that you might promise and give the said arras, notwithstanding that it exceeds the tenth part of your property."[49]

The bridegroom's position did not entirely compensate for his lack of wealth and social prestige. Ruy Gómez's influence with Philip, though obvious, was a commodity of uncertain long-term value, since Charles V was still in the prime of life and, while inter-mittent rumors circulated, there was as yet no strong hint that he would abdicate.[50] Moreover, despite his proximity to the prince, Ruy Gómez was not yet publicly acknowledged as a supremely influen-tial counselor. He held no governmental post, and there was no assurance that he ever would. There was no automatic connection between personal favor and political office. Charles V had not established a tradition of an all-powerful *privanza*, combining the functions of favorite and minister in one person. Since the time of the *comuneros* the emperor had tended to leave political admini-stration in the hands of bureaucrats, to the increasing exclusion of courtiers. This casts doubt on the theory, proposed by Maltby and others,[51] that this marriage was arranged primarily to serve the in-terests of the house of Mendoza. Spivakovsky bluntly asserts this view:

> Ana's father had instigated this marriage, acting upon the suggestion of his relatives. The extensive, power-hungry clan of the Mendozas planned to secure as their political ally the future King's favorite, whose influence over his master was practically limitless.[52]

This unsupported passage overstates Ruy Gómez's influence at the time and implies what contemporaries could not have known with any certainty about the future. More damning is the fact that the Mendoza "clan," largely because of its very extensiveness and the sometimes conflicting hungerings for power of various individuals within it, was not a unitary group that met in council to plan grand strategy. Had Ruy Gómez truly been the widely recognized marital catch that Spivakovsky's passage implies, many nobles—among them, doubtless, several Mendozas—would have been vying to marry their daughters to him. Furthermore, Ruy Gómez's father-in-law later insinuated that, far from being pressed by influential relatives to seek this match, he had been forced to sweep aside the objections of his own wife in order to conclude the marriage pact.[53]

At the same time Philip's clear interest in the match made it awkward if not impossible for the count of Mélito to refuse his daughter's hand to Ruy Gómez. Ana could not be placed in a convent to avoid the marriage, since there was no other heir to the house. Nevertheless, the count was not easily cowed by royal authority: a few years later he openly defied the regent and Charles V's sister.[54] While it might not be possible to reject Ruy Gómez's suit, pressed with Philip's backing, the count was a sufficiently strong character to exploit the bargaining position that remained to him. The emperor could not be expected to look favorably on his son's actions if they resulted in aggrieving a powerful subject or if they convinced other noblemen that the Crown would trample at will on their rights to marry their daughters as they saw fit. Thus Mélito was able to extract from Philip further concessions, which were not reflected in the formal marriage contract.

Although no existing document outlines the secret capitulations of the marriage agreement, their content can be deduced from subsequent events. In April 1554 the count of Mélito was named viceroy of Aragon by Philip, acting as regent of Spain.[55] On the first of March of the next year, as the two-year period for ratification of the marriage neared its expiration, Philip, now king of Naples, granted Mélito the Neapolitan title of duke of Francavila. Also at about this time some of his Castilian properties (including a number of villages whose possession was still being legally disputed by Mélito's second cousins) were amalgamated into the marquisate of Algecilla. Diego Hurtado de Mendoza was named the first marquis; thereafter the title would be held by the heir-presumptive of the house of Mélito. With these new titles Mélito was also accorded the coveted hereditary status of grandee of Spain.[56]

Like his forebears, Diego Hurtado de Mendoza seems to have

been eager to serve the Crown in proconsular offices. Unlike them, though, he had little talent for affairs of state. His tenure as viceroy in Aragon came to a disastrous end in 1556, when, in defiance of the Aragonese fueros, he had an accused bandit garroted in the Cárcel de la Manifestación in Zaragoza. This arbitrary act provoked a popular uprising and an unauthorized convocation of the *cortes* of Aragon. Mendoza took refuge in the city's castle and sent his secretary, Juan de Escobedo, to Valladolid to explain his actions to the princess regent. Both she and the Council of Castile, concerned about keeping Aragon loyal during the war with France, disavowed his actions and censured his behavior. Mélito, now known as Francavila because of his cession of the former title in 1555, was forced to retire ignominiously from Zaragoza, and no new viceroy was sent for three years.[57]

Despite this miserable performance Francavila was appointed to the Council of State and was named to head the Council of Italy upon its formation in 1558.[58] In 1564 he was sent once more to the eastern kingdoms, this time as viceroy in Catalonia.[59] The duke has been aptly described as "violent, thoughtless, incapable of prudence or reflection,"[60] and contemporaries thought him ill qualified for these prestigious and difficult posts. His merit was bluntly questioned by the Venetian ambassador Leonardo Donato, who doubtless came close to the truth with his observation, regarding the presidency of the Council of Italy, that Francavila "attained this position rather more through the son-in-law's favor than by his own ability." Donato added that Philip was well aware of the deficiencies of his appointee and thus had given him an assistant "who is always present in his stead in the council and expedites all its affairs."[61]

It appears, then, that Ana's father continued for many years to reap tangible benefits from this alliance. Francavila realized his good fortune, exclaiming in 1557 that "today one could hardly imagine a man in any kingdom more advantageously connected by marriage than I am in this realm."[62] The groom, Ruy Gómez de Silva, also profited from the private provisions of the marriage contract. On 13 March 1555 his father-in-law signed over to him his Italian estates and the title of count of Mélito. Ruy Gómez was to enjoy the income of these estates, except for a small allowance that would go to Mendoza, and, perhaps more important, would now be able to employ a noble title. In principle this was a perpetual donation, although in practice its duration was five years. Some practical and financial aspects of this transaction will be examined below.[63]

A royal document of 1555 states clearly that the cession of the Mélito title and estates to Ruy Gómez comprised part of his marriage contract.[64] It might be regarded as a sort of marriage portion, in kind rather than cash, for Ana. But since the original capitulations make it quite clear that her *dote* consisted of her claim to succeed to her father's estate, it seems more correct to regard the cession as part of a quid pro quo for the office and titles bestowed on the new duke of Francavila. The failure to make this agreement public probably stemmed from Philip's desire not to anger his father or other subjects by publicizing the favors he granted to secure his favorite's marriage. It is also very probable that the exact terms of the further concessions were left unresolved in 1553, since even Philip could not have been certain then that in two years' time he would be in a position to grant titles of nobility or major royal offices.

Ruy Gómez de Silva gained some further concessions from his father-in-law that had not been expressly agreed in the marriage contract. In March and April 1554 the count of Mélito signed over two sets of properties to his daughter's husband. The first set included Rapolla, Amendolea and the remainder of Mélito's claim to the 3,000 ducats of yearly revenue promised his father in compensation for Aliano. The second grant comprised three towns—Sacedón, Tamajón and Rotundas—with their jurisdictions and *banalités* in the New Castilian region of the Alcarria.[65] The transfer of the Italian towns and claim seems to have been designed to forestall or at least complicate future litigation over these properties that could be brought by Mélito's brother or by Lucrecia Caracciolo. An explicit reason was given for the second grant. Mélito declared that, in the marriage contract, no provision had been made for his daughter's *dote* except in the case that he were to have a son. Since she was still his sole heir, he said, nothing had changed on this score, but he felt an obligation to provide her with an allowance. This obligation had been "discussed" when the marriage was pacted, and now he was going to fulfill it by giving the three *alcarreño* towns to Ruy Gómez and Ana. This donation, "por via de alimentos para ayuda a sustentar las cargas de matrimonyo," was to take effect on the feastday of San Juan (June 1554) and would be valid "for all the days of my life or [that] of the lord Ruy Gómez."[66] It seems strange that Mélito was so punctilious in observing a monetary obligation that was not recorded in the contract, especially since (as will be seen abundantly below) the count was hardly a doting father. No proof of a connection can be found, but it is perhaps worth noting that these generous donations were made at the seat of Philip's court shortly prior to Mélito's appointment as viceroy of Aragon.[67]

The second donation provoked a response from Ruy Gómez that is interesting in two respects. After Mélito signed the donation the notary took a copy of the document to Ruy Gómez, who effused over its generosity and rushed to his father-in-law to kiss his hands. He then asked the notary to draw up a formal document of acceptance, which was duly signed and witnessed.[68] The latter gesture was not usual and lends some credence to the suspicion that the donation was part of an agreed quid pro quo. Be this as it may, Ruy Gómez's fawning response provides a glimpse of the characteristic methods of this courtier on the make.

A stronger taste of this aspect of Ruy Gómez's character is provided by a letter he wrote in August 1553 to the emperor's secretary, Francisco de Eraso. In this period the two men were developing the close and mutually self-serving relationship that they would maintain for many years.[69] "The favor that His Highness [*su Alteza*, i.e., Philip] made me in marrying me was great," Ruy Gómez wrote,

> but what has been said there [at the emperor's court] is not enough. It is true that His Highness did me the favor of promising me 6,000 ducats of income, which he is not [presently] giving me, from his household or in anything else; but he will settle with me when he can, as has been said there. From now until two years hence, when the marriage is to be effected, I don't have the right to ask anything from him, and not then either, if His Highness is not so kind as to give me something of his own accord.
>
> Your Grace should understand that if His Majesty [*su Magestad*, i.e., Charles] should not be pleased to show me some favor on this occasion, from which people might be satisfied that His Majesty approved of the *merced* that His Highness made me, I would be the most sorrowful man in the world, and thus I entreat Your Grace (since you go so seldom to His Majesty to [ask him to] shift me to another *encomienda* or to augment my income from it) that you might show how this might be accomplished, and otherwise I may well retire from here in a year. I leave Your Grace to consider it, and whether I should not be correct to presume that he does not value me.[70]

In a subsequent letter Ruy Gómez complained that "there will always be those who judge my affairs maliciously" and went on to protest that, regardless of what might be said in Brussels, he had received no further gifts from the prince. In fact, since the promised 6,000 ducats per year was not yet being paid, his current income barely allowed a monthly personal expenditure of 300 *escudos*, over and above the allowance for household expenses paid him as *sumiller*. "I offer Your Grace this account," he concluded to Eraso, "so that you may know that I am not so very well provided as not to be spending every bit that I receive and whatever else I can scrape together." He hoped that, with this in mind, the secretary would come to his defense "when you see me trampled on this score" and would plead his case for further *mercedes* from the emperor.[71]

Despite Ruy Gómez's protestations to Eraso, the prince did not delay long in fulfilling the promises made in the marriage capitulations. In February 1554 he donated to the couple the largely undeveloped lands between San Cristóbal and Santa Cruz on the island of Tenerife. This property was said to return an income of 8,000 ducats per year. This was an estimate, though, and probably a wishful one at that, since the governor of the Canaries was ordered to have the lands surveyed to determine how large a grant would be necessary to produce that amount of revenue. The grant included irrigation rights, but an additional provision stated that if insufficient irrigable land was found to exist on Tenerife, the grant could be rounded out with lands on La Palma.[72]

In the marriage contract Philip had promised the couple 6,000 ducats in revenues in Castile. The amount granted them in the Canaries was greater, in order to defray the added costs of administration outside the peninsula. It was stipulated that, if the Tenerife property yielded less than 8,000 ducats per year, the king would make good the shortfall from the "rentas de Castilla" at the rate of ¾ of the amount of the deficit.[73]

Nothing is known of the outcome of this donation, since it was superseded in 1558 by a grant of 6,000 ducats of yearly income from the yield of the *alcabalas* and *tercias* of the Castilian marquisate of Villena.[74] No clear reason was given for this substitution, but two explanations suggest themselves. First, the Tenerife properties may have been found to be worth much less than 8,000 ducats per year, especially in their unimproved state. Second, the management and improvement of the Canary lands would have demanded considerable supervision by Ruy Gómez or his agents. The original grant suggested that these lands would be suitable for sugar cultivation, which of course requires considerable capitalization and organization.[75] Ruy Gómez was a courtier, not an entrepreneur, and doubtless greatly preferred the lesser but guaranteed income from the Villena revenues, which would be collected and paid by the royal treasury, to the chancy prospect of developing an island wasteland. The initial grant, in Philip's view, must have seemed at least partially justified as an internal improvement project; the final form of the donation was simply an alienation of public revenues to a private person.

Although Philip fulfilled his promises, neither Eraso nor the emperor seems to have acquiesced to Ruy Gómez's plea for a sign of imperial favor. Given everything that the bridegroom stood to gain from the agreement pacted with the prince, his request for more seems shamelessly impertinent. Moreover, his threat to withdraw from public life was transparently hollow. Philip, not Charles, was his ticket to further honors and wealth; if he could maintain his relationship with the prince, the emperor would eventually become entirely irrelevant to his prospects.

Ruy Gómez de Silva must have realized this, and it is difficult to view his lamentations to Eraso as anything but symptoms of importunate greed for patronage. The prince's favorite, it appears, would not shrink from attempting to exploit any possible avenue of advancement, and he was not much concerned about the image that might result from such unbridled grubbing for favor. His further career illustrates the profitability of this approach and provides us with a glimpse of the workings of a court in which blatant spoilsmanship did not redound to the detriment of its practitioner, at least if the man on the make was as skilled as Ruy Gómez de Silva.

3

The King's Man

Early in the summer of 1554 the Infante Don Carlos, a boy of nine, was brought to the Castilian town of Benavente. There he awaited his father, Prince Philip, who would pass through en route to La Coruña and thence to England and his marriage to Queen Mary. The town had been richly decorated in preparation for this royal reunion and farewell. As they entered Benavente the members of the *infante*'s household were impressed by the great houses, some of them "very sumptuous," that lined the main street. They were particularly pleased by the facades of the houses on the right-hand side, which had been decorated with "very finished and beautiful effigies, in the style of medallions." On the upper level were depicted the emperor, Prince Philip and Don Carlos; below them were six portraits of court luminaries, including, in a central position, a likeness of Ruy Gómez de Silva.[1]

This was a striking indication of the public stature of the newly married Ruy Gómez. Evidently the count of Benavente and the leading citizens of his town numbered the Portuguese courtier among the handful of men closest to Philip. Only certain knowledge of the prince's partiality to Ruy Gómez could have induced them to have his portrait placed alongside those of men of much nobler lineage, like the count of Feria and the marquis of Pescara. His position was secure, at least to the extent that no one would openly question that he belonged in such company. This evidence is borne out by the events of the 1550s, for as Philip assumed the kingship of his far-flung realms, Ruy Gómez de Silva became ever more clearly his chief minister and confidant.

The ink was barely dry on his own marriage contract when Ruy Gómez de Silva set out for Portugal in the summer of 1553 to conclude a match between Prince Philip and the Portuguese Infanta María. That Ruy Gómez was entrusted with such a mission reflects the prince's confidence in him as well as his obvious qualifications as an emissary to the court of Lisbon. The negotiations were slowed, however, by wrangling over the dowry. Still, the marriage had nearly been agreed in August 1553 when Philip became aware of the opportunity presented by the accession of Mary Tudor to the English throne. The prince quickly and rather clumsily suspended the Portuguese negotiations and thus freed himself to seek the hand of the English queen.[2]

The arrangements for the English marriage were made in the subsequent fall and winter by representatives of the emperor's court in Brussels, most notably the imperial ambassador in London, Simon Renard. Neither the prince nor his advisers actively participated in the negotiations. Philip's misgivings about the match are well known, but, as an obedient son, in the end he resolved to play the part the emperor had assigned him. Nevertheless, he delayed half a year (purposely, in the view of many observers) before finally leaving Spain for England in mid-July 1554.[3]

Ruy Gómez de Silva was a member of the entourage that accompanied Philip to England, along with the other prominent household officials—Alba as *mayordomo mayor*, the *caballerizo mayor* Don Antonio de Toledo, the chaplain Fray Alonso de Castro—and a sizable portion of their staffs. A considerable number of grandees also elected to make the trip, doubtless attracted by the liberal *ayudas de costa* Philip promised all members of the retinue, and encouraged by the consideration that those who remained in Spain would be cut off from other forms of the prince's patronage.[4] Philip anticipated that his entire entourage would amount to about 3,000 people and 1,500 horses and beasts of burden. He seems to have regarded this as a rather austere following: "I am persuaded to take only the members of my household since, being few in number, it will be that much more possible to govern and get along according to the custom of the natives."[5]

This question of adaptability to English ways troubled a Spanish observer in London in early 1554. Don Juan Hurtado de Mendoza advised the bishop of Arras that Philip "must bring no soldiers, and only such courtiers as are prepared to be meek and long-suffering."[6] This was a tall order, given the temperament of the Castilian nobles. Not surprisingly, friction between the Spaniards and their hosts in England was considerable. Some felt slighted because the English household appointed by Mary had usurped many of their customary duties at Philip's side. Ruy Gómez de Silva complained that "if any of our number attempts to perform any service, they [the English staff] take it ill and do not wish to allow it to be done." The bulk of the household brought from Castile were left stranded along Philip's route inland and were not even present at the wedding in Winchester.[7] Obviously they were resentful at this exclusion from the festivities. One Spaniard grumbled that even Alba, the *mayordomo mayor*, was not being allowed to fulfill all of his duties. When the king dined in public, attended by Englishmen, the duke "did hand him the napkin, but did not act as master of the household nor carry his staff of office."[8]

The same writer expressed scorn for the great English lords. Pembroke and Arundel passed for "the greatest men of the realm at present, though their incomes are not more than 25,000 ducats."[9] This accusation was perhaps based on wishful thinking inspired by jealousy rather than on factual knowledge. Ruy Gómez de Silva was more concerned that the Spaniards would fail to impress the English with their grandeur. In late July he wrote Francisco de Eraso about his impressions of the English character and his anxieties on this score:

> Most seasonable was the grant of the Kingdom of Naples that His Majesty made to the King [Charles V gave Philip Naples and the Duchy of Milan as a wedding present[10]] and, as such, they [the English] have greatly appreciated it here. It was opportune because the greater the prospect of receiving more favors, the more content they are. Upon my faith, even though interest is a powerful motive in all lands, it is nowhere in the world stronger than here, where nothing is done well except with cash in hand. We have all brought with us so little money that, if they tumble to the fact, I do not know if we will escape alive; at the very least, we will be without honor, since in their disappointment they will flay us mercilessly.[11]

There is no further reference to the penury of the Spanish courtiers, but this condition, combined with their worries that the English household rendered them superfluous and compounded by linguistic difficulties, must have left the Spaniards anxious and uncomfortable during much of their stay.

They also feared for their personal safety and lamented the lawless nature of the English in terms reminiscent of the complaints of subsequent English travelers in Spain. "There are plenty of robbers on the roads here," wrote one Spaniard,

> and they have attacked several persons, among them a servant of Don Juan Pacheco, the marquis of Villena's son, from whom they stole 400 crowns and all the gold and silver objects he had with him. Not a trace has been found of all this property nor of four chests belonging to His Highness's household, though the Queen's Council do take certain precautions.

He concluded sadly that "the wise thing to do here is to imitate the English and go home early."[12] Ruy Gómez also took up this theme and compared the English with the Spanish brand of thievery. "There are some great thieves among them," he remarked to Eraso, "and they rob in plain view, having the advantage over us Spaniards that we steal by stealthy contrivance and they by main force."[13] Later in the summer it proved impossible to arrange suitable accommodation for all of the Spanish courtiers at Hampton Court, and the queen was apprised "that certayne disorderes hath risene in lodgeing of sundrye noblemen and gentlemen of the kinges trayne."[14] A joint committee of English privy councilors and Spaniards, including Ruy Gómez, determined to house part of the entourage in the neighboring countryside, at least in part "to protect them from the rapacity of the people."[15] Despite this attempt to alleviate friction the Spanish courtiers remained very uncomfortable; one wrote that "we are all desiring to be off with such longing that we think of Flanders as paradise." Many of the aristocrats who had accompanied Philip—among them the duke of Medinaceli, the marquises of Pescara and Las Navas, and the Netherlandish count of Egmont—applied for and received permission to leave England for the emperor's court. By 17 August only the key household officials, Alba and Ruy Gómez in particular, and the counts of Feria and of Olivares, remained as major figures at Philip's side. Joined by Don Pedro de Córdoba, these men seem to have comprised Philip's unofficial Spanish council thereafter.[16]

The shared discomfiture of the remaining Spaniards did not put an end to internecine rivalries. The ordinary strife of ambitious courtiers was complicated by the presence of another divided court at the emperor's residence in Brussels. Philip, though he now was king of Naples, duke of Milan and consort of England in his own right, was still clearly subordinate to his father.[17] At the same time the emperor's ill health (and intimations of his abdication) turned the thoughts of his servants to the coming reign and to strategies for enhancing or perpetuating their own influence within it. The intrigues of the time are confusing, not least because much of the pertinent documentation was lost,[18] but the courtiers, in England and Flanders alike, seem to have divided into two basic groups. One tendency was represented by the duke of Alba at Philip's court and, less overtly, by the bishop of Arras in Brussels. These seasoned courtiers seem to have staked their fortunes on a perception of Philip as a weakling who would be overawed by their experience and thus easily dominated. They counted on the notion that Philip's filial devotion would extend to his father's preferred counselors, and they probably believed that they would be even more indispensable to a young king. They desired and expected continuity in the personnel of government and the distribution of power at court. The other group, prominently including Ruy Gómez de Silva in England and Francisco de Eraso at the imperial court, acted on what may have been a more subtle appreciation of Philip's character. Their program was to exploit his resentment at the condescension of his father's servants and to build his confidence, hoping that Philip in power would be grateful to those who had helped him to assert his independence. They were the party of change, desiring the establishment under Philip of a new ministerial team, dominated by themselves.

A close analysis of all the personalities involved and of their positions on tangled issues of policy would not suit present purposes.[19] Instead, the focus here will be on the means by which Ruy Gómez secured the ascendancy over Philip that he enjoyed in the first years of the new reign. Although Ruy Gómez had enjoyed close personal relations with Philip at least since the late 1540s, his role in the actual operation of government had remained limited. In England, as previously in Castile, his principal rival for preeminence among the prince's entourage was the duke of Alba. Charles V, realizing his son's misgivings about the English marriage and hoping to avoid a repetition of the poor impression made by Philip during his tour of the northern kingdoms five years before, had entrusted Alba, as *mayordomo mayor,* with the task of maintaining discipline among the Spanish courtiers in England. "I implore you," wrote the emperor, "to take the measures you deem fitting to gain reputation and maintain the good opinion" of the English people.[20] In particular the emperor charged Alba with keeping an eye on Philip: "Duke, for the love of God, see to it that my son behaves in the right manner; for otherwise I tell you I would rather never have taken the matter in hand at all."[21]

Despite recent attempts to rehabilitate Alba, there is no reason to question the verdict of the Venetian ambassador who described the duke as "presumptuous, swollen with pride, consumed with ambition, given to flattery and very envious. . . . He is not well-liked at Court, for many there deem him heartless and imprudent."[22] Such a man seems a poor choice to appoint as a watchdog for a mature prince, jealous of his dignity and prerogatives. The emperor was not unaware of the duke's character. A decade previously he had warned Philip against becoming too dependent on Alba, who

> claims extravagant things, and attempts to swallow up all that he can, despite having appeared crossing himself, very humble and otherworldly. Observe, son, that he will place himself near you who are younger. You must guard against placing him or other grandees in the inner circle of government, since he and they will proceed by all possible means to get their way from you, which will cost you dearly later.[23]

Charles proved an apt prophet, and Alba's haughty demeanor angered the prince even as a youth.[24] The duke grew no more tactful as Philip matured and became increasingly conscious of his regal status. Alba habitually addressed Philip, even when the latter had become king, as "son." This condescension was not made more palatable by the duke's explanation that it was a sign of his great personal affection for Philip.[25] The proud prince was prepared to accept paternal guidance from Charles V alone.[26]

As a young man Philip had far less personal contact with Antoine Perrenot de Granvelle, the bishop of Arras, but nonetheless he conceived a dislike for him as well. At least in the 1550s Arras was less bluntly patronizing toward Philip than was Alba; it has been justly noted that "he did not hesitate to stoop to the lowest forms of flattery in order to curry favour." Still, the prince remained cool toward him, and many years were to pass before Arras (Cardinal Granvelle from 1561) was valued by Philip as he had been by Charles V. Arras enjoyed both a keen intelligence and a very high opinion of himself, and he may well have initially alienated Philip by condescending to him in 1549 during the prince's painful progress through the Low Countries. That the prince disliked Arras should not be surprising; the arrogant bishop had made many enemies during his precocious rise to power.[27]

One such enemy was the secretary Francisco de Eraso, who was Arras's principal rival at the court of Brussels by the time of the English marriage. The power struggle between these two men, envenomed by a bitter personal enmity, persisted for more than a decade and left its marks on Philip's policy in the Netherlands and elsewhere.[28] Eraso had strengthened his position vis-à-vis Arras by maintaining access to Charles V during the emperor's severe illness and depression in 1553 and early 1554—for months, Charles effectively refused to see anyone except the secretary and his sister Mary.[29] The canny secretary had also begun to exploit, to Arras's detriment, a rift between the bishop and his countryman Simon Renard (both were *franche-comtois*), which arose in part from their conflicting claims to credit for arranging the English marriage.[30] Meanwhile, looking ahead to the inevitable succession, Eraso had cultivated an alliance with the one man at Philip's court whose long-term interests most neatly dovetailed with his own—Ruy Gómez de Silva.[31] Even before the English match Ruy Gómez and Eraso had schemed to minimize Arras's influence over Philip.[32]

Arras and Alba also shared an obvious common interest in maintaining their influence through the transition between reigns.[33] Both men could count on continuing to prosper under Charles but might face different circumstances under Philip. In Alba's case, arrogance seems to have dulled the recognition that things might change when Philip came to power. Arras made some attempt to woo the prince—or at least to rehearse for the leading role he envisioned for himself in the coming regime—by adapting to Philip's well-known predilection for Spanish ways and interests. Alone among the emperor's Burgundian intimates, Arras went to the trouble to learn Castilian and began to expound an hispanocentric vision of the empire similar to Alba's. These gestures failed to win the prince's affection and succeeded only in straining relations between Arras and the Burgundian and Flemish courtiers, who were already arrayed in ethnic mistrust of the Castilian heir-apparent and his peninsular advisers.[34] Alba hardly tried and Arras failed to overcome the personal traits that had alienated the prince. At the same time, neither the duke nor the bishop was as well situated to know and exploit the prince's feelings and resentments as was Ruy Gómez, who assisted at Philip's dressing and undressing and slept in his antechamber, nor were they as close to the emperor in his last years as was Eraso.[35] In any case, Alba and Arras did not work together to maintain their positions half as effectively as Eraso and Ruy Gómez toiled to supplant them. For the most part these senior counselors seem to have assumed that power over Philip was their due and would fall into their hands like a ripe fruit. They were mistaken, and they did not comprehend until it was too late that Eraso and Ruy Gómez had darted in to snatch the prize from their grasp.

During Philip's first stay in England (July 1554 to September 1555) Eraso and Ruy Gómez de Silva labored assiduously to project a positive image of Philip's behavior and acumen in his sensitive role as Mary's consort. In contrast to the more pessimistic dispatches of Renard and others and to his own private observations on the Spaniards' reception in England, from the very outset of the English sojourn Ruy Gómez sent glowing reports of Philip's actions to Brussels:

> The Queen is very happy with the King, and the King with her; and he strives to give her every possible proof of it in order to omit no part of his duty. . . . [T]he best of it is that the King fully realizes that the marriage was concluded for no fleshly consideration, but in order to remedy the disorders of this Kingdom and preserve the Low Countries.[36]

and

> his [Philip's] dealings with the English lords are such that they themselves say that England has never had a King who has so rapidly won the hearts of everyone. . . . I believe what they say because of what I see of His Highness's actions towards them. In every letter he writes, His Majesty [Charles] should not fail to praise his son for this nor to urge him not to tire in such behavior, for it is certain that he [Philip] knows how to behave marvellously if he so desires.[37]

In another passage Ruy Gómez lauds Philip's treatment of Mary and incidentally gives a glimpse of his own intimacy with his master, who must have been telling tales out of school:

> He skillfully amuses the Queen and well knows how to pass over her defects from the standpoint of the carnal sensibility. He maintains her in such happiness that, in truth, the other day when they were by themselves she very nearly spoke loving endearments to him, and he responded in kind.[38]

Clearly these words of praise were meant for the emperor's ears and wider circulation at court. In the same vein, Ruy Gómez contended a few weeks later that Philip's arrival in London had quieted the inhabitants' unrest, attributed rather dubiously to their resentment at being denied the presence of their beloved king.[39]

In these months rumors circulated widely that the emperor meant to retire soon.[40] His work habits had become extremely lackadaisical, with his secretary for Italian affairs complaining that Charles had refused to resolve individual petitions from the peninsula for nearly four years.[41] By September Arras seems to have believed that Charles had in fact decided upon abdication.[42] Although he had been very close to Charles during his illness and thus was alert to the emperor's weariness, Eraso was less certain that the retirement was imminent, and Ruy Gómez, hearing the rumors, excoriated the secretary for keeping him and Philip in the dark. It appears, however, that Eraso was correct—Rodríguez-Salgado concludes that "abdication gradually emerged in the course of 1555 as the most suitable option"[43]—and the allies continued to act on the assumption that Charles would delay his abdication until he was convinced that Philip was competent to assume his responsibilities. The emperor's charge to Alba to watch over Philip clearly demonstrates that he had serious reservations about his son's aptitude for governing northern European subjects.[44] The prince's comportment in England would be eagerly studied by his tired father for signs that he could conscientiously lay down his regal burdens. Therefore, Ruy Gómez and Eraso set out to present Charles with evidence of his son's competence. At the same time, other courtiers, like Arras, might find themselves better served were the abdication postponed as long as possible.[45] Via Ruy Gómez, Eraso had received assurance that Philip would retain him in a major administrative post;[46] others had no such guarantees. The dynamics of this situation—complicity between Eraso and Ruy Gómez, the mounting success of their campaign on Philip's behalf, the emperor's paternal and self-interested desire to think well of his son's capabilities and Arras's discomfiture over this issue—are illustrated in a letter from Eraso to Ruy Gómez of 29 November 1554. The secretary had recently been in England carrying despatches from the court; upon his return to Brussels he informed Ruy Gómez that

> I made a verbal report to the Emperor of such things as seemed to me essential in praise of our master [*nuestro amo*, i.e., Philip], touching upon the skillful manner in which he conducts himself and manages all affairs, and the care and steady tenacity with which he negotiates, and the rapid resolutions and decisions he makes, and his excellent desires and designs and their execution insofar as it lies within his power, and the prudence with which he handled the religious question. . . . I told likewise of the peaceful state of affairs that prevailed over there, and of how beloved and well-liked the King is, by the illustrious and the commons alike, and of the good treatment that he accords everyone, as well as the fact that he has acquired much credit for his management of justice.[47]

The reference to Philip as "our master" is suggestive, given that Eraso had for years been one of the emperor's closest advisers.[48] Charles V's response to the secretary's paean must have been deeply gratifying to these allies who so clearly had cast their lot with Philip:

> His Majesty [Eraso continues] heard all these things very attentively and with singular satisfaction, and he was even more content that the King should enjoy such great credit with the Queen, and that everyone knows it to be so, and that he goes out among the public very freely and they marvel at this, which is one of the reasons why they hold him in such esteem. Finally, having gone over all this with His Majesty, he responded that he gave great thanks to God for the favor shown him in this, and that truly the King had changed greatly.

This triumph was made more delicious by the opportunity to repeat this happy report to some of his adversaries at the court:

> And at this point the Queen [Charles's sister Mary], M. de Prats [Praet] and the bishop of Arras came in, and His Majesty ordered that I should repeat for them the points I had made; and even though the speech was in "coarse Castilian" ["çafio castellano"] I emphasized everything in such a manner that I think there was no lack of comprehension of that which suits us.[49]

Presumably the emperor stood by, beaming with paternal pride, while Eraso clearly relished the telling. One can imagine that Arras viewed this scene with a sinking premonition of his future and had to struggle to mold his features to the proper cheerful aspect. Resentment at Burgundian condescension resonates in Eraso's remark about "coarse Castilian." It was sweet indeed that Philip's Spaniards were winning the struggle for Charles's heart and that Eraso should be there to break the news to the haughty courtiers.

Eraso also reported that he had sung Philip's praises widely in the governing circles of the Netherlands and assured Ruy Gómez "that the King enjoys here so great a reputation and such positive opinion that they desire nothing better than to see him here, and that he should govern them, and I think it is necessary [that he should]."[50] This seems a dubious proposition, and it is unlikely that either Eraso or Ruy Gómez were so taken in by their own propaganda as to believe that the Netherlanders awaited Philip with eagerness. More likely this claim was meant to bolster Philip's ego. As will be seen, Ruy Gómez de Silva was in the habit of showing Eraso's letters to Philip; part of the allies' game was, of course, to offer the prince proofs of their devotion, while simultaneously strengthening his confidence and resolve.

This campaign of encomiums for Philip was effective and incidentally helps to illuminate the nature of the alliance between Ruy Gómez and Eraso in the mid-1550s. Although the two men had corresponded for several years,[51] it is difficult to imagine that their bond was one of personal affection. Since they operated at two separate and widely removed courts, they cannot have met often nor spent a great deal of time together. Moreover, Eraso's personality was notoriously harsh and unpleasant.[52] Consonance of policy views might provide an explanation of their alliance, except that the correspondence between the two men in this period is seldom focused on large issues or ideology. Instead, it seems clear that the Eraso–Ruy Gómez entente was firmly based on the perception of mutual self-interest and mutual usefulness. Both were extremely ambitious, self-made men in ardent pursuit of royal favor and the power and wealth it could bring. And, in certain obvious ways, they could help each other while simultaneously helping themselves.

Ruy Gómez de Silva was extremely close to Philip, and the French ambassador in England deemed him "the person by whose judgment [the prince] was chiefly guided."[53] Philip's advancement could only mean an access in his own position and influence. In the waning years of Charles's reign, though, the rise of Ruy Gómez de Silva was structurally blocked. Despite his pleas he received no special favors from the emperor at the time of his marriage (and no other imperial *mercedes* have come to light). Thus it was very much in his interest to proclaim Philip's readiness to govern. Eraso, a strong voice at Charles V's court, could broadcast these advertisements for the prince (and, incidentally, for his *sumiller*[54]) where they would do the most good. Moreover, Ruy Gómez de Silva had little experience in administration or government. If he hoped to play a major role in affairs of state, he would need the guidance of an experienced ally within the bureaucracy. For protection in these tangled affairs of state, wrote Ruy Gómez, "I need Your Grace's shield and sword."[55]

In turn, Eraso stood to gain from Ruy Gómez's influence with Philip. The secretary, of undistinguished *hidalgo* origins, had served the emperor since 1523 but had attained a significant post only in 1546. In 1554 he was in his mid-forties. The course of his career, particularly its disgraceful latter stages, indicates that he was motivated by a greedy drive for power and wealth.[56] Already in 1557 the Venetian Badoero, perhaps confused but more likely punning, referred to him as Secretary "Crasso."[57] In many ways Eraso was a perfect example of one style of Habsburg bureaucrat, of what has been described as "the predatory, arrogant, avaricious secretary of the new age."[58] Eraso was hardly the man to go quietly into retirement at the peak of his long climb simply because Charles V chose to relinquish power. Moreover, Eraso nursed long-standing grudges against other powerful figures at the imperial court, including Arras, Juan de Figueroa and Gonzalo Pérez, who had for years scorned his abilities and obstructed his rise.[59] It was unlikely that he would gain satisfactory revenge while Charles ruled, since the emperor was a master at balancing and massaging the massive egos of his counselors. If, however, Eraso could gain a privileged foothold with the new king, all might be very different, and his former tormentors might find the tables turned. Better than any other member of the prince's entourage, Ruy Gómez could secure for the secretary a pledge of Philip's future favor.

A letter of 12 August 1554 illustrates well what Ruy Gómez de Silva could do for Francisco de Eraso. Ruy Gómez wrote:

> His Highness has seen your letters and was very glad to hear the news you sent me in them. By the way, I showed him [one letter in particular] . . . in order to be able to speak about you and see how he feels about you. I do not think he lacks desire to show you favor and keep you in your honorable position. Do not fail to make up your mind as to what you want, and I will see what can be done for you.[60]

This was not an isolated episode. A month later, for example, Ruy Gómez reported that "I showed Your Grace's letter to the king, and His Highness was not content to see just that one but demanded to read all the others as well."[61] These letters neatly illustrate what would always be the basis of Ruy Gómez's influence with Philip. In an early modern monarchy private access to the ruler was power: the favorite could set part of the agenda during his daily conversations with the prince and could turn the discussion to topics that aided his friends and harmed his enemies. Ruy Gómez once claimed that "I have never interfered in nor spoken about any matter that lies outside my métier, which is to dress His Highness in his jacket."[62] This seeming self-deprecation throws a thin veil over the possibilities inherent in such a relationship: a trusted favorite could furnish his master's mind even as he clothed his body.

The pro-Philippine campaign soon began to bear fruit. On 7 December 1554 one of the first crucial steps toward abdication was taken when Charles wrote to Philip praising the behavior that Eraso had described. The emperor urged his son to come to the Netherlands as soon as possible. Such a visit, which Charles had previously discouraged, was a necessary preliminary to the turnover of power.[63] Philip had been emboldened, perhaps by Eraso's glowing reports of his repute in the Low Countries, to press harder for permission to come to his father's court; in the meantime Charles had gained a better impression of his son's abilities.[64] No less than the emperor, the allies Ruy Gómez and Eraso must have been heartened by Philip's growing assertiveness in these months. In addition to expressing his desire to take a hand in Flemish affairs, Philip had begun to complain that the imperial court was not showing him proper deference in matters relating to his states of Naples and Milan.[65] The prince was clearly developing the temperament of a king.

Mainly because of the hopes aroused by Mary Tudor's false pregnancy,[66] Philip's journey to his father's court was delayed until September 1555. In the interim Ruy Gómez de Silva and Francisco de Eraso were entrusted with primary responsibility for maintaining communication between the two courts at London and Brussels. Ruy Gómez made three trips to Brussels at Philip's behest between December 1554 and August 1555. During the same period Eraso made the opposite journey at least twice. The two allies managed liaison between the courts as preparations went on for Philip's journey to the Netherlands and Charles's abdication. By March 1555 Arras was forced to entrust requests for favors from Philip to Ruy Gómez.[67]

One reason for Ruy Gómez de Silva's increasing prominence was that the duke of Alba was ordered away from Philip's court in the early months of 1555. The prince, asserting his sovereignty over Naples and Milan, ordered Alba to take up the government of Italy, which was being threatened by a French army.[68] William Maltby has interpreted this appointment as the result of an intrigue masterminded by Ruy Gómez, who stood to benefit from the removal of his rival. Maltby does not, however, explain just how Ruy Gómez managed this coup.[69] The surviving evidence does not allow certainty, but a plausible scenario of these events can be sketched. Contrary to Maltby's image of Alba accepting the bitter cup of command in Italy against his own inclinations and out of a sense of duty to his clientele and to the dynasty, it appears that Alba's own ego and ambitions propelled him into this assignment, with hardly a nudge from Ruy Gómez de Silva.[70]

What emerges from the diplomatic correspondence is that in the fall of 1554 and the ensuing winter there was a bitter competition for the appointment to command in Italy involving three principal claimants—Ferrante Gonzaga, Emmanuel Philibert, duke of Savoy, and the "reluctant" duke of Alba. The open jockeying began when Gonzaga, governor of Milan since 1546, appeared in the Netherlands in the fall, eager to dispel criticism of his administration and to solicit subsidies and rewards for his service. Rodríguez-Salgado suggests that Alba was behind the allegations of corruption leveled against Gonzaga in 1553, which would seem to weaken the case for the duke's disinterest. In October Gonzaga crossed to England to pay court to Philip and seek a vote of confidence for the continuance of his tenure at Milan.[71] Meanwhile, at the imperial court, conflict had arisen between Gonzaga and the duke of Savoy, whose principality was under French occupation and who desired the Milanese command for himself. Gonzaga returned to the Continent at the end of October, having been richly feted but promised nothing. Savoy journeyed to England to press his own claims at the end of the year.[72] Resolution of these conflicting claims posed a tricky problem for the emperor's servants, compounded by the fact that Philip had proclaimed his desire to make decisions concerning Italy for himself. Still, Arras had not internalized this latter fact, and he encouraged the merry chase of the claimants to London as a means of buying time for the emperor to make a decision on the choice of a commander.[73]

It would appear that Alba's appetite for preferment was further piqued by the parade of contestants through London. By lavishing attention on Ferrante Gonzaga during his October visit, Ruy Gómez de Silva may have played a part in exciting Alba's jealousy and interest. Alba's temperament was not such as to view with equanimity displays of favor toward another captain. Moreover, his family had extensive interests in Italy. In any case, Alba was complaining of boredom in England and lobbying Philip for the command at least by late November.[74] By the end of the year Philip was determined to entrust Alba with unprecedentedly broad powers in the peninsula, but the emperor continued to balk, in part from distrust of Alba and also to avoid shabby treatment of his longtime comrade Gonzaga. The public decision on the post was thus postponed until late February, when, with apparent concurrence between Charles and Philip, it was granted to Alba. Still, Charles did not sign Alba's commissions until April.[75] This turn of events clearly outraged Gonzaga and allegedly disgusted Italian opinion, but it also provided a solution for several outstanding problems.[76] The rivalry between Gonzaga and Savoy had made it impossible to appoint either of them without offending the other's supporters and thus sowing discord among pro-imperial elements in northern Italy at the very moment of a serious French threat.[77] The choice of Alba posed the risk of offending all Italian opinion but allowed pacification of the other rivals on relatively equal terms. Savoy's disappointment was allayed by the offer of the government of Flanders and by imperial support for a grand match with the duchess of Lorraine.[78] Gonzaga, whose potential disaffection was a less serious threat to Spanish interests (but perhaps of greater personal concern to the emperor), was first threatened with disgrace if he did not step aside and then fobbed off with cash and praise. The case that Alba openly competed for the Italian command is reinforced by the evidence of Gonzaga's lasting enmity toward the duke and also by the fact that he demanded compensation for the loss of his governorship in the form of Alba's post as *mayordomo mayor* in Philip's household. This demand was rejected, and Gonzaga had to content himself with a variety of gifts and subsidies, the promise of prestigious lodgings in the palace, and vague assurances that he stood next in line for a major military post.[79]

Another problem was resolved by the despatch of Alba to Italy. The presence of the imperious duke in England had become an irritant to Philip and indirectly a threat to the success of the pro-Philippine campaign of the prince's allies. This is the import of Ruy Gómez's letter to Eraso of 15 April 1555, which is cited by Maltby as his principal evidence of an intrigue against Alba. For reasons that will emerge, however, this letter can be regarded as a relatively straightforward account of events, rather than as the hypocritical poison-pen missive that it appears to Maltby.

In the letter Ruy Gómez de Silva claims to write on Philip's behalf in order to apprise Eraso of the prince's fears regarding Alba's probable behavior when he reaches Brussels on his way to Italy. "You are to know," he wrote,

> that the Duke, after having thrown himself at the King's [Philip's] feet, as I told you, in order to secure these appointments, now that he has attained them asserts that he is being made to take them, complaining in every quarter that he is not being treated according to his deserts. In all this, he uses his accustomed skillful arguments in order to draw the water to his own mill. . . . As for the Duke's interests, the King says he has got away with more than there was any good reason to give him.[80]

Still, Alba had complained bitterly about "the scanty favour that is shown him," even though he had received about 40,000 ducats for his services in England. Eraso needed to know the truth in order to be able to counter Alba's laments at the imperial court.[81] Beyond this, there was reason to fear that Alba would try to destroy the image of Philip's competence as a ruler that had been so painstakingly fostered by the allies:

> The King says that the Duke may intimate that affairs in England are not being handled with all due care. As for this, the King remarks that he has not wished to conclude certain business before having got the Duke out of this country, because he, his friends and his wife have permitted themselves to say that once the Duke had left everything would go to ruin, he having been the mainstay in all these matters and the King not being equally vigilant. As they have been talking like this here in the King's Court it is quite possible that they will do the same when they reach the Emperor's, and if everything that had to be accomplished had been terminated before the Duke left, he would have been able to attribute all the merit to himself. Therefore, the King decided to wait until the Duke was out of the way, although the Duke greatly insisted, again and again. This is what the King wishes me to write to you, begging you to take particular care to keep him informed of what happens.[82]

Ruy Gómez also feared a personal attack:

> Now that the Duke has spoken to me about the appointments to Naples and Milan . . . and has assured me that he is eternally obliged to me for them, I am afraid that when he sees his Majesty [Charles], he may not treat me as tenderly as he is accustomed to do. . . . Therefore I implore you to do what you can to protect me, for I certainly am afraid of him. He is a dead shot.[83]

This letter would seem to clarify several points about Alba's appointment. The duke had lobbied for the position and had enlisted Ruy Gómez to help his candidacy with Philip.[84] At the same time Alba's behavior, particularly his tendency to claim the credit for all achievements, had rankled the prince. Philip's desire to be rid of an overweening adviser surely was a major factor in the decision to give Alba his desired appointment. Alba's departure from England was by no means unwelcome to Ruy Gómez de Silva, but it is difficult to see in this situation the clear-cut intrigue against Alba posited by Maltby. The further charge, lately resurrected by Maltby, that Ruy Gómez and Eraso conspired to deprive Alba of adequate funds during his Italian tenure,[85] is still less tenable. The evidence cited for this purported deprivation—"an act of irresponsibility bordering on treason," according to Maltby—comes above all from Alba's letters. As any reader of the *Epistolario* can attest, the duke never ceased to complain about his finances in the most bitter terms; surely this evidence must be taken with a grain of salt. In addition, although Eraso was very much involved in disbursements in the period of Alba's tenure in Italy, Ruy Gómez de Silva had no official position in the financial bureaucracy until 1557, near the end of the duke's viceregal term. Moreover, Maltby produces no evidence of collusion between Ruy Gómez de Silva and Eraso on this matter, despite his contention that these allies plotted to deny Alba the wherewithal to defend the king's interests in Italy. To the contrary, the most recent study argues that Eraso was more Alba's victim than vice versa and that neither he nor Ruy Gómez could possibly have controlled all of the persons and institutions responsible for remittances to the duke. It would seem more logical and more just to analyze Alba's problems, insofar as the duke's complaints had foundation, in terms of the increasingly straitened circumstances of the Crown finances. Throughout the monarchy in those years, royal obligations far exceeded the capacity of the treasury.[86] Ruy Gómez himself provides eloquent witness to this financial strain: "More money we must have though it cost us the very blood in our veins," he exclaimed in December 1554. "May God cradle our affairs in His hands, since we no longer know how to hold anything in our own."[87]

Faulty interpretation on these points is primarily the result of the unfounded belief that the bitter enmities between Philip's advisers that emerged later in the reign were fully developed in the period prior to Charles V's abdication.[88] A great deal has been written on the topic of the struggle of factions led by Ruy Gómez de Silva and the duke of Alba at the court of Philip II. There is abundant evidence that deep divisions within Philip's Council of State became clearly delineated in the first years after the emperor's abdication and thereafter played a major role in politics. One must be careful, however, not to project too far back in time the sharp rift and personal venom between the king's principal counselors that pervaded the court in the late 1550s. The phenomenon that truly polarized the court—the elaboration and intensification of animosity between Ruy Gómez de Silva and the duke of Alba—postdated the period of Philip's sojourn in England.

Maltby argues plausibly that even before 1550 Alba was "a true *caudillo,* a soldier with a large political following." He was the head of an old and wealthy family, whose members were well positioned in the church, the military and at court. But no such case can be made for Ruy Gómez's influence, at least outside the court, despite Maltby's contention that "by the 1550s his following equalled that of Alba." Maltby relies on the dubious theory that, by virtue of his marriage, Ruy Gómez de Silva somehow became the political head of the Mendoza family.[89] No evidence exists to support this notion. Moreover, even were it true, this clan leadership would have been of little use to Ruy Gómez during Philip's stay in England. While Alba could count on the support of kinsmen and friends at both of the northern courts, few members of the putative Mendoza network had come to England with Philip or were in Flanders with Charles. Insofar as Ruy Gómez had a functional clique in this period, it consisted of Eraso and perhaps Diego de Vargas in Brussels and the count of Feria in England. None of these men can plausibly be associated with the Mendoza clan; nor, more important, is there any evidence that they regarded Ruy Gómez as their chief rather than as their ally. In more ways than one, Ruy Gómez de Silva was alone with Philip during the English sojourn.[90]

And that—his relationship with Philip—was of course the basis of his influence. In fact until 1555 and formally until Philip formed his own Council of State in 1556, Ruy Gómez's position was strictly that of a favorite and an informal "household councilor."[91] Alba, on the other hand, was a true counselor of state, a man of wide experience and stature throughout the monarchy. He was the emperor's adviser and could believe, with some justification, that Charles had given him a commission to oversee Philip's affairs. Ruy Gómez, the friend and valet of the prince, shone only by virtue of the latter's reflected glow. Until Philip was king the two men were not overt rivals for the directing hand in affairs of state. Their competition prior to Philip's accession was essentially limited to the sphere of the household, where both had been officials since 1548. Even there, Alba held the senior post of *mayordomo mayor.*

It may be presumed from his collusion with Eraso, and it became abundantly clear later, that Ruy Gómez de Silva had aspirations to act as a major figure in government as well as in the household. Before the formation of Philip's Council of State, however, Alba could not (and could not justly be expected to) regard as a serious competitor a man so far beneath him in lineage and station, a man who, moreover, had no experience or official status as an officer of government. On the contrary, Alba seems to have regarded Ruy Gómez as a useful conduit to the prince and as a potential ally. This is borne out by the fact that before and during his tenure in Italy Alba wrote repeated friendly letters to Ruy Gómez de Silva, relating the news and asking for favors and intercession with Philip.[92] In Carande's words, Alba saw Ruy Gómez de Silva as "su confidente cerca de don Felipe."[93] The surviving evidence reveals that Alba's civility was reciprocated by Ruy Gómez.[94] Of course, the good faith that underlay this apparent cordiality must not be overestimated. Certainly Ruy Gómez sought to become a power in the state as well as the household, and an increase in his influence would necessarily come at the expense of Alba, among others. Moreover, as was seen above, Ruy Gómez was critical of Alba's character and motives in his letters to Eraso. On 6 June 1555 he went further and denounced Alba to Eraso as "a great rogue."[95] Nevertheless, the fact remains that in these final months of Philip's apprenticeship the relationship between the future rivals was free of public animosity. The clash of factions had not yet emerged. Alba, who had a substantial clientele, was seemingly unaware of any need to direct it against Ruy Gómez de Silva, who as yet had no grand following of his own. This situation, however, would be altered drastically during Alba's tenure in Italy. Although it cannot be demonstrated that Ruy Gómez orchestrated the duke's appointment as viceroy, there can be no doubt that he exploited the opportunity afforded by Alba's absence.

Alba's biographer, on uncertain evidence, argues that by late 1554 the duke was Philip's "chief spokesman" and had "assumed the dominant role" in Spanish policymaking in England.[96] At least that Alba believed this to be the case may be inferred from Ruy Gómez's letter quoted above. There is in fact little reason to believe that any of the Spaniards played a considerable role in English affairs. Philip himself and Simon Renard had the ear of the queen, who was the only effective instrument of Habsburg influence. The few Spanish counselors who remained were handicapped by their unpopularity with the populace and by their undoubtedly shaky understanding of English politics.[97] Among them only the count of Feria and perhaps Ruy Gómez could speak English at all.[98] Despite a recent charge that his ignorant advice harmed Philip in his relations with the English, Ruy Gómez seems at least to have gotten along well with some of the English aristocrats, notably Charles Lord Howard of Effingham, and he won a prize from the queen's hand in a joust on 4 December 1554.[99]

All in all, though, Alba, Ruy Gómez de Silva and the rest of the band of Spaniards who remained with Philip seem to have stood on the sidelines of English affairs. Their principal role was to provide Philip with companionship and to handle his communications with Brussels. Ruy Gómez played an important part on both counts from the outset of the stay in England; and once Alba was gone, he was indisputably the most active of Philip's advisers. As noted above, he made repeated trips to the Continent on the prince's business. Important correspondence from Brussels was routed to Philip through him. On 23 August 1555, for example, Arras wrote Ruy Gómez regarding the state of military affairs in Flanders. "I wished to inform you of what was happening," Arras concluded, "in order that you might report to the King and making sure that you will do this I am not writing to him."[100] Ruy Gómez still had no formal position outside his household office[101] but clearly was regarded as a de facto minister of state. Ruy Gómez also managed the arrangements for Philip's departure from England in September 1555. At the final stage he had six ships outfitted in Calais and returned with them to Dover, where he met Philip and a sizable English retinue. Despite fears of French mischief the royal crossing was made without incident on 4 September 1555.[102]

Thereafter events moved swiftly, and with them the trajectory of Ruy Gómez's ascent. Once Philip arrived in the Low Countries the complex process of Charles's abdication was set in motion. On 26 September 1555 the emperor issued orders for the Estates-General and the leading officials of the Netherlands to convene in Brussels in the following month. Before this assembly, on 25 October, Charles turned his title to rule in the Low Countries over to Philip. Much less ceremony attended Philip's investiture as king of Castile, Aragon and Sicily on 16 January 1556. Charles simply handed the acts of abdication for the Spanish crowns to Francisco de Eraso. This was strangely fitting, in light of the efforts made by Eraso and Ruy Gómez de Silva to clear the way for Philip's elevation. Over the next few months Charles divested the remainder of his hereditary territories. Without clear authority to do so, the emperor made Philip and his heirs perpetual vicars of the Italian lands of the Holy Roman Empire in March 1556. The Franche-Comté was made over to Philip on 10 June. Power in the empire (and in 1558 the imperial dignity itself) went to Charles's brother Ferdinand.[103]

Having received his patrimony, Philip II set about to organize his government. The king chose to revive as a key institution of government the Council of State, which his father had reduced to an honorific and inactive body.[104] Philip named his councilors of State shortly after his assumption of the Spanish crowns in early 1556. Ruy Gómez de Silva was one of the dozen or so men from throughout Philip's lands elevated to the council.[105] The choice of councilors was doubtless dictated by several considerations. Some names—Ferrante Gonzaga, Andrea Doria—were included primarily as a nod to the honor of men whose loyalty, rather than their advice, was crucial to the new king. The bulk of the list, however, reveals an attempt to forge a unified ruling institution comprising, on the one hand, the principal advisers inherited from the previous reign and, on the other, the key figures among Philip's own men, primarily officers of his household. The outstanding members of the first group were Alba, Arras, the duke of Savoy and Don Juan de Figueroa. Among the second were Ruy Gómez de Silva, Don Antonio de Toledo, the count of Feria and a rather surprising choice, the obscure Gutierre López de Padilla, one of the king's *mayordomos* and identified by Cabrera de Córdoba as a friend and client of Ruy Gómez.[106] The council was rounded out with men who had caught Philip's eye as good administrators or diplomats—Don Bernardino de Mendoza, skilled in naval and financial affairs, Don Juan Manrique de Lara, who had been ambassador at Rome, and the count of Chinchón, a man who was to rise steadily for decades in Philip's service and estimation.

While Philip II governed from Brussels in 1556 and 1557 six of these men emerged as the true Council of State. Ruy Gómez de Silva, Mendoza, Arras, Feria, Manrique and Don Antonio de Toledo met twice daily (in the mornings until noon and again from 2:00 P.M. until dark) to debate the principal affairs of state. Ruy Gómez seems to have been the principal minister, a situation underlined by the fact that the meetings of the council were often held in his lodgings.[107] Thus Ruy Gómez had gained a lofty position in the mechanism of state to complement his personal influence with the king. At the same time his ally Eraso had been promoted to a position of power unrivaled among the secretaries, who actually transacted the business of government. Along with his constitution of a Council of State, Philip had reshuffled secretarial appointments. Eraso emerged as secretary of Finance (*Hacienda*) and of the patronage bureau, the Cámara de Castilla, as well as secretary to the administrative Councils of Inquisition, Orders and Indies.[108] His ally Ruy Gómez must indeed have put in a good word for him, and the secretary had reason to be well pleased. His position allowed him to sit in on meetings of the Council of State and to have a major voice in a wide range of policy decisions, as well as giving him tremendous influence in the granting of state patronage and of the *encomiendas* of the military orders. Now he could truly act upon his predisposition to enrich himself, aid his friends and harm his enemies.[109]

Nor could Ruy Gómez de Silva complain about the preferment shown him by Philip. Despite its prestige and attendant power, the position of councilor of State carried no stipend, while the relatively small allowance he received as *sumiller de corps* was mostly earmarked for entertainment expenses.[110] Philip II soon made good this deficiency. In February 1556, at Antwerp, the king granted Ruy Gómez the town of Eboli, in the southern Italian principality of Salerno.[111] The revenues of the town, 1,958 Neapolitan ducats per year, were granted to Ruy Gómez to make up the shortfall in the 3,000 ducats per year promised to the estate of Mélito by Charles V.[112] At this point no title was attached to the grant. Badoero reported that "Don Ruy Gómez . . . does not call himself Duke [of Eboli], but is addressed by the title of Excellency."[113]

In March 1556 Ruy Gómez was favored with the grant of the *encomienda* of Herrera in the Order of Alcántara. Eraso as secretary in charge of the patronage of the orders countersigned the king's gift, and Ruy Gómez was invested with his new and lucrative *encomienda* in a ceremony at a Brussels monastery on 7 April.[114] Both his political position and his economic position were further enhanced on 30 January 1557, when Philip II named him *contador mayor* of Castile and the Indies.[115] In this position, Ruy Gómez stood (along with the two other *contadores mayores*) at the top of the financial administration of the Castilian sphere of the monarchy. Some of his duties and activities in this post will be examined in the next chapter. As *contador mayor* he also enjoyed a small salary and more substantial dues (*derechos*) amounting to more than 531,000 *maravedís* (1,416 ducats) per year.[116]

Thus the efforts of Ruy Gómez de Silva and Francisco de Eraso to bring about the abdication of Charles V and the accession of their "master," Philip II, paid rich dividends as soon as the new reign began. Through the grateful patronage of Philip II the allies gained preponderant positions in the councils and the financial administration. They received new honors, incomes and salaries in addition to the personal financial opportunities presented by their offices. Still, victory had not been total. Philip had not seen fit to dispense entirely with the trusted counselors of Charles V. Once Philip announced the composition of his Council of State, Arras was able to drop the pretense, adopted in the period of the abdication, that he hoped to retire to his estates. The bishop remained an active member of the government. Nevertheless, he was not trusted or consulted by Philip as he had been by Charles, and increasingly his influence was restricted to the internal government of the Netherlands, where he served as chief adviser to Savoy, the governor.[117] According to the Venetian ambassador, Ruy Gómez de Silva was disappointed that Arras retained even these vestiges of his former influence.[118] Alba had also been granted a seat on the Council of State, but, absent in Italy, he had little say in the central administration in the first years of the reign. Upon his return the duke would find that Ruy Gómez had grown into a serious rival indeed. Alba's dismay at finding another man ensconced in what he believed to be his rightful position as first minister would touch off the personal and factional conflict of the late 1550s and 1560s.[119]

Ruy Gómez de Silva and Eraso were Philip's men, and as such they won great advancement at the outset of the reign. Nevertheless Philip, though still young, was already in many respects the Prudent King. He was willing to exalt his own creatures over his father's counselors, but he refused to place his government entirely and irrevocably in the hands of the allies who had served him so well. Old counselors, men of experience and now clearly rivals of the upstarts, were kept in the wings to provide the king with a check against domination by the men he had elevated. Ruy Gómez de Silva had extended his sphere of influence from the household to the halls of government; now he would have to maintain his position at the pinnacle of Philip's administration. The supplanted counselors stood ready to topple him, and they were soon joined by younger men on the make. In his turn, Ruy Gómez de Silva would find that staying on top could be just as difficult as climbing.

4

The *Privado*

Ruy Gómez de Silva stood at the height of his ascendancy in the first years of the reign of Philip II. As the king's *sumiller de corps* he enjoyed constant private access to Philip. His voice was dominant in the Council of State, largely because his special personal relationship with the king was widely acknowledged. Meanwhile, as *contador mayor*, Ruy Gómez aggregated supervision over the Crown's finances to his privileged position in policymaking and the royal household. In reporting to the doge and Senate regarding his tenure in Brussels in 1556 and 1557, the Venetian ambassador Federico Badoero graphically described the extent of Ruy Gómez's supremacy among the advisers of Philip II:

> [T]he main title that everyone gives him is that of *rey* [king] *Gómez*, in place of Ruy Gómez, since it seems that no one has ever been so privy with a prince of such great power, nor as well beloved by his lord as he [Ruy Gómez] is by His Catholic Majesty.[1]

In these first years of the reign Ruy Gómez attained the status of a true *privado;* his role as a friend and private *hombre de confianza* of the king burst forth beyond the personal sphere of the household to encompass a substantial role in the public exercise of kingship. He was the only true *privado* of the reign of Philip II, or indeed of the entire sixteenth century in Spain.

The *privanza*, in the sense of the combination in one person of unmatched royal favor and a principal role in government, had been a common feature of the late medieval Castilian monarchy. The weak kings of the fifteenth century, notably John II and Henry IV, were accustomed to govern through all-powerful favorites (or, alternatively, were powerless to govern without them). The perception that *privados* like Alvaro de Luna ruled the country in their own interest rather than that of the Crown was a critical precipitant of the civil wars that wracked Castile until the end of the 1470s. Because of this, and also because they delighted in active kingship, neither the Catholic Kings nor Charles V had revived the institution of the *privanza*. The personal favorites of these monarchs had for the most part been restricted to a private role in the household, while the tasks of governance fell increasingly to secretaries who were the king's servants rather than his friends.[2]

The preeminent position of Ruy Gómez de Silva at the outset of the reign of Philip II thus amounted to a partial reversal of a trend toward more impersonal and bureaucratic administration. The king's dual personality—as a man and as a ruler—was reintegrated in the public sphere in the person of Ruy Gómez. The source of the *privado*'s power lay in the perception that he spoke and acted for the king, as a physical extension and indeed substitute for the royal presence. This concept of the *privanza* was later clearly institutionalized in the form of the *valimiento* conferred by the seventeenth-century Habsburgs on their favorites. Philip III, for instance, decreed in 1612 that the written or verbal orders of his *privado,* the duke of Lerma, would enjoy binding force utterly equivalent to his own royal signature or pronouncements. Thereby a royal alter ego was legally created.[3]

Philip II never went so far as to define the status of his *privado,* and indeed, after the first decade or so of his reign, the king seems to have rejected the notion of a *privanza* altogether. By the late 1560s Philip's ruling style revealed sure signs of a return to government through personal direction of secretaries whose private relationship with the monarch was thoroughly circumscribed. Philip's initial reliance on a *privado* and subsequent retreat from the *privanza* delimited the contours of Ruy Gómez's public career after 1556. The king's personality and manner of governance evolved and matured over the course of the first decade of his reign, first creating and later closing off political opportunities for his favorite.

We are accustomed to envisioning Philip II as a fixed and timeless personality, the Prudent King ensconced in his study at the Escorial, coldly and purposefully directing a grand plan to make Spain the arbiter of a re-Catholicized northern Europe. To the degree that it is accurate at all, however, this vision of the "Spider of the Escorial" holds true only for the last decades of the reign. The confident and aggressive monarch who set in motion the Invincible Armada and risked all the formidable resources of his monarchy in a reckless bid to upset the French succession must be contrasted with a very different younger self. The mature Philip was single-minded, supremely sure of himself, and voracious in his appetite for the exercise of power. When he came to the throne, however, Philip II was a diffident young man, a somewhat timid son awed by the example of a legendarily bold and omnicompetent father. Perceptive foreign observers agreed on this point. Philip's disposition was "phlegmatic and melancholic," his constitution "extremely delicate"; he was physically weak, slept a great deal and detested vigorous activity. When confronted with a crisis, the king exhibited "a rather timid spirit" and despite his intelligence and ability to comprehend complex issues, "did not possess the vigor and liveliness for the measures requisite to the good government of so many kingdoms and cities." Philip was constitutionally

> more inclined to tranquillity than to action, more to repose than to labor. Consequently, even though he is of an age at which ordinarily are manifested bellicose enthusiasms and insatiable desires for glory and power, up 'til now all of the efforts of His Majesty have been directed, not at the warlike expansion of his estates but rather at their conservation through peace.[4]

It was also reported in these years that the king, although unfailingly courteous and regal in bearing, found it difficult to converse on matters of substance. He disliked going out in public and preferred "to stay in his room speaking of private matters with a few favorites." In conferences with ambassadors and ministers, Philip remained aloof and gave little indication of his own views on the matters under discussion.[5]

Geoffrey Parker has remarked of Philip's early years as king that "for some time he continued to stand in the shadow of his father." Throughout 1556 this paternal presence was physical, since Charles remained in Brussels until the end of the year, intermittently intervening in his son's government.[6] Thereafter the emperor's influence, though intangible, was no less real. Philip took to heart his father's written instructions and precepts of government. From them he absorbed a strong sense of the responsibilities of kingship and an exalted notion of the standard set for him by the emperor. He also seems to have attempted to comply with Charles's advice that as king he should trust no one and should dissemble his own feelings and opinions, always reserving the right to make decisions contrary to the advice of his counselors.[7]

Conflicts thus arose between the king's natural timidity and diffidence and his ingrained commitment to active, responsible kingship. Philip's shyness, which rendered him awkward in public, in combination with his suspicion of others (both innate and encouraged by his father), made it impossible for the king to attend to his duties in the gregarious personal style that had suited the emperor.[8] Moreover, Philip rejected the incessant itinerancy that had characterized the reigns of Ferdinand the Catholic and, especially, of Charles V; he insisted that "traveling about one's kingdoms is neither useful nor decent."[9] In the long run Philip resolved these contradictions by developing a method of ruling through the written word rather than through personal contact and debate. The capacities and inclinations that would eventually make Philip the "king of paper"[10] were evident from his youth. "It was well said of him," Merriman reports, "that from his childhood days he preferred to communicate by writing rather than by word of mouth." Already in the first years of the reign, the king's propensity for secluded reading and study had been remarked by the Venetian Badoero.[11] Even as late as his mid-thirties, though, the king still lapsed into lethargy at times, unable to force himself to attend to the daily press of paperwork.[12]

As a young king, then, Philip II was a shy, passive, sedentary man miscast in a regal role that for forty years had been played by the active and extroverted Charles V. It would take Philip more than a decade to perfect his own governing system as the secretary-king ruling far-flung dominions with pen and ink alone. In the meantime Ruy Gómez de Silva acted as the king's eyes, ears and voice. While Philip for the most part held back, aloof from public contacts and personal direction of affairs, his *privado* traveled for him, spoke for him, and presided over the Council of State in his place.

Philip's unease with his regal position was exacerbated in the late 1550s by a sense of geographical displacement. He never felt comfortable outside Spain,[13] but the momentum of events conspired to keep him in northern Europe for three and one-half years after his accession. Although Spanish hopes for the future of the English alliance were permanently dimmed by the disappointment of Mary Tudor's false pregnancy (1555), Philip remained obliged to pay some attention to his wife's affairs. It was war rather than love, however, that truly compelled his continued presence in the north. Despite the king's attempts to forestall hostilities by concluding the Truce of Vaucelles with France in early 1556, general conflict erupted in the first year of the reign. Further negotiations between Ruy Gómez de Silva and the constable of France (Anne de Montmorency) broke down in July 1556, primarily because of French intransigence. Pope Paul IV, chiefly infuriated that Philip had opposed his election, offered dire provocations that led to the invasion of the Papal States by Spanish forces under Alba in September 1556. The truce with France wholly evaporated at the end of the year, when Henry II allowed the duke of Guise to lead a French army across the Alps to aid the pope, who was essentially defenseless in the face of Alba's army. The war spread to the north with Henry's declaration of war at the end of January 1557.[14]

The outbreak of war was the occasion of a major diplomatic and financial mission entrusted to Ruy Gómez de Silva. On 2 February 1557 Philip instructed his *privado* to undertake a journey to England and thence to Spain. In England Ruy Gómez was to convey a written message from Philip to the queen and to inform her verbally of the king's plans to visit the island. (Philip landed, on what was to be his final visit to England, on 18 March 1557 and stayed until 6 July 1557.[15]) He was also to inform Mary of the provocations of the pope and the king of France and of the measures Philip proposed to take in response. Ruy Gómez was to encourage the course of events that Philip expected—that the English would also break with France— primarily by taking William, Lord Paget into his confidence and urging Paget to prepare the ground so that the king would find English aid forthcoming upon his arrival.[16]

Ruy Gómez de Silva left the Netherlands for England early in February 1557. Presumably he accomplished his mission at Mary Tudor's court with dispatch, since he wrote from Greenwich on 16 February that he was leaving to go on to Spain. Philip II had ordered a ship prepared to convey Ruy Gómez from England to Iberia, and it landed (probably at Laredo) in early March. Ruy Gómez arrived in Valladolid at the court of the regent, Princess Juana, on 10 March 1557.[17] There, aided by his *criado* Gutierre López de Padilla,[18] he set about the principal tasks assigned to him by the king. Ruy Gómez's main mission was to arrange and expedite the provision of men and money from Castile for the military campaigns that would have to be undertaken against the French in Flanders and Italy. The widening conflict demanded increased support from the peninsula. Ruy Gómez's official appointment as *contador mayor de Castilla*, designed to give him authority to command the fiscal apparatus in Spain, was granted on 30 January 1557,[19] the very day Henry II declared war. The power of the *privado* qua *privado* declined in proportion to Ruy Gómez's distance from the king; an appropriate official appointment could be expected to bolster his informal prestige in his dealings with Castilian officials and notables.

The Crown's Spanish finances were in a wretched state at the beginning of 1557.[20] The extravagant borrowing undertaken to support Charles V's initiatives and campaigns in the 1550s burdened the treasury with short- and medium-term debt of nearly seven million ducats by the end of 1556.[21] Service on these debts consumed that portion of the revenues of Castile which was not already pledged to the holders of long-term *juros*.[22] In December 1554 a Castilian treasury official had calculated that revenues would fall short of required debt payments by at least 4,300,000 ducats over the period 1555–1560, and by 1556 all predicted revenues through 1560 had been committed in advance.[23] By 1557 the outlook was even worse. The debt had continued to increase, while Castilian revenues had suffered a severe blow from Pope Paul IV's revocation (effective in 1556) of the *cruzada* and *subsidio* collected under papal dispensation from the Spanish church. Now, to compound these problems, Philip II had to have large sums from Castile in 1557 in order to meet the expense of warfare, since none of his other kingdoms was willing to provide significant subsidies. Thus he sent Ruy Gómez de Silva to extract the needed revenue through a variety of expedients; meanwhile, as Ruy Gómez reached Spain, the king himself set in motion the grandest expedients of all, by ordering a rescheduling of debts to the Crown's creditors and further by directing the officials of the Casa de Contratación in Seville to confiscate all treasure arriving from the Indies for private persons.[24]

While in Spain Ruy Gómez de Silva was to make sure that the

revenues released by the rescheduling or suspension of payments were expeditiously dispatched to the fronts in Flanders and Italy. Philip's orders were blunt: he instructed his *privado* that, immediately upon arrival, "you are to insist with the Princess [regent] that before anything else she should order the drafting and dispatch of the decrees necessary" to effect the transfer of the bullion confiscated at Seville to the agent (Agustín de Santander), who would move it to northern ports for transshipment to Flanders.[25] The king needed these funds—he specified a sum of one and one-half million ducats—in a hurry: "In the matter of the money, you must lose neither an hour nor a speck of time, since more rides on this than on all the rest."[26] Ruy Gómez was ordered to dispense with the time-consuming task of assaying the treasure and instead to send two Spanish metal-founders to the Netherlands along with the bullion. Philip suggested that it might also save time to send the money in up to three discrete shipments, rather than waiting for the whole amount to be collected at the port.[27] Meanwhile, Ruy Gómez was to ensure that an additional 600,000 ducats were transferred from Seville to Barcelona and from there to Italy to meet the needs of Alba's army. Philip assigned his *privado* an additional responsibility in connection with this shipment. En route to Italy the bullion would be transported from Castile into the Crown of Aragon, and Ruy Gómez de Silva had to make sure that the viceroy of Catalonia was apprised of this transfer in advance, so that he could arrange with the customs officials to forgo collecting duties on the treasure. "Since it is our own Hacienda," the king wrote, "it is not necessary to do this [i.e., collect the customs]."[28] This directive affords a sharp glimpse into the peculiar federal structure of the Spanish monarchy. In effect, Philip II ordered his adviser and plenipotentiary to order one of his proconsuls to order some of his customs officials not to collect his duties on his own money being transferred between his realms. One suspects that Philip saw nothing strange in this unwieldy process. It is in a way impressive that the king remembered this detail, which was but one of a myriad of complications that had to be borne in mind in order to rule his dominions effectively.

Besides money the king needed soldiers and warships, and Ruy Gómez was directed to see to the provision of both. Castile was to provide eight thousand troops and the rations for their trip to the north; in addition, a fleet of thirty ships was to be assembled at

Laredo. Divided into two squadrons, the fleet would ferry the bullion and the soldiers from Cantabria to the channel ports. Overall supervision of this mobilization fell to Ruy Gómez. One of his principal tasks was to arrange for the victualing of the fleet on its runs between Spain and the north. He was empowered to arrange for the commercial transfer of grain from southern England to Laredo to provision the fleet, if this proved viable.[29] Although the actual victualing arrangements have not come to light, the suggestion that English wheat might be brought to Laredo more economically than Castilian grain gives an interesting indication of contemporary perceptions of the relative costs and convenience of sea and land transport for bulky goods.

The king also asked Ruy Gómez de Silva to visit Charles V in his retreat at Yuste, in order to deliver a letter and to put Charles in the picture regarding the affairs of the monarchy. This aspect of the mission was complicated by Philip's evident insecurity; he wanted his *privado* to convince the retired emperor to resume an active political role in this crisis. Ruy Gómez should implore Charles V, "supplicating most urgently and humbly

> that His Majesty might be inclined to exert himself in this conjuncture, aiding and assisting me not just with his opinion and advice (which is the greatest resource I can enjoy), but also with the presence of his person and authority, leaving the monastery [of Yuste] for whatever place may be most amenable to his health and the business at hand, dealing with such affairs as may arise by the means that cost him least affliction. [This is critical] since the common good may well depend on his decisions, for once the world learns of his resolution I am quite sure that my enemies will greatly alter their conduct in these affairs.[30]

This instruction provides a revealing glimpse of Philip's psychological state at the outset of the first great crisis of his reign. Clearly the king thought his own authority a laughable deterrent to his adversaries, while on the other hand his father's merest exertion would cause all Europe to tremble. Despite his vested authority, the king's self-image remained that of a mummer disguised in the oversized robes of the emperor.

Ruy Gómez de Silva spent about ten days in Valladolid, consulting with the princess regent and setting the financial machinery in motion, before embarking on the rather arduous journey to Yuste.

Toward the end of March he stayed with the emperor for several days, presenting Philip's plea for help. The tone of these meetings may have been awkward, since both men doubtless recalled the strenuous efforts of Ruy Gómez and Eraso to convince Charles of his son's independence and competence to govern alone. In any case, the emperor staunchly refused to leave his retreat. Charles did grudgingly assent to another of Philip's requests: he postponed the formal renunciation of his imperial title pending the outcome of the year's campaigns in Flanders and Italy. Philip had feared that a complete transfer of power in the Empire would erode his authority in these nominally imperial territories.[31]

Although Ruy Gómez de Silva was unable to convince the emperor to come out of retirement, he did obtain Charles V's counsel on a number of pressing matters. The presidency of the Council of Castile was vacant, and in Valladolid Ruy Gómez had begun to urge that Don Juan de Vega, the former viceroy of Sicily, be elevated to fill the vacancy. The emperor concurred in this choice, and Vega got the post, to the severe annoyance of the marquis of Mondéjar, who had openly campaigned for the appointment.[32] Ruy Gómez's role in the selection of Vega incidentally provides a refutation of the argument that he was the court patron of the house of Mendoza, since in 1557 Mondéjar was the most visible representative of that house.[33]

Another issue was determined in the consultations at Yuste. Philip had hoped that Ruy Gómez might bring Don Carlos, the eleven-year-old crown prince, back to the Netherlands with him. There the prince could gain experience of statecraft and firsthand knowledge of his future territories. It is also possible (Cabrera, at least, believed so) that the king had heard rumors of a budding "romance" between his son and his widowed sister the Princess Juana (born 1535), and that he wanted to remove Don Carlos from the temptations of this inconvenient attachment. In any case the emperor convinced Ruy Gómez that the time was not yet ripe for Don Carlos's debut on the world stage. The young man remained too willful and disorderly. Ruy Gómez likely had already observed the prince's behavior for himself. He dropped the notion of taking Don Carlos to the Netherlands; instead, he busied himself in a search for new guardians and tutors for the prince, men who could ensure that the youth "might observe actions and pictures that elevate his spirit with thoughts and deeds of majesty [and] that will generously stimulate him to grandeur, glory and triumphs."[34] The new tutors, in common with those they succeeded and others yet to come, were to enjoy little success in improving the mind and character of their pathetic charge.

Upon leaving the emperor at Yuste Ruy Gómez de Silva turned his attention to what was perhaps the most sensitive and difficult aspect of his mission in Spain in 1557. During Philip's absence from Spain the privileged orders of the realm had become increasingly uncooperative and belligerent in their attitudes toward agents of the royal fisc. This was particularly true of the high clergy who, emboldened by the pope's revocation of the *cruzada* and *subsidio*, haughtily refused all pleas for contributions to the treasury. Juan Martínez Siliceo, the archbishop of Toledo, turned a deaf ear to official pleading that the church should contribute to the state in the interests of common welfare. To underscore his defiance Siliceo sent sizable sums in 1556 to Pope Paul IV, the king's enemy. The archbishop's actions formed a prime example of what Braudel termed the "crisis of insubordination" afflicting Castile in the mid- and late 1550s.[35] In order to quell this insubordination and raise funds from the privileged orders, Philip II instructed Ruy Gómez de Silva to implement another expedient. What the lords and prelates refused to pay as taxes would be claimed from them "in the form of a *donativo* [free gift], in appearance voluntary, but in truth obligatory and compelled." Upon departing for Spain the *privado* was provided with sixty signed letters from Philip II, addressed to the wealthiest figures in the realm and asking for financial aid. Ruy Gómez also carried additional copies of the letter with the recipients' names left blank, to use as he saw fit.[36]

Through April and into May, Ruy Gómez de Silva attempted to coerce the *donativo*. This was a ticklish job, since the members of the privileged orders jealously guarded their exemptions from taxation and resented any challenge to them. The prelates, in particular, remained reluctant to contribute, citing the impropriety of using church funds to subsidize warfare against the pope. The stubborn Siliceo's control of the immense wealth of the Toledan see was still a principal stumbling block. Ruy Gómez met with the archbishop to attempt to convince him to donate the sum he had previously pledged for a North African expedition (now postponed) and to arrange for the churches to grant a *subsidio* notwithstanding Paul

IV's orders. Siliceo stalled, and he died, without having promised any contributions, on 12 May 1557. The government of the princess regent immediately ordered the sequestration of Siliceo's estate and an embargo, for the king's use, of the dues that would be paid to the papacy for succession in the see of Toledo. In essence the archdiocese and its revenues were placed in receivership under the control of a secular magistrate.[37]

This situation was the occasion for what seems to have been an attempt to bribe Ruy Gómez de Silva. After Siliceo's death the cathedral chapter of Toledo, anxious to win an ally who might be able to lift the sequestration of the archdiocesan revenues, confirmed Ruy Gómez in his possession of the title of *adelantado mayor* of Cazorla. The *adelantamiento* of Cazorla (a jurisdictional unit in northeastern Andalusia) had been the object of a protracted legal battle between the see of Toledo and the heirs of Charles V's great secretary, Francisco de los Cobos. In the 1540s Cobos had secured papal bulls granting the *adelantamiento* to his son. With the emperor applying pressure on the ecclesiastical hierarchy, the territory had subsequently been incorporated into Cobos's *mayorazgo* of Camarasa. The see of Toledo objected, arguing that the position of *adelantado* was in the archbishop's gift and could not be perpetually alienated. In the early 1550s Archbishop Siliceo, ignoring the incumbency of Cobos's heir, had named Ruy Gómez *adelantado*, doubtless hoping to benefit from his influence with Philip, who was then regent of Castile. Ruy Gómez's interest in wresting the title from the house of Camarasa was intensified by the fact that his father-in-law's house of Mélito had been adjudicated a portion of the property of the *adelantamiento*, and possession of the title might bolster a claim to the remainder.[38]

The sources disagree as to whether Ruy Gómez de Silva accepted reconfirmation in this post from the cathedral chapter in May 1557. Cabrera de Córdoba asserts that he did not; Salazar y Castro, that he did. In either case they concur that the *privado* urged the archdiocese to pay the Crown its due, and no evidence exists that Ruy Gómez raised objections to the sequestration.[39] It is impossible to know what really happened, but it is not difficult to believe what Salazar y Castro implies: that Ruy Gómez took the bribe but declined to exert the influence it was meant to purchase. The fact that the next archbishop, Carranza, further confirmed Ruy Gómez's possession of the title—despite Paul IV's order to revoke it—may indicate either that the see of Toledo was not displeased with the outcome of the bribe or that, regardless of the sequestration, Ruy Gómez remained the person best situated to combat the claims of Cobos's heirs. In the coming years Ruy Gómez did intervene on behalf of the Toledan see in the suit brought in Rome to restore the gift of the title of *adelantado mayor* to the archbishop. Despite a favorable ruling by the pope in 1559, however, actual possession of the *adelantamiento* remained with the house of Camarasa until the early seventeenth century. Eventually Ruy Gómez de Silva ceded his rights to Cazorla to the house of Alba, which after lengthy litigation finally won possession in the seventeenth century.[40]

Despite Ruy Gómez's rather murky dealings with the Toledan chapter, the death of Siliceo presumably enabled the Crown to extract some subsidies from the revenues of his archdiocese. Difficulties persisted with the other dioceses, however, and Ruy Gómez made another pilgrimage to Yuste on 18 May 1557 to enlist the emperor's aid in his attempts to coax a *donativo* from the recalcitrant prelates of Castile. On this occasion Charles V agreed to lend his authority to the effort, and Ruy Gómez returned to Valladolid with letters from the emperor addressed to some of the least tractable bishops. Chief among this group was Fernando de Valdés, archbishop of Seville and inquisitor-general. The princess regent had summoned Valdés to a personal audience in March, where she and Ruy Gómez had asked him to supply 150,000 ducats for Philip's campaigns. Valdés—once described by the normally affable count of Feria as a "treacherous malcontent"[41]—stalled for two months in the face of further importunities and responded to the emperor's letter in May by pleading that alms-giving had exhausted his income. Moreover, he upbraided a treasury officer for having the temerity to dun a prelate. Ruy Gómez reported to Charles V that, despite Valdés's protestations of poverty, six mules heavily laden with the archbishop's revenues had just passed through Valladolid. The emperor wrote once again to Valdés, more sternly this time. After more dithering the archbishop grudgingly promised 50,000 ducats to the Crown, with even this sum to be reduced by the arrears owed Valdés from previous loans. This pattern, of obstruction, delay and, finally, payment of a reduced share of the sum asked for the *donativo*, seems to have been typical of the behavior of the prelates and lords from whom Ruy Gómez sought contributions. Finally, though, more generous giving was stimulated when Philip, at the end of his patience, threatened to sequester Valdés's archdiocese in order to collect an amount (100,000 ducats) he considered reasonable. With this prod, the *donativo* solicited by Ruy Gómez de Silva may in the end have realized as much as two million ducats for the king; this was a remarkable success, when the resistance of most of the contributors is borne in mind.[42]

Ruy Gómez completed his mission in Spain in midsummer and left Valladolid on his return journey on 30 July 1557. Despite the king's February injunction to "come back as quickly as you can" and the regent Juana's urgings that he hasten back to the Low Countries to advise her brother that he must return to Spain, the *privado* had been absent from court for nearly six months. He was further delayed awaiting embarkation at Laredo until the end of August.[43] Regardless of these delays, though, Ruy Gómez's mission had succeeded. In June Philip had received significant remittances and reinforcements brought from Spain by Don Antonio de Velasco. A month later, 550,000 ducats were delivered to the duke of Alba in Italy. When Ruy Gómez sailed in August, it was at the head of a squadron laden with more troops and some money (perhaps 100,000 ducats[44]). The financial machinery he had set in motion continued to operate through the fall and winter, and a final installment of at least 200,000 and probably as much as 800,000 ducats was brought to Flanders in the spring of 1558 on the fleet of Don Pero Meléndez de Avilés. Although the expedients employed, particularly the confiscation of private American treasure, did not realize the grandiose sums projected by Philip II, the success of the crucial summer campaigns of 1557 in both Italy and Flanders owed a great deal to the timely infusions of cash and manpower from Spain.[45] In the north the campaign culminated in the great victory of St. Quentin (the crucial assault came on 27 August, just as Ruy Gómez de Silva was leaving Laredo). Cabrera de Córdoba credited Philip's *privado* with a crucial role in this triumph: "Rui Gomez arranged the provision of the money in such a way and with such abundance that it sustained an army of 80,000 combatants" throughout the summer and at the siege of St. Quentin.[46]

Ruy Gómez had performed well in a series of difficult tasks, and he had largely succeeded in imposing the king's authority in financial matters in Spain. His efforts had provided enough support to enable Philip's armies to prevail (barely) over those of the similarly strapped king of France, but they were of course not of a nature calculated to rectify the long-term problems of royal finance. Funds were too scarce to allow decisive action to follow up the victory at St. Quentin, and by November the king was reputed to be essentially bankrupt. His bankers, reeling from the suspension of payments, refused further credit. Suriano, the Venetian ambassador, reported that Spain was in turmoil, its resources "exhausted by the forced exactions ("li partiti extremi") levied for war by Don Ruy Gómez." Philip was forced to rely on the Estates-General of the Netherlands for further revenue; with considerable justice, the delegates remonstrated that the king's demands were unreasonable.[47] Ruy Gómez played a major part in the king's unsatisfactory quest for new sources of revenue in this period. He was the sole *contador mayor* at Philip's court in the late 1550s—Bernardino de Mendoza had died in the last days of the siege of St. Quentin, and the third *contador*, Gutierre López de Padilla, remained in Spain and did not long survive him. Mendoza had been the most competent man of finance among Philip's inner circle, and his expertise was sorely missed in the last years of Philip's stay in the north.[48] Meanwhile, the king and Ruy Gómez toyed with desperate expedients, involving

> a German in Malines [Mechelen] who, by mixing one ounce of some powders of his with sixteen ounces of quicksilver, fabricated sixteen ounces of a metal that is resistant to the touch and to the hammer, but not to fire. It was proposed that this silver be employed for payment of the army; but the estates [of the Netherlands] did not wish to acquiesce in this. . . . At all events, since that invention greatly pleased the king and Ruy Gómez, it may well be believed that in case of necessity his Majesty would make use of it without scruple.[49]

The activities of the alchemist, Peter Sternberg, were overseen by Ruy Gómez's secretary, a man named Calderón. The secretary was a shifty character who was not above selling his master's secrets to the Venetians, and he turned his superiors' fascination with alchemy to his own profit if hardly that of the treasury. Sternberg received at least 1,200 ducats from the king as a reward for his efforts, while Calderón received 800 ducats for himself. The royal confessor (Don Bernardo de Fresneda) opposed this pathetic expedient from the outset, and his appeals to Philip's conscience, if not his common sense, seem to have prevented the counterfeit scheme from progressing beyond the stage of expensive demonstrations.[50]

While these quicksilver dabblings reveal one of the whimsical facets of the collaboration between the king and his favorite, the mission of 1557 provides clear illustration of several more central aspects of the *privanza*. Both in England and in Spain Ruy Gómez acted as the personal representative of the king. Except in the limited sphere of his role as *contador mayor*, his authority rested not on vested office but on broad authority conferred by his special relationship with Philip II. No bureaucratic or diplomatic commission in the Habsburg repertoire would suffice to empower the bearer to perform all the roles—among others, advance man at the court of St. James, coordinator of policy with the emperor and the princess regent, expediter of funds between and across jurisdictions, fundraiser for the *donativo*—that were discharged by Ruy Gómez de Silva in 1557. The king remained in the Netherlands, but Ruy Gómez traveled as an embodiment of his kingship, licensed to deal with rulers and mighty subjects on terms and with broad discretion provided not by his personal stature but by the aura of reflected and delegated majesty that surrounded him. Ruy Gómez doubtless trod on many toes in Spain, not just those of the social superiors he hectored to contribute to the royal fisc, but those of officials of the military and fiscal administration as well. His success in these dealings outside the chain of command and against the grain of the social hierarchy owes something to his own considerable skills, but primarily it reflects the grudging recognition by lords, prelates and bureaucrats that Ruy Gómez wielded the crosscutting authority of Philip II himself.

The description of the mission provided by Philip's early biographer Luis Cabrera de Córdoba bears examination for the impressions it provides of the *privanza* as a symbiosis of the king and his favorite, a delegated reproduction of some of the attributes of incarnate kingship. Cabrera wrote that the king

> sent . . . Rui Gómez de Silva to take steps to arrange this provision [of men and money from Spain], to raise 8000 infantrymen, to visit the Emperor, to confer on affairs of state, determine the best course to be followed, assess the state of the kingdoms and determine what must be remedied, since he [Philip] could not then visit them; moreover, he was to bring the Prince Don Carlos back to the Low Countries

in order that he might see those lands and be sworn as heir to them, and in order to steer him away from encounters with the Princess his aunt, and principally in order to set the Prince on the right path through his example and presence, since he [Ruy Gómez de Silva] understood his [Don Carlos's] habits as well as though he were of the same flesh and blood.[51]

As described by Cabrera, Ruy Gómez's mission comprised not just the execution of a series of public tasks but also the performance of some of the king's most sacred personal duties. Since Philip could not come to Spain, his *privado* would assume the royal function of evaluating the state of the kingdom and the imperatives of just government. Even more striking was Ruy Gómez's insertion into the affairs of the king's family. In Philip's place the *privado* would tie together the Habsburg generations, reporting to the emperor like a son and supervising Don Carlos like a father.

Ruy Gómez de Silva remained an intimate of Philip II for most of the remainder of his life, but seldom after 1557 did he appear so unmistakably as the royal alter ego. During most of the rest of his *privanza* Ruy Gómez operated in the midst of envious and hostile competitors for power and influence. In 1556–1557 his ascendancy among Philip's men stood out in sharp relief; thereafter it was more a matter of degree. Only rarely after 1557 did he stand alone on the public stage in an obvious position of command; in later years his power was wielded in the more private world of a closed court. For the most part he appeared at public functions as one among a shifting cast of courtiers and magnates. His dominance was exercised behind the scenes, and it surfaces in the records of the reign like the voice of a lead singer emerging by subtle counterpoint from the confused roar of an enthusiastic but ill-conducted choir.

Thus it is that we find him in 1558–1559 taking a leading but not solo role in the negotiations that led to the Peace of Cateau-Cambrésis. At the beginning of 1558 he, along with the bishop of Arras, was named by Philip to treat for peace with the pope with Cardinal Carlo Caraffa, the papal nephew and legate. Later in the year the negotiations expanded to encompass a general peace among the Habsburgs, France and England. On 11 October 1558

Philip designated his commissioners: Ruy Gómez de Silva; the duke of Alba; Arras; William, prince of Orange; and Viglius van Aytta of Zwichem, head of the Netherlands Privy Council.[52] Because of his linguistic aptitude Arras was probably the principal voice of Philip's delegation during the negotiations, which lasted in two stages until April 1559. Meanwhile Ruy Gómez de Silva acted as envoy between Philip II and the talks; during the parley he made several journeys to confer with the king on important issues and secured royal approval of the final draft at the end of March.[53]

Once the treaty was concluded Philip sent his *privado* to Paris to carry the wedding jewels to his affianced bride, Isabel de Valois, and to inform her of his plans to return to Spain and send for her to join him there. This was the sort of highly visible ceremonial task that fell to Ruy Gómez de Silva in his capacity as *sumiller de corps.* His grand public roles were often colored by an overtone of the menial. Here he was both an emissary of the king and his master's bearer. Likewise in the case of the elaborate obsequies staged in Brussels in 1558 to commemorate the passing of Charles V: Ruy Gómez stood with the king at the ritual focus of the procession, but he was there to carry the six-yard-long train of Philip's robes of state.[54]

Ruy Gómez de Silva arrived in Paris on 5 July 1559. This was a critical moment, since Henry II lay dying from the wound he had suffered on the last day of June during the tournament celebrating the wedding and the peace. Philip II feared that if the French king died his successors would renounce the peace and annul the marriage; foreign observers reported that the Spanish contingent in Paris was immensely saddened and anxiety ridden as a result of the king's perilous state. Philip instructed his *privado* to extend his sympathy to the royal family and, more important, to demand guarantees of French compliance with the terms set at Cateau-Cambrésis. Andreas Vesalius and another surgeon arrived with Ruy Gómez, sent by Philip to attend Henry II. The party had ridden straight through from Brussels by post-relay and, still booted and spurred, Ruy Gómez was ushered into the king's chamber ahead of Vesalius. He remained closeted with the dying king for two hours, presumably seeking assurances that the pact would be honored.[55]

Within a matter of days the *privado* learned that Catherine de' Medici was suffering the complementary fear that Philip II would seize this opportunity to back out of the treaty and attack France in its weakness. Seeking further advantage, Ruy Gómez reacted non-committally to Catherine's discreet inquiries about the Catholic King's intentions. The desperate pleas of the duke of Guise and other leading figures on the morning after Henry II's death (11 July) provoked a similarly inconclusive response.[56] Despite the fears this behavior aroused among the French, there is no evidence that Philip even considered renouncing the peace. If nothing else, his finances demanded an end to warfare. Thus, regardless of Vesalius's failure to save Henry II, the peace was ratified. Ruy Gómez's coyness in Paris was simply standard operating procedure for an envoy scenting possible further advantage. He gained no concrete concessions, but he managed to extract from the new governors of France relief and gratitude for an outcome that his master had desired all along.

With the conclusion of the treaty Philip II, in Ghent, proceeded with his preparations to return at last to Spain. Ruy Gómez de Silva sought and received permission to precede the king, and he left directly from Paris for Spain on 26 July 1559; by 7 August he was back in Valladolid.[57] Again, Philip hoped that his *privado* might convey Don Carlos to the Netherlands to act as governor there, but this plan was abandoned in view of the prince's evident incapacity, and Ruy Gómez stayed in Spain to await the king's return. During his absence from Philip's side his place as *sumiller de corps* was filled by Don Juan de Pimentel.[58] According to an English agent at Ghent, Philip was occupied in the last weeks of his stay in the north with the provision of *mercedes* for his retainers. "His rewards given to retain his private ministers of late are great and right notable," the agent reported. He cited an *ayuda de costa* for Alba amounting to 150,000 ducats, and another of 80,000 for the duke of Sessa (governor of Milan). Compensation for their efforts went "to certain other Spanish Lords after the like rate."[59] While Ruy Gómez de Silva may or may not have shared in this banquet of largesse (and it is impossible to be certain), he had already received a striking reward from his king.

On 1 July, as Ruy Gómez prepared to leave Brussels for Paris, Philip II had granted him the Neapolitan title of prince of Eboli. In the privilege Philip II acknowledged his esteem for and gratitude to his *privado:*

In consideration of the remarkable and eminent virtues, and endowments of valor, of the Illustrious Ruy Gómez de Silva, Count of Mélito, our much beloved counselor of State and *sumiller*, and of his Noble and resplendent family, and [his] much-noted knowledge of other affairs, in both the Civil and the Military sphere, in addition to the embellishments of most elevated fortune, virtue, prudence and ingenuity, all of which we know to be abundant and remarkably honored; and to leave to one side the continuous and important services that since his adolescence he has performed with consummate fidelity, application and labor, services which would take too long to recount here, in view of the fact that he has always been with us as our companion in affairs public and private, and in other arduous and very secret expeditions in wartime, times of difficulty and travels; for which reason, with no wrongful motive whatsoever, moved by these and other considerations, we judge him worthy to be adorned with the Title and honor of Prince, in order that we may manifest with unmistakable signs the singular heartfelt affection ["afecto de ánimo"] that we bear him, and so that his descendants may know that he was pleasing and meritorious in our sight.[60]

The document's phrase—"he has always been with us as our companion in affairs public and private"—neatly sums up Ruy Gómez de Silva's status as *privado* to Philip II.

The privilege elevated the town of Eboli (near Salerno, in the Kingdom of Naples[61]) and the lands Ruy Gómez held surrounding it to the status of a principality. Philip's *privado* received the title of prince for himself and his heirs by primogeniture in perpetuity.[62] This title was not as grand as it may seem. Gaspar Muro noted that the Spanish Habsburgs granted various Italian princely titles but that, "far from constituting a more elevated hierarchy, the recipients were not even considered the equals of dukes, grandees of Castile." He quoted the seventeenth-century genealogist López de Haro to the effect that the title of prince in the Kingdom of Naples was roughly equivalent to that of marquis in Castile.[63] Ruy Gómez himself appears to have valued the title more highly than that of a Castilian count. He immediately dropped the appellation of count of Mélito, which he enjoyed in those years by virtue of his father-in-law's cession, in favor of prince of Eboli. Of course, this may well have reflected his pleasure in a title truly his own rather than an evaluation of the respective merit of the two titles.

Around the same time Philip enlarged his *privado*'s principality by granting him the town and marquisate of Diano and the fief of

Lago Picholo in Campania, on condition that he redeem a lien, in the sum of 36,666 escudos, held against these properties by the prince of Astillano. Presumably Ruy Gómez paid off Astillano, since he held these properties until 1567, but even with this addition the principality of Eboli was more valuable for its title than for its revenues. Eboli was a dusty town of 600 hearths, according to the fiscal census of 1648, and had an assessed revenue in 1556 of 1,958 Neapolitan ducats per year. This was slightly increased by a supplementary grant of Crown revenues in 1559. Diano had 150 hearths in 1648, with a net return to its lord in 1558–1559 of 1,876 ducats. Both towns offered additional "donations" or *servicios* to Ruy Gómez in the mid-1560s: 2,000 ducats from Diano and 3,000 from Eboli, to be paid in installments over three years. In the late 1560s Lago Picholo was leased out yearly for a lump sum of around 1,400 ducats— a beneficial arrangement, given that remittances from the fief had amounted to a mere 85 ducats in 1558–1559. It would be surprising if these properties taken together (and without regard to the outlays for redemption from Astillano) were ever worth more than 7,000 ducats per year to Ruy Gómez de Silva; by comparison, the estate revenues of a Castilian duke in that era fell in the range of 40,000 to 100,000 ducats annually.[64]

Back in Spain the new prince of Eboli continued to play a leading role in government in the years after 1559. As he had in Brussels, he spoke for the king in the Council of State, first at Toledo and after 1561 at Madrid. His alliance with Eraso was renewed and strengthened, and at various times in the 1560s it seemed that the two of them controlled the entire governmental machine.[65] As the sole *contador mayor*, Ruy Gómez was paramount in the financial bureaucracy to a degree unmatched since the glory days of Francisco de los Cobos. Assisted by Eraso, Eboli dominated the Council of Hacienda and thus exerted great influence both on the direction of policy and on the flow of salaries, grants and *mercedes*. The combination of his intimate influence over Philip and his official powers in the Councils of State and Hacienda made Ruy Gómez de Silva the crucial stopcock in the pipeline of royal patronage throughout much of the decade of the 1560s. "Because of the king's regard for him, Ruy Gómez always has the last word in matters of honors, rewards, favors and payments," according to the Venetian Antonio Tiepolo.[66]

Meanwhile, particularly after the court was established at Madrid, Philip II retreated even farther from public view, firmly establishing the reclusive brand of kingship that would characterize his long reign in Spain. For contemporaries, just as for modern historians, the king was barely visible in the early 1560s. He stayed away from his councils, and his meetings with foreign envoys were rare and taciturn.[67] In the eyes of the ambassadors at court, the *privado* was an indispensable source of access to the king and of information on Philip's wishes and disposition toward their affairs. In some ways Eboli's function was analogous to that of the chief of staff to a modern executive: as *the* man who saw the king on a regular basis and thus could largely control the flow of information to and from the source of power and preference, the *privado*'s pronouncements and gestures carried great weight and were eagerly parsed by those who had business at the court of Spain.[68] Ruy Gómez de Silva stood at the center of the affairs of the court, like a lens collecting rays of aspiration emitted by the competing interests gathered at the seat of government, focusing some onto the king and refracting others away from their target and into oblivion.

A wide range of contemporary observers acknowledged the *privado*'s vast influence as a conduit to the king and a crucial broker in affairs of government and patronage. For the French ambassador Saint-Sulpice, presentation to Ruy Gómez de Silva was one of the first matters on the agenda when he arrived in Madrid in 1562.[69] At the end of 1563 the powerful secretary Gonzalo Pérez informed the duke of Sessa that, among all the grandee's friends at court, none but Ruy Gómez de Silva could help him in a bid for royal *mercedes*.[70] While offering similar advice to his protégé the baron de Bolwiller in 1564, Granvelle observed that, in "a question of finances and matters of state," Ruy Gómez enjoyed "more power over the king than anyone else alive."[71] Granvelle's brother Thomas de Chantonnay also placed his trust in Philip's *privado:* "through your aid and intercession with His Majesty I may hope to gain fit compensation for all the years and the private resources I have spent in [the royal] service."[72]

The outcome of Chantonnay's petition remains unknown, but perhaps he benefited from the same sort of persuasive energy that

Ruy Gómez expended on behalf of his longtime friend and client, Count Persico Broccardo. In 1565 the *privado* asked the duke of Alburquerque, captain-general in Milan, to expedite the audit of the expenses Broccardo had reported as arising from his recent mission to Rome for the king. "Several times," Ruy Gómez began,

> I have informed Your most illustrious Lordship of what a great friend of mine is Count Broccardo, whom I value both for his services to His Majesty and for his personal merits. . . . [Lately] he has performed services that deserve a much better reward than bearing on his own account the expenses he had there and in his travels to and fro. And although I am sure that you have ordered that the audit of these expenses should be carried out immediately, as His Majesty has commanded . . . [still] I implore Your Lordship to order once again that these harassments come to an end. . . . For it is a great shame if it is not enough for a gentleman to risk his life and honor, without consuming his fortune as well.[73]

Alburquerque, he concluded, should resolve Broccardo's problem "without regard for the subtleties of lawyers or the slanders of those persons in that state [Milan] who do not wish him well."[74] Throughout the 1560s and into the next decade Ruy Gómez exerted influence on behalf of Broccardo.[75] He seems truly to have liked the count, once exclaiming that "if one could accompany him, a trip to Italy would be a great delight," and he may also have found Broccardo a useful advocate in his personal affairs in Italy.[76]

According to Sigismondo Cavalli, Ruy Gómez "is the recourse of all the men of affairs and of the whole court" ("è il ricorso dei negozianti e di tutta la corte").[77] Cavalli's successors agreed: when it was impossible to gain an audience with the king himself, "we met with signor Ruigomez in preference to any other."[78] The prince of Eboli knew how to get things done. When Viceroy García de Toledo obstructed attempts by agents of the admiral of Castile to export grain from Sicily under a previously obtained royal license, the admiral's man of affairs turned to Ruy Gómez for help. The *privado* learned that the matter had been referred to the Council of Italy, and he wrote to one of the regents of that body, asking him to present the case to his fellows in a manner favorable to the admiral. Confident of the desired outcome, he wrote to the conciliar secretary, Diego de Vargas, telling him to be prepared to send the compliance decree to García de Toledo without delay. Then Ruy Gómez instructed his *criado,* Juan de Escobedo, to visit the regent in order to reinforce verbally his own written request. Finally, Escobedo was directed to speak to Vargas's assistant, "inducing him to open the letter that is coming" so that his master would be sure to read it immediately.[79] This episode reveals some of the reasons why Ruy Gómez's support was so prized by petitioners at the court. The *privado* once remarked, regarding the conduct of business in Philip's administration, that "matters here progress *a la española,* that is to say, in a sluggish and ill-considered fashion."[80] Over time, however, Ruy Gómez became a master of circumventing bureaucratic obstacles and manipulating the system for his own benefit and for that of his friends and clients.

The *privado* was not only an expediter of bureaucratic process and the conduit of requests for the king's favors but also acted as a funnel for dissent. For example, when Fernando Francisco Dávalos, marquis of Pescara, objected to Philip's decision to establish a resident embassy in Turin, he made his disagreement known to Ruy Gómez, who passed it on to his master.[81]

Of course, relatives also reaped the benefits of Ruy Gómez's skilled intercession. His younger brother, Hernando de Silva, held the post of governor of Asti and was furnished with a considerable stipend authorized by the duke of Sessa, while the latter served as captain-general in Milan and himself enjoyed the patronage of Philip's *privado.*[82] Instead of posts and emoluments, some family members requested special pleading in criminal matters. Doña Ana's aunt, the dowager countess of Concentaina, asked Ruy Gómez to intervene with the king on behalf of her son. On Corpus Christi day, 1562, the young count had been involved in a sword fight on the streets of Valencia, had fled the officers of justice, and now was confined in the archbishop's palace awaiting disposition of his case. "What I ask of Your Lordship," his mother wrote, "is that His Majesty should know the truth . . . and see that the count was forced to do what he did and is blameless in this."[83] On occasion, family loyalties compelled the *privado*'s intervention on behalf of total strangers. In one such instance, Ruy Gómez tried to influence the judicial officials of Alcántara (Extremadura) to release a Portuguese named Joan Rodrigues from their jail. "My father informs me," he explained, "that he [Rodrigues] is a man of honor but they don't know him there [in Alcántara] and thus for their lack of respect he could receive a stiff sentence." He sent Escobedo a letter requesting amnesty for Rodrigues, with the address left blank, instructing his *criado* to learn the identity of the responsible judge in Alcántara and to forward it to that official with the proper salutation. Meanwhile Escobedo should contact Licenciado Medellin, presumably an official of justice at court, and "ask him for the love of me to take this matter in hand."[84]

Not just the king's powerful subjects and the *privado*'s demanding relatives, but foreign royalty as well recognized Eboli's crucial position at the Spanish court. To ensure Ruy Gómez's goodwill toward her daughter, Philip's queen, Catherine de' Medici saw fit to send him a personal note enclosing a diamond for Doña Ana.[85] Emanuele Filiberto of Savoy fairly gushed that "I am so very obligated to Your Lordship that, while the Duke of Savoy lives and breathes, the Prince Ruy Gómez will possess in him a true friend, and so I have written and signed this [affirmation] with my own hand, for now and forever."[86] And even Teresa de Avila, who conducted a great deal of business at court in the course of her efforts to reform the Carmelites, recalled that "in all matters it was well to secure the favor of Ruy Gómez, who enjoyed so much credit with the King and with everyone."[87]

The public stature of Ruy Gómez de Silva, established during Philip's years in the north, thus remained very prominent after the return of the court to Spain. Meanwhile, to all appearances his private life was also marked by the blessings of fortune. By the late 1550s the generosity of Philip II had bestowed on Ruy Gómez, in addition to his princely title, yearly revenues from the royal treasury in the amount of 26,000 *escudos* (24,266 ducats).[88] Most of these grants of income took the form of *juros* situated on the royal *alcabalas* of various towns and jurisdictions of the Crown of Castile. The largest single grant was doubtless the 6,000 ducats per year, secured on the marquisate of Villena, that Ruy Gómez enjoyed as part of his marriage settlement.[89] The composition of another 13,000 ducats per year of the *juros* granted by Philip II to his *privado* can be reconstructed from records compiled in 1661 by the estate administrators of Ruy Gómez's great-great-grandson, the fourth duke of Pastrana (see Table). This impressive income was the fiscal measure of Philip II's devotion and gratitude toward his favorite and was further enhanced by the emoluments of his post as *contador mayor* and as a *comendador* of the military orders. In addition to these revenues, en-

Table. *Juros* Granted to Ruy Gómez de Silva and Still in the
Possession of the House of Pastrana in 1661

Situation (Revenue type and site)	Amount (ducats per year)
Alcabalas, Marquisate of Villena	441
Alcabalas, Marquisate of Villena	316
Alcabalas, Alcaraz	2,773
Alcabalas, Granada	1,367
Alcabalas, Granada	751
Alcabalas, Jaén	200
Alcabalas, Mérida	4,218
Alcabalas, Segura de la Sierra	1,008
Alcabalas, Segura de la Sierra	1,032
Alcabalas, Guadalcanal	645
Alcabalas, Llerena	288
TOTAL	13,039

Source: Archivo Histórico Nacional, Madrid, Sección Osuna, legajo 2281², no. 3, folios 277–281. In the source the value of the *juros* is given in *maravedís*. I have converted the figures to ducats of 375 *maravedís*, rounding off to the nearest even ducat. The precise total is 13,042 ducats, 61 *maravedís*.

joyed at the king's pleasure, the prince of Eboli had another source of income that was seemingly more secure. Between 1555 and 1560 he collected the revenues of his father-in-law's Italian estates, which he and Doña Ana could expect eventually to inherit.

In addition to his public position and his growing wealth, Ruy Gómez de Silva had another reason to rejoice in the period of his *privanza*. His family was growing rapidly in the 1560s, as Doña Ana presented him with one child after another. Their marriage had been consummated during Ruy Gómez's mission to Spain in 1557. Doña Ana had become pregnant at that time, but the child, christened Diego, died in infancy before his father returned from the north. Once Ruy Gómez was back in Spain, however, the family grew rapidly, and by 1566 the prince and princess of Eboli had five live children. The eldest was a daughter, born in 1561 and named Doña Ana after her mother. Next came a boy to stand as heir to his parents: Don Rodrigo, born in 1562. The name was probably chosen as a Castilianization of his father's. Then, in 1564–1566, three more boys were born, Don Diego, Don Pedro González de Mendoza, and Don Ruy Gómez de Silva. The first two were obviously christened in honor of their mother's lineage, while the last, born in 1566, bore his father's name with no apologies for its foreign origins.[90]

Thus Ruy Gómez de Silva could count himself a favored child of fortune in the first decade of the reign of Philip II. From unpromising origins he had risen to become the king's friend, counselor and *privado*, a man of wealth and influence, and a husband and father linked to one of the great houses of Castile. But the people of that age knew man's fortune to be remarkably volatile, and Eboli's career was still to provide an illustration of this truism. In words that might have served as an admonition to Ruy Gómez de Silva in the years of his glory, Philosophy counseled Boethius to take account of the nature of his life's trajectory:

> If you hoist your sails in the wind, you will go where the wind blows you, not where you choose to go. . . . You have put yourself in Fortune's power; now you must be content with the ways of your mistress. If you try to stop the force of her turning wheel, you are the most foolish man alive. If it should stop turning, it would cease to be Fortune's wheel.[91]

The privado of Philip II had indeed ridden a favorable wind to the pinnacle of worldly success. Then, in the final chapter of his life, he was spun about by a gale that threatened to wreck him on the inhospitable shore of failure. In the depths of this great crisis of his life he would prove himself to be not a foolish man but instead a true man of the Renaissance. Ruy Gómez de Silva would oppose the forces of fate with the exercise of *virtù*, and in the end he would succeed in stopping and then reversing the turning wheel of fortune.

PART TWO

CHALLENGE AND RESPONSE

[I]f it happens that time and circumstance are favourable to one who acts with caution and prudence he will be successful, but if time and circumstances change he will be ruined, because he does not change his mode of procedure. No man is found so prudent as to be able to adapt himself to this, either because he cannot deviate from that to which his nature disposes him, or else because having always prospered by walking in one path, he cannot persuade himself that it is well to leave it; and therefore the cautious man, when it is time to act suddenly, does not know how to do so and is consequently ruined; for if one could change one's nature with time and circumstances, fortune would never change.

Niccolò Machiavelli, *The Prince,* ch. XXV
(Ricci translation, 1950)

Introduction to Part Two

In the last fifteen years of his life Ruy Gómez de Silva faced altered circumstances and, in the end, mastered fortune by redirecting the focus of his endeavors. Perhaps, as Machiavelli argued, Ruy Gómez could not change his nature, but he did shrewdly adapt his behavior and goals to meet the challenge of troubled times and difficult conditions. Throughout his life he had prospered in dependence, as the king's servant and as the beneficiary of a marriage to the daughter of a man whose hereditary wealth and social prestige were much superior to his own. In a monarchy tending toward absolutism and a society that was rigidly stratified primarily on the basis of birth, such dependence was the normal price of favor and upward mobility. And through most of his life Ruy Gómez de Silva reaped the rewards of extremely adept self-subordination. During the course of his ascent to the *privanza* his dependence was transmuted into power and influence. His servitude was the office that bestowed all others and made him one of the high and mighty of the court of Spain. No matter how lofty his titles and exalted his responsibilities, Ruy Gómez remained at root the *criado* or *criatura* (servant and creature) of Philip II and the son-in-law of the duke of Francavila. His status, wealth and influence were not inherent attributes of his being but rather were transmitted through the links of a patron–client network, and consequently there was always the danger that they could be extinguished at their source. Successful subordination had meant startling upward mobility, but it also implied constant insecurity.

If insecurity was the concomitant of dependence, independence was the prerequisite of long-term security. In the last phase of his life Ruy Gómez's status was threatened with erosion in both the public and the private spheres. He eventually overcame these threats by establishing his personal independence in the only way practicable in a society of orders governed by an absolute monarch.

At the end of his career, Ruy Gómez de Silva froze the transit of fortune near its perihelion by insinuating himself into the Castilian aristocracy. Within its ranks he and his lineage were shielded from the whims of his benefactors and from the intrigues of his enemies by walls of inviolable privilege.

In the modern sense of the word, of course, Ruy Gómez had lived a life of tremendous privilege ever since his conquest of Philip's favor. But no matter how close his relationship to the king, his perquisites remained functions of bestowal rather than entitlement and thus, in the terms of his age, were no privileges at all. By contrast, aristocratic privilege was an inseparable aspect of aristocratic *being*, an essential personal attribute of its holder. Privilege was intrinsic status rather than the borrowed grandeur of an elevated client. True privilege made lofty status—*grandeza* or greatness—essentially irrevocable and was therefore a formidable rival of the forces of political modernity, a puissant survival of a social order inimical to the sweeping sovereign claims of kings. As a tendency absolutism aspired to make all men clients; those subjects who proclaimed a stature based on privilege could boast with considerable justice that they were no man's client and that their absolute rights of command and ownership differed from the king's in degree rather than kind.[1]

The rise of Ruy Gómez de Silva from obscurity to become the *privado* of the most powerful monarch in Europe was an extraordinary testimony to his ability to seek advantage and seize opportunity within the social world of clientage and deference. His final triumph was even more extraordinary, since by converting himself into a *grande de España* Ruy Gómez in effect liberated himself from the milieu of subordination. He transferred the position and the goods that had come to him in a lifetime of service across a frontier of social jurisdiction into the charmed realm of individual and familial independence and security. This sort of triumph of social mobility was extremely rare, and it usually marked the culmination of a gradual multigenerational ascent; for Ruy Gómez de Silva, however, it was the achievement of a lifetime.

5

Rivalry and Retreat

The erosion of his position that caused Ruy Gómez de Silva to change the direction of his career was a gradual process. Over the decade between the mid-1550s and the mid-1560s, his vulnerabilities as a public figure were discovered, explored and exploited by rivals at the court. Eventually his enjoyment of the unparalleled favor of Philip II was imperiled. Growing uncertainty in his private life compounded his insecurity.

The most persistent threats to the public stature of Ruy Gómez de Silva arose as a consequence of the development and elaboration of bitter antagonisms within the court, beginning in late 1557. These antagonisms have traditionally been represented as a struggle, largely played out within the Council of State, between political factions headed by the duke of Alba on one hand and Ruy Gómez de Silva on the other. Several scholars have depicted the Alba–Eboli dichotomy as something akin to a party system that shaped and dominated debates over policy in the Council of State from the 1550s until the eclipse of Alba and the disgrace of Antonio Pérez in the late 1570s. The principal disagreements among modern students of the subject have concerned whether and to what degree the factions represented either opposed and coherent political ideologies or the rivalries of great families for precedence, royal favor and patronage.

Through his study of contemporary sources, Leopold von Ranke correctly identified the existence of a strong personal antagonism between Alba and Ruy Gómez. He went beyond this, however, to discern a component of ideological disagreement in their conflict. Alba, in his view, "had the aristocrat's inclination to help despotism" and was a forceful exponent of the belligerent extension of royal power throughout the Spanish monarchy. Ruy Gómez, on the contrary, "gave the empire itself a pacific tendency; in doubtful cases he was always for peace."[1] Writing a century later Gregorio Marañón expanded the notion of an Alba–Eboli antagonism to encompass factions comprising kinship networks engaged in a rivalry for "the conquest of Power (supreme motor of History), reducible in those times to the conquest of royal favor." Still, the families composing the factions—the Mendozas and their allies, rather loosely defined, on the side of Ruy Gómez, and the house of Toledo arrayed around the duke of Alba—were not mere alliances of related spoilsmen but heirs and perpetuators of "conservative" and "liberal" political ideologies originating in the period of *comunero* strife. Alba's *bando* was "the strenuously traditionalist force, partial to absolute power, rigid, and hostile in principle to change and influences from abroad." Eboli's partisans represented "the force open to progress, revisionist, inclusive, flexible and favorable toward moderation in the use of power."[2]

John H. Elliott endorsed Marañón's findings in his *Imperial Spain* (1963), identifying the *albistas* with "'closed' Castilian nationalism" and the *ebolistas* with an "open Spain" ideology. Moreover, he linked the factional struggle to his general conception that the crucial dynamic of early modern Spanish history was a contest between centralizing and federalist-centripetal forces and ideologies.[3] Where Marañón had clearly favored his "liberal" *ebolistas* over Alba's "conservatism," Elliott's sympathies were more complex. Alba had some merit as a proponent of centralization but was simultaneously a retrograde "Castilianizer." Conversely, Eboli's party avoided the pitfall of narrow chauvinism, but it failed to perceive the dangers of clinging to an archaic federal structure.

In 1979 Helen Nader bolstered the Marañón-Elliott thesis with her compelling demonstration that the Mendozas were indeed traditionally "cultured and cosmopolitan,"[4] but she also sounded a warning note (generally unheeded to date) regarding the facile equation of the *ebolistas* with the Mendozas. She observed that during the period of Ruy Gómez de Silva's prominence a predilection for an "open" Spain could not plausibly be attributed to the main stem of the Mendoza family (the house of Infantado and its cadets), but only to those branches founded by the great cardinal.[5] In practical terms this reduced the universe of ideological "liberals" to the house of Mélito, a rather slender reed to support the weight of an "open Spain" ideology. Moreover, Nader's research incidentally called in question the etiology of factionalism proposed by Marañón, by demonstrating that the houses of Toledo and Mendoza had been allies in the political struggles of the early sixteenth century.[6]

Meanwhile, Paul David Lagomarsino studied a key episode of factional division in his dissertation, "Court Factions and the Formulation of Spanish Policy towards the Netherlands (1559–1567)." His conclusions obliquely undermined the notion that an "open–closed" philosophical dichotomy lay at the root of disagreements over Netherlands policy. Instead, personal ties—linking Eboli to various Netherlands nobles and Alba with the nobles' *bête noire*, Granvelle—and the bitter personal enmity between Granvelle and the secretary Francisco de Eraso emerged as principal determinants of the alignments on this issue.[7] The effect, if perhaps not the intent, of Lagomarsino's work was to discredit the notions, stemming from Marañón, that turmoil at the Spanish court had much to do either with grand ideological visions or with the struggle for precedence of large and unitary family blocs.

In his 1983 biography of the duke of Alba, William Maltby rejected the ideological interpretation of the factional rift in favor of a conflation of two explanations: personal antagonism between Alba and Eboli and bitter competition between the kinship networks of the houses of Mendoza and Toledo. Maltby's pithy debunking of the substantive differences in political philosophy posited by Marañón and Elliott is definitive, and, building on Lagomarsino's contribution, he assigns due importance to the jockeying of rival schools of secretaries as an influence on the actual formulation of policy.[8]

To sum up, it is safe to say that the evolution of the historiography has cast grave doubt on the ideological thesis advanced most forcefully by Marañón and endorsed in part by Elliott and others. Indeed, in a recent article José Martínez Millán aptly characterized this interpretation as "stale."[9] The other principal argument, that the factions essentially represented a clash for patronage between two great kinship networks, the Toledos and the Mendozas, is also in important respects untenable. Commentators have always restricted the roster of Alba supporters to close relatives, and this is generally just: the duke certainly was the outstanding leader of his clan. In this regard it is, however, important to remember that the Toledos were a relatively small clan by the standards of the great aristocratic houses of Spain. A graver difficulty is posed by the notion that Ruy Gómez de Silva led and spoke for a close-knit alliance of the huge and widely ramified Mendoza family. Such an idea, though repeatedly asserted, is for the most part unsupported by documentary evidence. Maltby follows Erika Spivakovsky in the dubious assertion that Ruy Gómez de Silva was "courted . . . with almost indecent haste" by the vast Mendoza clan, whose political spokesman and lobbyist he became by virtue of marriage to Doña Ana.[10] I have found no evidence that the Mendozas as a clan sought an alliance with Ruy Gómez or recognized him as their leader. Indeed, as will be seen below, grave doubt must exist that Ruy Gómez was consistently able to dominate even the house of Mélito, the single, comparatively small branch of the Mendozas to which he was closely related. Moreover, the identification of family with faction is contradicted by a pattern of recurrent friction between Ruy Gómez de Silva and such prominent Mendozas as the marquis of Mondéjar. John Owens, in his study of legal wrangling at Philip's court, was puzzled by these contradictions and concluded that "family was obviously not the only basis of the factions despite what many historians have indicated."[11] While it would be absurd to deny that Alba was the head of the Toledo family or that Ruy Gómez sometimes found allies among or performed favors for members of the Mendoza family, the clash between Alba and Eboli cannot be adequately explained as the jostling of family champions for position around the royal pork barrel.

What, then, is left, if neither ideology nor family rivalry suffices to explain the Alba–Eboli conflict? The problem troubled Maltby. Echoing Ranke, he waved it away with the assertion that

> The truth of the matter is that none of this [kinship networks, ideological differences, the more cosmopolitan intellectual tradition of the Mendozas] was as important as the personal equation. Alba and Ruy Gómez were antithetical personalities, and . . . the antagonism between them was deep and visceral.[12]

This is undoubtedly true, at least for the period after 1557, but it raises another set of questions. In what senses were these two "antithetical personalities"? What was the root of their "deep and visceral enmity"?

While often manifested in rather petty episodes, the split between Ruy Gómez de Silva and the duke of Alba reflected strongly held notions of the proper constitution of society and government.

A clash of mentalities, if not of coherent factions or systematic political ideologies, emerges from close examination of the conflicts between these polar figures of the court of Philip II; the two men represented and protagonized conflicting visions of who was socially qualified to collaborate with Philip II in the government of his monarchy. The social distance between the duke of Alba and Ruy Gómez de Silva created the potential for the electrical charges of antagonism that were exchanged between them. This distance largely determined their beliefs and the stormy nature of their interaction. Alba, from head to heels the paragon of Castilian aristocracy, would not and could not accept a position of political and courtly parity with a man so evidently his social inferior. Self-interest reinforced the grandee's instinctive belief that the lords of the earth were born, not created by kings. As was natural, Eboli, the king's man, accepted as right and just the force that had propelled his own ascent. His career had been a demonstration of the sovereign power of monarchs to override social convention. The denouement of the career would, however, provide testimony to the persistent strength of the old order.

Ruy Gómez disembarked in the Low Countries in September 1557, having sailed from Spain with an escorting squadron ordered by Philip II to protect his *privado* from French warships. He rejoined the king at the fortress of Ham in Picardy, which had recently fallen to Habsburg arms.[13] He received a warm welcome from Philip, but the court had changed in ways that threatened the maintenance of his supremacy among the king's advisers. The change was aptly symbolized by the location of Philip's establishment and retinue in the midst of a military camp at Ham. Ruy Gómez de Silva had left for Spain just as the war was beginning; not surprisingly he returned to a court whose composition reflected a preponderance of aristocratic warlords. From the Netherlands, Germany, Spain and Italy, the military elite of the Habsburg world had congregated around the Catholic King. The great lords were joined by hordes of gentleman-adventurers attracted by the opportunities of fighting, booty and preference. The roster assembled in the Netherlands by

1558 was astounding in its length. A list of only the most glittering dignitaries would include the Spanish dukes of Alba, Arcos, Sessa, Francavila and Villahermosa, plus the Netherlandish prince of Orange, counts of Egmont, Horn, Arenberg and Hoogstraten and lords of Berghes and Montigny. From Germany came the duke of Brunswick and Count Mansfelt; and from Italy, the dukes of Savoy and Parma, Semenara and Atri.[14]

Ruy Gómez de Silva had assumed his *privanza* in England and the Netherlands, at a court of comparatively small size, relatively underpopulated with great aristocrats and primarily occupied with peacetime administration rather than the prosecution of warfare. Returning to a court of strutting warriors, he was faced for the first time with two troubling threats to his position of preeminence. First, by necessity the king was much engaged with military questions and was surrounded by aristocratic generals infinitely more qualified than his *privado* to offer advice on such matters. At this very juncture an ambassador noted of Ruy Gómez that "neither his taste nor his studies incline him towards matters of war, and up to now he has not taken part in any military expedition."[15] Second, Ruy Gómez began to face the enmity, envy and resentment of aristocrats, gathered for the first time around their new king and hopeful of gaining his ear and patronage, who saw with dismay that their sovereign was under the spell of a man of much inferior social origins. The Castilian grandees in particular were haughty, scornful and jealous of the *privado*, who was no aristocrat, no warrior and, perhaps even worse, no Castilian. A perspicacious contemporary cited as evidence of the affable manner of Don Antonio de Toledo the observation that he "never has shown himself envious—as have other Spaniards, some of rank less elevated than his—of the honors and favors which he [Philip II] has heaped on Ruy Gómez."[16]

This enmity based on social distance pervaded the atmosphere of Philip's entourage from the time Ruy Gómez de Silva rejoined the court, and the *privado's* activities reflected his attempts to combat this unfavorable constellation of circumstances. Rather predictably, he soon established himself as an advocate of peace with the papacy and with France.[17] What better way to reduce the influence of the men of war than to bring the war to an end? In addition to expediency, some degree of conviction doubtless underlay Ruy Gómez's promotion of peace. For example, in the concluding weeks of the negotiations for the Treaty of Cateau-Cambrésis Ruy Gómez urged the English commissioners to accept the agreement, even though it would leave Calais in the hands of the French. He grounded this argument on the basis that the treaty would give the new queen (Elizabeth) a period of peace, "which is a thing much to be esteemed and wished for of princes at their first advancement to the crown."[18] In addition to expressing some rather mundane political wisdom, Philip's *privado* may have been hinting at personal regret that his king had gone to war so early in the reign, just when his own favor seemed to have been established as paramount.

Beyond pursuing peace, Ruy Gómez sought to defend his position by winning allies among the assembled aristocrats. He seems to have had considerable success among the Netherlanders.[19] The Castilians, more dangerous competitors given Philip's predilection for Spaniards,[20] were more difficult to win over. Ruy Gómez did manage to forge a strong alliance with the count (from 1567, duke) of Feria, Don Gómez Suárez de Figueroa, with whom he had enjoyed friendly relations during the court's sojourn in England. Ruy Gómez wasted no time in setting about to cement this earlier bond of amity. Rejoining Philip at Ham in September 1557, he immediately asked the king to grant a favor to Feria. Before he left Valladolid the marquis of Villanueva had died, leaving vacant the *encomienda* of Segura of the military order of Alcántara. Ruy Gómez prevailed on the king to name Feria to replace the deceased Villanueva.[21] The *privado*'s solicitude paid off, and Feria became a staunch friend and ally, but the expediency that underlay this tentative of friendship did not escape the Venetian Michele Suriano: "Don Ruy Gómez," he wrote, "perhaps from fear of inability to resist single-handed so many who envy him, is uniting himself with the Count de Feria [*sic*], whose repute augments daily."[22]

Although he was no more than "ordinary in intelligence" and physically frail, Feria was generally popular because of his warm disposition and modest manner. He was well liked by Philip II and enjoyed military stature as commander of the king's Spanish Guard.[23] His devotion to Ruy Gómez provided the latter with a valuable and socially legitimizing friendship with at least one of the great Castilian nobles. Badoero thought their relationship worthy of remark when reporting to his masters in Venice:

> Calm and amiable, [Feria] does not know envy, and even though greatly superior in lineage to Ruy Gómez, he has never given any sign of being jealous or resentful of his advancement. On the contrary,

> there exists between them such mutual understanding that he is well
> satisfied to see Ruy Gómez employed, even in preference to himself,
> on secret matters [of state]; for his part, it does not trouble Ruy Gó-
> mez that Feria keeps his head covered in public, even in the king's
> presence, a privilege he enjoys as a grandee of Spain, while he himself
> [Ruy Gómez] has to hold his cap in his hand.[24]

The implication is clear. The attitude of Feria, as a grandee, toward
Ruy Gómez de Silva was noteworthy because it was distinct from
that of other men of his class. Feria was content with the *privanza* of
a man of vastly inferior rank. This attitude was the exception rather
than the rule among the fraternity of the *grandeza*, that crème de
la crème of the Castilian aristocracy whose members cherished the
outward symbols of their supremacy (the right to be addressed as
"cousin" by the king and to cover their heads in the royal presence)
as well as a belief that they were by birthright entitled to monopo-
lize the king's ear and the high offices of state. Other grandees were
much less tolerant of the position and the pretensions of the Portuguese courtier who stood among them, hat in hand.

Among the grandees the most formidable was the duke of Alba,
"presumptuous, swollen with pride, consumed with ambition,
given to flattery and very envious."[25] The duke prided himself on
his long military career, and he was in his own eyes and in those of
some observers the greatest general of the Habsburgs. Other contemporaries were less impressed and depicted him as a timid general, unfit for independent command.[26] Alba was an imposing man,
but not particularly likable. Few dared criticize him to his face, but
he was the subject of pasquinades long before his notorious tenure
in the Netherlands (1567–1573). One lampoon of the 1550s parodied
Alba as a blowhard, subverting in its preamble his punctilio regarding his titles: "To the very illustrious lord, the lord duke of Alba,
Captain-General for both of their Majesties in time of peace, and in
time of war Grand Steward of the Court."[27]

Whatever Alba's merits as a general,[28] there could be no question
about his lofty pedigree or his exalted sense of aristocracy. From his
birth he had imbibed a strong noble ethic of service and entitlement.
"Among the dukes of Alba," according to Maltby, "this tradition was
unusually strong and they were exceptionally ruthless in using it to
mold the characters of their offspring."[29] The duke's sense of his
own dignity, and of his singular fitness as a grandee and a general

to advise the king, was a pronounced characteristic of his personality. With psychological insight, Gregorio Marañón wrote of Alba that "he was excessively sensible of his lineage and the mission of the aristocracy, and it pained him to see men sprung from nothing rise and engross the royal favor."[30]

Thus it was not surprising that immediately upon his return to Brussels in January 1558 the duke of Alba became embroiled in a series of bitter disputes with Ruy Gómez de Silva. The rivalry that began to flare upon Alba's return involved personal disputes, but it must also be seen as a particularly virulent manifestation of the awkward difficulties that had surrounded Ruy Gómez de Silva since his own return to Philip's side in the autumn of 1557. Until their reunion in Brussels in early 1558, the two men had maintained generally cordial relations, at least in public, though there is little doubt that Ruy Gómez had long regarded the duke as a formidable obstacle to his own ambitions. When the duke left for Italy in 1555 Ruy Gómez had still been, in his eyes at least, little more than a superior valet to the prince, useful as a conduit to the shy Philip but hardly a rival as a minister of state. Alba returned, eager for rewards for his service in Italy, to find a Portuguese upstart ensconced as the king's *privado*, arrogating the position of principal adviser that he craved for himself. This situation was intolerable to a man as proud and jealous of the authority of his caste as the duke of Alba. As Ruy Gómez himself had recognized years before, no matter how many honors might be showered upon the duke, he would remain "dissatisfied because he doesn't enjoy the whole" of the king's favor.[31] Alba soon became the embodiment of grandee resentment against the king's *privado* and the prime instigator of attempts to humble Ruy Gómez de Silva.

Some at the court had anticipated that there would be trouble upon the duke's return; in November 1557 the Venetian ambassador reported that "on the Duke of Alva's arrival, some great novelty will possibly be witnessed."[32] Alba was eagerly awaited by others, his relatives and those who hoped to see the flow of favor diverted from Ruy Gómez. Meanwhile, Suriano reported that the *privado* dreaded Alba's arrival and described his attempts to buttress his position in preparation for that event.[33]

When Alba arrived in Brussels on 22 January 1558 he was met with great pomp by the principal figures of Philip's entourage, "with the single exception of Don Ruy Gómez, who from indisposition, real or feigned, did not go out of doors."[34] If his absence was indeed calculated, it may reflect a blunt snub to Alba or, more likely, a desire to evade an occasion where his low birth would make Ruy Gómez seem a small fire in the dazzling sunlight of a gathering of aristocrats. Alba, with a public show of great solicitude, went to visit the *privado* in his lodgings. Maltby drily remarks that Ruy Gómez "was not noticeably cheered by the visit." Among contemporaries, the Venetian ambassador at least was not deceived by this display of amity: "[O]ne cannot believe that between these two such great rivals, there can be any true union."[35] This suspicion was amply justified by events, since Alba and Ruy Gómez immediately fell into a series of disputes.

The first of these involved the disposition of the rich duchy of Bari, which had fallen to Philip II upon the death in November 1557 of its last lord, Bonna Sforza, dowager queen of Poland. The papal legate and peace negotiator in Brussels, Cardinal Carlo Caraffa, staked an early claim to the duchy on behalf of his brother, the dispossessed duke of Paliano.[36] Alba, while still in Italy, had promised Paul IV (Gian Pietro Caraffa) aid in securing this prize for his nephews. Indeed, it appears that this was the keystone of a deal that the duke, exceeding his authority, had made with the pope, under the terms of which Paul IV undertook to restore lands he had confiscated from the Colonna family, Philip's allies and Alba's relatives by marriage. The duke also negotiated with the pope for the grant to himself of some military-order lands in Spain, an arrangement designed to circumvent Philip's supreme authority over the orders.[37]

In late 1557 the king had gotten wind of Alba's maneuvers and was angered by them; as a result, he had postponed a decision on Cardinal Caraffa's claim to Bari until Alba should arrive at court and give an explanation of his conduct. Meanwhile, Alba himself, double-crossing the Caraffas and perhaps scenting further personal advantage, urged Philip to reject the cardinal's claims. For his part the cardinal opposed the restoration of the Colonnas and wanted Bari without any quid pro quo.[38] His displeasure would be heightened tremendously when Alba appeared in Brussels. The duke was hardly dismounted from the saddle before he began to beseech Philip to grant Bari to him, as recompense for his service in Italy.

At this juncture Ruy Gómez de Silva, who had conducted Philip's negotiations with Caraffa (in regard both to the peace and to the issue of Bari), pressed his own importunities on the king, pleading that the duchy should be his.[39] The *privado* had been quite willing to see Bari go to the house of Caraffa but clearly did not want it to fall into the hands of his rival the duke. According to Cabrera de Córdoba, Ruy Gómez claimed Bari not as recompense for any particular service but "for the advance of his clientage and favor."[40] This analysis of motive comes close to the mark. Because of Alba's unexpected claim the disposition of the duchy had gained symbolic importance as a test of the relative strength of Philip's devotion to his *privado* and to his victorious general. Already alarmed by the prospect of Alba's renewed presence at court, Ruy Gómez was not prepared to allow the duke an uncontested victory in a matter of royal patronage, a victory that might be interpreted as a sign that the king's favor was shifting away from his *privado*.

According to Cabrera de Córdoba, these claims and counter-claims

> cast peace from the King's household and provoked secret jealous rivalries founded on issues of individual power, authority and interest, conducted with discretion insufficient to prevent their traces from emerging publicly.[41]

Philip II was placed in an exceedingly awkward position in all this. Ingeniously, the king resolved the dilemma by asserting that he was unsure of the legitimacy of his own inheritance of Bari. To buy time he sent a commission to Poland to inquire into the matter with the counselors of the deceased Bonna Sforza and fobbed off Caraffa with some lesser concessions. When at length his ownership of Bari, never truly in doubt, was confirmed, the duchy was granted to no one but instead remained part of the king's own Italian patrimony. Both Caraffa and Alba were openly angry at the rejection of their claims; Ruy Gómez greeted the decision with greater equanimity, most likely because his primary goal had been to thwart Alba's bid for a signal acknowledgment of royal favor.[42]

By March the news of dissension in Brussels was current at the French court. Henry II had "heard that King Philip's ministers had not a good understanding together" and expressed the view that this situation rendered a serious peace parley unlikely, since the duke and Ruy Gómez each "pretend that they are [*sic*] to be the chief in every negotiation."[43] The French king proved an apt analyst. The duke, smarting from his failure to win Bari, cast himself in heated opposition to Ruy Gómez's ongoing peace offensive, which in early 1558 took the form of an impassioned speech in the Council of State imploring Philip to conclude a peace and then to return to Spain forthwith. Perhaps he quoted the gloomy views that Gutierre López de Padilla had shared with him:

> If the king tries this time to achieve more than has already been accomplished [in the previous summer's campaign], he will likely reproduce what his father did on other occasions, which was ... to enter France dining on fat fowl but then return grubbing for roots.[44]

Meanwhile, Ruy Gómez argued, the peninsular kingdoms needed to see their ruler and anyway were more important to the king than were the troublesome northern lands. Most likely his primary interest was to remove Philip from the war zone and the influence of his generals. If the war had to continue, perhaps Alba could be left behind while the king and his *privado* returned to Iberia. According to Alba's biographer, Antonio Ossorio, "the military men and those who had more desire of glory than of returning to the fatherland listened with displeasure to this discourse." Alba championed their views, arguing that the war could and must be prosecuted to a successful conclusion and that the king's reputation would suffer grievous harm if he abandoned the fighting or the personal leadership of his armies. To urge the king to leave the Netherlands now was to counsel pusillanimity. Philip longed to return to Spain and is said to have preserved a stony silence during the debate. But if his *privado*'s arguments tempted him, he nevertheless chose to accept Alba's counsel on this issue. Again according to the hostile Ossorio, Ruy Gómez de Silva did not accept his defeat with good grace but instead continued to lobby for the king's return to Spain, and he carried his displeasure so far as to impede intentionally the preparations for the campaign of 1558.[45]

This clash rather neatly foreshadowed the next decade's dispute over policy toward the rebellious Netherlands, which above all else has given rise to the notion of an ideological split between *albistas* and *ebolistas*. Both in 1558 and in 1565–1566 it is, however, difficult to discern much beyond self-interest in the vaunted "pacifism" of

Ruy Gómez de Silva. The idea that this pacifism was a matter of personal principle does seem at first glance to find support in Suriano's observation that Ruy Gómez placed more trust in the 1558 peace offers of the papal legate than did the other lords surrounding Philip II, "because he above all of them has always peace and quiet at heart."[46] Still, the context—a comparison with the attitudes of Philip's generals[47]—is significant. Ruy Gómez's "pacific tendency," such as it was, is perhaps best understood in relation to another remark of Ranke's: "In matters of war indeed Alva always had a decisive voice."[48] In peacetime Ruy Gómez de Silva could expect to exercise a preponderant influence on his king; in wartime he could not. This simple truth was enough to make him an advocate of moderation and nonbelligerence.

These first rounds of sparring between Alba and Ruy Gómez had essentially ended in a draw. The *privado* had successfully blocked Alba's bid for the *merced* of Bari but had himself been thwarted in an attempt to remove the king from the theater of war. On the latter issue, Philip characteristically had revealed himself more susceptible to the call of duty and glory than to an appeal to comfort and expedience. The king doubtless recognized the undertones of self-interest in both positions in the debate over the war. Ruy Gómez de Silva ought to have sensed a warning in the fact that Philip remained sufficiently an aristocrat to find Alba's self-interested arguments more honorable than his own. Still, the king soon showed himself willing to defy Alba's wishes in other spheres. The duke's victory on the issue of abandoning the Netherlands was followed by a setback; in April Alba was infuriated by Philip's choices to fill the Italian proconsular posts that he had left. Perhaps Alba had hoped to return to these powerful positions. Certainly the duke did not approve of the king's dispatch of Juan Manrique de Lara to Naples to serve as temporary lieutenant there until a permanent viceroy could be named. Manrique de Lara had angered the house of Toledo in 1555 by reporting (accurately) that Alba's uncle, the cardinal-archbishop of Santiago, Juan Alvarez de Toledo, had contravened royal instructions to oppose Gian Pietro Caraffa in the papal conclave (Caraffa was elected as Paul IV). Even more galling was the fact that the new lieutenant was being sent to Naples to replace Alba's son, Fadrique de Toledo, whom the duke had left in charge when he returned to the north.[49] The reasons for the duke's opposition to the choice of the duke of Sessa as governor of Milan are less evident, although the bishop of Limoges noted in 1560 that the two men had fallen out during Alba's period of command in Italy.[50] Moreover, Sessa's candidacy had probably been supported by Ruy Gómez, as part of his search for aristocratic allies, and this was enough to set Alba in opposition to the choice. The fact that both Manrique de Lara and Sessa subsequently looked upon Ruy Gómez as a patron supports the surmise that Philip's *privado* lobbied for their appointments.[51] In any case, the court interpreted these appointments as a royal rebuke of Alba, and the angry duke, employing a tactic to which he would recur time and again, threatened to leave court and retire to his estates in Spain. Such a course of events, according to the Venetian ambassador, would "render Don Ruy Gómez absolute lord of everything," an outcome that surely would have pleased the *privado*.[52] Alba soon dropped his threat to leave and seems to have moderated his behavior for a time, perhaps chastened by this clear demonstration that Philip had the force of character to thwart his own powerful will.

Whatever tensions continued to exist between Alba and Ruy Gómez, their conflict escaped public notice during the remainder of the court's sojourn in the Netherlands. The two rivals, along with Feria, had the leading voices in the Council of State and coexisted there and as counselors during the peace negotiations without major incident.[53] The status differential between Ruy Gómez and the aristocrats was, however, underlined repeatedly in the summer of 1559. Alba was chosen to stand proxy for the king in the wedding ceremony with Isabel de Valois that sealed the treaty of Cateau-Cambrésis. Ruy Gómez had beseeched Philip to entrust him with this mission, to no avail; such an exalted ceremonial post demanded lofty aristocratic credentials.[54] Alphonse de Ruble, himself a nobleman and thus perhaps sensitized to the ceremonial protocol of an earlier age, remarked that Philip's choice in this matter

> wavered between Frederick [*sic*] of Toledo, duke of Alba, and Ruy Gómez de Silva. . . . The former was a grand seigneur; the latter a petty gentleman whom the king's favor had raised to the first rank. The King of Spain was made to perceive that propriety imposed upon him the nomination of the former.[55]

Meanwhile Philip sent the duke of Arcos—in the king's words "a person of such quality and authority as is required in such a case"—

to express his condolences to the royal family upon the death of Henry II.[56] For similar reasons Ruy Gómez de Silva was passed over, in favor of Alba, Arcos, the prince of Orange and Count Egmont, in the selection of the ritual hostages who were dispatched to Paris in June 1559 to guarantee fulfillment of the peace terms. The "hostages," whose duties in practice consisted of submitting to a round of dazzling fetes, had to be men of the highest honor—that is to say, aristocrats. Once the proxy wedding had been celebrated Ruy Gómez was allowed to carry Philip's wedding gift of jewels (valued at 133,000 ducats) to Isabel, but another aristocrat, the count of Feria, was delegated to escort the royal bride to Spain.[57]

Philip's grant on 1 July 1559 of the title of prince of Eboli was perhaps intended in part to provide Ruy Gómez with the semblance of aristocratic credentials. If so, the strategy did not succeed very well. Rather than diminishing, aristocratic envy and rancor toward Ruy Gómez de Silva rose to unprecedented levels. After Philip's departure from the north in the fall of 1559 the English diplomatic agent in Antwerp reported a rumor current there that Ruy Gómez de Silva had been imprisoned in Spain. In some versions the *privado's* offense was reputed to be that he had usurped aristocratic privilege by engaging in hunting; others had it that Ruy Gómez had fallen afoul of the Inquisition. The Englishman was skeptical: "if he be so imprisoned it is of envy and cruel malice, for many of the great do not brook his greatness, as the Duke of Alva."[58] The rumor proved groundless, but the suspicion of malice is borne out both by the identity of the gossipmongers and by the nature of the offenses they ascribed to Ruy Gómez de Silva. The principal sources of the tale were the secretary Gonzalo Pérez, at that time a staunch Alba partisan, along with various "men and women of blood and reputation" among the Spanish community in Antwerp.[59] Moreover, the accusations cast Ruy Gómez either as a baseborn upstart overthrown by an attempt to ape his betters or as a heretic uncovered by the Inquisition. The former calumny was a wildly exaggerated slur on Ruy Gómez's origins, since, although he was no grandee, he was undoubtedly a nobleman and thus entitled to hunt. The latter charge of heresy was serious slander in any case and perhaps should be interpreted as an ethnic insult as well, given the traditional Castilian conviction of the religious laxity of the Portuguese.

Ruy Gómez left France laden with gifts of jewelry from the young King Francis II.[60] He and the other luminaries of Philip's court grad-

ually reassembled in the imperial city of Toledo during the fall of
1559. Perhaps in hopes of diluting the rancor between his principal
subordinates, the king summoned an enlarged Council of State,
over which he would personally preside. This was not to be an oner-
ous task, since, owing to the difficulties encountered in assembling
the sixteen councilors, the Council of State met only twice between
November 1559 and the summer of 1560.[61] An ineffective advisory
board, the expanded council proved equally useless as a device to
reduce tensions at court. Alba was reportedly affronted by the very
notion of a council:

> [H]e cannot stand being put on the same footing with the others in
> the deliberations [of the council], and (so they say) would like the
> king to make him chief and supreme member of the government,
> renouncing the whole burden to him.[62]

As the other councilors made their way to Toledo, the duke, true to
form, sulked in his ancestral tent.[63]

Alba emerged from his estates only in order to accompany Philip
to his formal marriage to Isabel de Valois, which was held in Guadalajara's Infantado Palace at the end of January 1560. The wedding
festivities were conducted with full ceremonial pomp amid a notable gathering of the elite, including

> the Cardinal of Burgos, the Dukes of Brunswick, Alba, Infantado, Ver-
> agua, the Admiral of Castile, Count of Benavente, Marquis of Cenete,
> Marquis of Denia, the grand priors of Castile, the grand master of
> Montesa, the Count of Alba [de Liste], Marquis of Soria, Duke of Es-
> calona, Prince of Sulmona, all [of them] grand seigneurs, and various
> other marquises, counts, and lords who are neither counted nor
> placed in the rank of the grandees, and a great number of ordinary
> gentlemen as well; and you may be sure that each one had been posi-
> tioned in proper order [of precedence].[64]

Alba and his duchess served as *padrinos*,[65] while Eboli attended—
and, indeed, had helped to arrange the spectacle. Despite his newly
minted title, though, he had to hang back in the caparisoned throng,
outside the charmed circle of the grandees. Doubtless this galled
Ruy Gómez de Silva as much as it delighted the duke of Alba.[66]

This sort of satisfaction was not, however, sufficient to pacify the
duke for long. The king returned to Toledo from his brief honeymoon to find that Alba had escalated his demands. Paolo Tiepolo,

the ambassador of Venice, reported on 16 February 1560 that "Alva gave it clearly to be understood that he would not go to the Court if Don Ruy Gómez was there (and this has been the chief cause of Alva's absence hitherto)."[67] Philip, placed in a quandary, attempted to appease the duke, but not at the price of banishing his *privado*. Tiepolo, who held Alba's talents as a counselor in high regard, believed that Philip II was disgusted with the duke's behavior but felt the need of his advice. "Therefore," he wrote to his masters, "it is under compulsion rather than voluntarily that he holds the Duke in account."[68]

The king, then, would try to lure Alba back to court with flattery and favors. In the meantime, though, while the duke again withdrew to his estates, preponderant influence in the day-to-day operation of the government fell increasingly to Eboli and to Francisco de Eraso. The two old allies collaborated smoothly and were able to wrest control from the unwieldy Council of State.[69] Ruy Gómez was firmly in charge of the government's most ambitious project of 1560, the drafting of a new apportionment (*encabezamiento general*) of the *alcabalas*. The *privado* supervised a survey of the population and wealth of Castile, and the tax burden was redistributed among the administrative districts of the kingdom on the basis of the new figures. This was a complex and sensitive task, and it was carried out smoothly by Ruy Gómez and his collaborators. The new *encabezamiento* went into effect in 1561 and met none of the popular outcry that greeted the next reapportionment, in 1575. The burden evidently was computed realistically, since the *alcabalas* returned the prescribed 456 million *maravedís* per year throughout the fifteen-year term of the *encabezamiento*, a success seldom duplicated in the history of Habsburg Spain.[70] Ruy Gómez was richly rewarded for his achievement; the king, appreciative of this bright spot in an otherwise gloomy financial picture,[71] granted his favorite the proceeds of the excise on inheritances of 100,000 *maravedís* or more, collected during the term of the *encabezamiento*.[72] The records of this revenue have been lost, so the value of the *merced* is unknown. Nevertheless, even allowing for lax collection practices, the amount must have been considerable.

Philip's blandishments brought Alba back to the court, then summering at Madrid, during June and July 1560, but the duke's sojourn was brief. He could not tolerate the fact that Eboli and Eraso dominated the business of state. This situation was not simply an affront to Alba's belief in his own indispensability, reported Tiepolo; it also offended a more general principle. The duke was enraged because he could not "suffer others, unworthy to be compared with him, to have power equal to his, and superior to it in some respects."[73] In other words, Alba believed that there should be a strict correlation between social rank and the distribution of political influence within the monarchy.

The vehemence of this belief was demonstrated in a remarkable scene enacted in the *alcázar* of Madrid during that summer. One day, in June, Alba presented himself at the royal chambers, only to find the king closeted in his study with Francisco de Eraso. The duke tried the key that he held as *mayordomo mayor*, but found it blocked by another inserted from within. He then knocked on the door and demanded entry. Without opening the door, Eraso responded that he could not come in. Alba flew into a rage at being denied and shown up before the other gentlemen waiting in the anteroom. Shouting from the hallway, he hurled abuse at Eraso and demanded the king's leave to retire from court, on the grounds that he could no longer bear such humiliation. Philip II attempted to calm the irate grandee but finally granted Alba permission to leave for a few days. Two months later the duke still had not returned to court, despite repeated royal summons. Once again the king resorted to flattery and urgent pleas for advice in an effort to draw Alba back to court.[74] Tiepolo's argument in justification of the king's behavior, that Philip desperately felt the need of Alba's counsel, is somewhat weakened by the fact that he had governed successfully without it during the majority of his reign. On the contrary, it is hard to avoid the suspicion that the king still felt intimidated by this imposing general who had served his father; otherwise, it is next to impossible to account for Philip's equanimity in the face of Alba's temper tantrums and repeated ultimatums.

While the haughty duke raved and fumed in the halls of the court, these were years of quiet desperation for Ruy Gómez de Silva. If Alba continued to fail in his efforts to exalt himself above all rivals, he and his allies had at least succeeded in ensuring that Ruy Gómez, no matter how strong his favor with the king, could never forget their scorn for his origins. In 1558 the *privado* had viewed a return to Spain as a solution to his problems with envious aristocrats. Once his wish was granted, though, he found that he had exchanged one unenviable position for another. On their home ground the grandees' rancor and jealousy intensified and were magnified by the presence at Toledo or Madrid of their large retinues of retainers and relatives, which had been absent in the Netherlands. At the court of Castile Ruy Gómez de Silva was immersed in an environment more overtly hostile than he had experienced in the north.

Simultaneously, in the first years back in Spain, Ruy Gómez was harassed by illness. During the negotiations at Cateau-Cambrésis he had been stricken by a severe fever (a "quartan ague" in the parlance of the day), which recurred for years afterward.[75] By early 1560 it was evident that the tandem onslaughts of animosity and sickness were exacting a heavy personal toll. An ambassador who called upon the king in the second week of February to congratulate him on his marriage found Philip "accompanied by Don Ruy Gómez, who is suffering much from his fever, but yet more from the recent and violent persecution of many of these chief personages [of the court]."[76]

In a report drafted in September 1560 the French envoy to the court of Spain—the bishop of Limoges, Sebastien de l'Aubespine—described the campaign being waged against Ruy Gómez. By his account the origins of the current struggle lay in the resolution of the old allies Alba and Arras, taken while Philip's court was still in the Low Countries, to regain control of the business of the monarchy. Once Alba was back in Spain "he labored to engross the affairs of state, to respond to the ambassadors, and generally, after the person of the king his master, to do singlehanded what I have seen my lord the constable of France do."[77] This ambition set him on a collision course with Philip's *privado*, and in order to humble Ruy Gómez the duke enlisted the aid of his peers. Alba

> thoroughly captivated and drew to himself the grandees of Spain, who then broadcast widely, and remarked even in the presence of the Catholic King, that all the kingdoms hum with gossip about how he lets the likes of Ruy Gómez govern.[78]

The grandees objected that the *privado* "was a poor gentleman, [and] a Portuguese foreigner," and they went beyond this scorn to more serious charges, "engaging in a multitude of inventions to calumniate him . . . and even attacking him for his religion and wishing to entangle him with the Inquisition."[79] De l'Aubespine believed that Ruy Gómez's quartan ague was a physical manifestation of the anguish caused by the grandees' assaults on his character and position.[80]

Paolo Tiepolo, who represented the Most Serene Republic at Philip's court from mid-1558 until the end of 1562, provided another revealing account of Ruy Gómez's troubles in his retrospective report to the Venetian Senate, read on 19 January 1563. According to Tiepolo, immediately upon his return to Spain the *privado* was forced to recognize that many of the Castilian grandees, spurred by Alba, were envious and bitter toward him "for being a foreigner of the kingdom of Portugal and not very highly born."[81] Another observer noted Ruy Gómez's kindness to the French ladies who had accompanied the new queen to Madrid and attributed the *privado*'s empathy to the circumstance that he was "himself a foreigner and in the same position as the others, so much do some lords here at times make war against him."[82] Ruy Gómez greatly feared their personal attacks and malicious gossip. Tiepolo's description of his attempts to parry this threat suggests that Ruy Gómez adopted a two-pronged defensive strategy. First, he altered his political behavior. The *privado*'s very visible exercise of power had excited envy; in an effort to neutralize this irritant, Ruy Gómez lowered his political profile. Initially, he

> judiciously retired, and remained for a time away from the court, sometimes by reason of his quartan fever and other times for some other reason, so that for the most part the occasion of speaking about him was removed.[83]

When he was at court Ruy Gómez adopted a more deferential role in the formal processes of decisionmaking. Since Philip's accession to the throne Ruy Gómez had exercised power openly, as dominant minister in the councils of the government. Now he began to retreat from this exposed public position and reverted to the safer ground of private influence with Philip, which had been the sole basis of his power prior to 1556. The high tide of his *privanza* had been reached as Eboli's personal favor swept forth to overrun and engross more and more public power. Now, around 1560, the tide began to ebb. Under pressure from his rivals Ruy Gómez retreated from the public sphere to the refuge of the royal household. This process is encapsulated in Tiepolo's description. At the Spanish court, Eboli

> has not wished to return to the business of state as in Flanders, where everyone was in the habit of coming to him, and insofar as possible he has escaped it; and he has often waited to be asked to go in to the council, where, when he has entered, he has offered little opposition, indeed almost deferring to the others ["riportandosi quasi agli altri"], showing himself well-contented to be chief of the Council of Hacienda. . . . But nevertheless on the matters that weighed upon him, he has not ceased doing one on one *in camera* with the king all that he might want.[84]

This withdrawal from a provocative prominence that excited envy and malice was accompanied by another behavioral adaptation. As his overt interest in matters of state and administration diminished, Ruy Gómez began to evince a greater concern with "his own comforts and pleasures, and particularly gaming with balls, cards and dice."[85] While Eboli assuaged the grandees' injured sensibilities by seeming to defer to their desire to dominate the constituted organs of government, perhaps he could win some social acceptance by enthusiastically engaging in their private world of leisure. Here perhaps is the first subtle evidence of an incipient design to escape his torments by joining the ranks of the tormentors. This interpretation is reinforced by the fact that, in this period, Ruy Gómez began to scout properties that might be suitable for a private estate outside Madrid. In March 1561 the count of Buendía complained of Ruy Gómez's repeated absences from the meetings of the Council of Hacienda. The count felt that his business before the council was being slighted; meanwhile, Ruy Gómez was supervising some construction that he had undertaken in the rural village of Estremera.[86]

In Tiepolo's opinion, by the end of his ambassadorial tenure in Madrid this strategy of withdrawal had enabled Ruy Gómez "for the most part to avoid and extinguish that envy which had nearly overwhelmed him."[87] Eboli weathered this crisis, but only at the price of acquiescing in the grandees' demands that he should recognize the social distance that separated him from the truly great figures of Castile. The king had not withdrawn his favor, but neither had he extended it to include a warning or rebuke to Alba or his allies for their obstreperous antagonism toward his favorite. Philip's rather dispassionate and evenhanded arbitration of the disputes between Alba and Eboli, his remarkable patience with Alba's repeated provocations and his failure to intervene when invidious rancor threatened to destroy his favorite, should perhaps be seen as further confirmation of the king's innate conservatism and punctilio regarding (in Elliott's phrase) "inherited obligation and . . . the bonds of legality."[88] In elevating Ruy Gómez de Silva to the status of a *privado*, Philip had, perhaps inadvertently, issued a challenge to the traditional authority, perquisites and sensibilities of the aristocracy. When they rose to this challenge, he had in essence acknowledged the justice of their grievances by allowing them to heap his creature with scorn. He had shown himself unwilling to defy the customary pretensions of the aristocrats by forcing them to accept the legitimacy and social prestige of an authority that derived from his own sovereign will rather than from inherited position and privilege.

The struggle between Alba and Eboli, then, though played out sometimes on issues of policy and sometimes on questions of patronage, was in its origins not so much a conflict between factions as a means of conducting a debate over precedence and propriety in the structure of the top echelon of government service. The actual contestants were a number of the grandees, championed by Alba, and the king, Philip II. Ruy Gómez's role was more passive than active; he was in a sense the issue in the conflict, or at least its most visible embodiment. At stake were the legitimacy of his *privanza* and, more generally, the king's right to exalt lowborn courtiers to positions of equality or precedence over the members of the traditional aristocratic elite.

This is not to say that the clash did not give rise to a polarization within the Council of State that was augmented and compounded by preexistent rivalries between the major "schools" of royal secretaries. The rise of the factions, though, was a product not of diametrically opposed policy viewpoints nor of the patronage struggles of great kinship networks. Instead, factionalization was a natural consequence of the animosity that arose between Alba and Ruy Gómez less because of differences of opinion than because of differences in social stature. Their struggle for precedence inevitably poisoned personal relationships within the government. As Suriano noted, anyone who sought or received the favor of one of the two great rivals lost the friendship of the other; to agree with Alba on any issue meant to draw the ire of Eboli, and vice versa.[89] In de l'Aubespine's words, "these lords are so divided among themselves that what one of them likes is made abominable to the other."[90] Agreement on matters of principle or ties of blood relation or similarity of social status might predispose one or another figure to identify either with Alba or Ruy Gómez, but, as Lagomarsino has demonstrated, factional allegiance was prone to sudden and repeated shifts; it is thus better explained as a matter of day-to-day expediency than of devotion to clearly enunciated party programs.[91] Factional identification, then, was a nearly inevitable concomitant of existence in a court dominated for years by a dramatic tension between its most prominent individuals. Shifts in this identification were largely reflections of betting on the outcome of the struggle, of individual reactions to the subtle, oscillating indications of Philip's opinion about who—the *privado* he had elevated or the chief of the Castilian grandees—should be first minister of his government.

6

Safely into Port

Although Philip II refused to force Alba to recognize Ruy Gómez de Silva as his chief minister or to intervene to put an end to the sniping of jealous aristocrats, he nevertheless showed no signs during this period that his personal affection for Eboli was waning. On the contrary, one observer wrote, in the midst of Alba's outbursts in 1560, that

> it is evident that his Majesty's mind towards Don Ruy Gómez is not in the least changed, and that he loves him as heartily as he ever loved him[;] many persons are of the opinion that in secret Ruy Gómez will always have greater favour and authority with the King than anyone else.[1]

But be this as it may, Ruy Gómez had been deeply wounded by Alba's attacks, and he remarked to the bishop of Limoges that the duke was "a melancholic enemy of men, who would ruin their court and their master."[2] The *privado's* withdrawal from the public stage of the court was a response to this hurt, but Ruy Gómez also professed to hope that it would help to bring down his enemy. "He was well-satisfied," reported de l'Aubespine,

> that all matters were remitted to the Duke of Alba, and well pleased to see every day the anxieties and importunities of a thousand persons, expecting that in the end, since this nation is scurrilous in its envy, rancor and deceit against favorites, the said duke would suffer the same penalty that he had.[3]

Meanwhile he kept to himself, continuing in private his supervision of the finances and, observers believed, plotting with Francavila, Eraso, Mondéjar (from 1561 president of the Council of Castile) and the king's confessor against Alba. The duke, despite "lamenting . . . the fortune of those who carry the burden of public affairs," seems in 1561 to have been the paramount public front man for Philip's government.[4] Ruy Gómez's hopes were doubtless raised that sum-

mer by the rumor circulating in Madrid that his nemesis would be
sent to Naples as viceroy—it was remarked that the duke's departure would leave Eboli and Eraso "kings" at court—but Alba held
fast to the position that he would never leave Spain except to accompany the king.[5]

In the following year, though, the tide began to turn against Alba.
The early months of 1562 saw the court convulsed by a rather obscure intrigue precipitated by the death of the count of Alba de
Liste. Alba coveted his deceased kinsman's post as *mayordomo mayor*
to the queen. Ruy Gómez operated behind the scenes promoting
candidates of his own, first the duke of Medinaceli and then Alba's
own relatives, García de Toledo and Antonio de Toledo. Presumably
Eboli hoped to sow discord within the house of Toledo, and the
outcome—Alba was named acting *mayordomo,* but Philip procrasti-
nated in selecting a permanent successor—seems to have rankled
the duke.[6] Alba's frayed temper was stretched past the breaking
point in August 1563. Convinced that Philip was slighting him in
order to bestow lavish *mercedes* on Ruy Gómez de Silva, the duke
stormed off to his estates once again.[7] This time the breach was
prolonged; a year later the secretary Vargas reported to Granvelle
that Alba had not consulted with the king in the interim.[8]

With his rival once more out of the way, Eboli was clearly the
chief figure in the government during the king's visit to his Aragonese kingdoms in the fall and winter of 1563–1564.[9] Foreign observers again remarked on his great favor with Philip.[10] Still, Granvelle at least realized that, despite Ruy Gómez de Silva's apparent
victory in this round, the struggle was hardly decided. He praised
Eboli to Gonzalo Pérez for using "his grandeur and *privanza* very
modestly" but observed that it was still the case that, "if some are
content with his grandeur, others are not."[11] Although Ruy Gómez
de Silva had begun by 1563–1564 to recover from the low ebb of his
fortunes, the continuing strength of his enemies, coupled with the
king's growing reluctance to bestow his favor unconditionally,
meant that Eboli was never again to attain the great heights of
power that he had scaled in the 1550s.

During these years Ruy Gómez demonstrated a mastery of courtly skills unmatched by any of his contemporaries at the court of Spain. His dual achievement of the early 1560s—moderating "that envy which had nearly overwhelmed him" without any real help from his protector the king and simultaneously maintaining Philip's favor— comprised a triumph of the artful style of the Renaissance courtier. Beginning in his youth Ruy Gómez had labored to perfect this style; his rise to power and prominence had been effected through masterful courtiership, employed first to attract the prince's eye and then to impress Philip and others with his ability to maneuver within the environment of the court and household. By middle age Ruy Gómez had become a model courtier who might have stepped straight from the pages of Castiglione. "Look at the Spaniards," exclaimed Calmeta in the *Book of the Courtier,* "who seem to be the masters in Courtiership."[12] A brief examination of the courtly style of Ruy Gómez de Silva will perhaps confirm this observation.

He was favored by nature for the role. Castiglione's prescription for the physical size and appearance of the courtier called for a body neither too large nor too small but well-proportioned and fit for "agile exercise." "And hence I would have him well built and shapely of limb," the writer continued, "and would have him show strength and lightness and suppleness."[13] Compare Badoero's description (1557):

> Ruy Gómez is . . . of medium height. His eyes are bold and full of lively intelligence, his hair and beard black and curly, his frame delicate but his constitution robust. . . . He is graceful in all his movements and very courteous, with certain innate qualities that win him affection and esteem.[14]

The Venetian commented further on Ruy Gómez's "subtle frame", while another observer remarked on his "handsome aspect."[15] Portraits of the prince of Eboli indeed reveal a thin, lithe and handsome man, with a straight nose, dark watchful eyes and full beard, dressed stylishly in a velvet doublet and tights, a flat cap, lacy ruff and jeweled chains.[16] All in all, he might have embodied the perfect courtly specimen described by Count Ludovico in *The Book of the Courtier,* a man

> endowed by nature not only with talent and with beauty of countenance and person, but with that certain grace which we call an "air,"

which shall make him at first sight pleasing and lovable to all who see him.[17]

For Castiglione, a principal benefit of physical beauty and agility was their utility in attracting admiring public notice. In particular the courtier should show himself adept in gentlemanly competitions; in

> jousts, tourneys, stick-throwing, or in any other bodily exercise—mindful of the place where he is and in whose presence, he will strive to be as elegant and handsome in the exercise of arms as he is adroit, and to feed his spectators' eyes with all those things that he thinks may give him added grace. . . . [H]e will take care to have a horse gaily caparisoned, to wear a becoming attire, to have appropriate mottoes and ingenious devices that will attract the eyes of the spectators even as the loadstone [*sic*] attracts iron.[18]

And indeed, throughout his career Ruy Gómez cut a prominent figure at tournaments and jousts. He debuted at Valladolid in 1543 in a splendid display of finery, participated in the round of tourneys that marked Prince Philip's progress through Italy and the Low Countries in 1549–1550, won a prize from Queen Mary at an English joust in 1554 and was still competing in 1560 at Toledo.[19] Badoero observed that, prior to 1556 and his assumption of a major governmental role, Ruy Gómez's "only study was to serve the king in his chamber, to please the king in everything, and to shine in jousts and tourneys."[20]

Hunting provided another opportunity for distinction in courtly and aristocratic circles, and Ruy Gómez was eager to make a good showing in this arena as well. For example, in 1563 he went to considerable lengths to outbid Don Antonio de Toledo, Alba's kinsman and Philip's master of the horse, for the prized hunting greyhound "Marugan." Ruy Gómez may have been more intent upon depriving his rival of this flashy animal than on hunting with it. The breeder at least seems to have suspected as much, and Eboli's reply did not entirely dispel this notion: "Since I have great affection and desire for this sort of hunting, if the occasion arises I shan't fail to take advantage of your offer [of more dogs], but for now this one will suffice."[21]

Tourneys, mounted bullfights, hunting and the like were of course a sort of mock military exercise, but they also provided the courtier with a chance to demonstrate his equestrian skills:

> I wish our Courtier [wrote Castiglione] to be a perfect horseman in
> every kind of saddle; and, in addition to having a knowledge of
> horses and what pertains to riding, let him put every effort and dili-
> gence into outstripping others in everything . . . [22]

Although he never rode to war, Ruy Gómez was a dedicated horseman. No record of his proficiency has come down to us, but his
interest is attested by the fact that he maintained a large stable of
riding horses, carriage teams and mules. Already in 1557 his agent
wrote that the horses in his string were "the finest that exist now in
Spain." At his death Ruy Gómez's stock included a small white pony
named "La Polonia" and a prancing black horse suitable for ceremonial processions and perhaps for use in mounted bullfighting. One
of Eboli's finest mounts was "the silver-gray horse that is called Ribera," likely an Arabian. He also maintained a number of carriages,
and he undoubtedly cut a fine figure on the streets of Madrid in his
leather-covered coach, upholstered in cochineal-dyed satin.[23]

For Castiglione, in addition to these physical attributes and skills,
the ideal courtier should be "more than passably learned in letters,
at least in those studies which we call the humanities," and should
enjoy some familiarity with the classical languages and fluency in
the principal vernaculars.[24] In this realm Ruy Gómez's courtly credentials were less imposing. His education remains a mystery. Some
authors, on uncertain evidence, imply that he was educated alongside the young Prince Philip.[25] If so, his role in accompanying the
prince was undoubtedly more that of a servant than a fellow pupil
of Juan Martínez Siliceo, Philip's tutor and a rather uninspired hu-
manist.[26] No evidence exists that, as a youth, Ruy Gómez received
any formal education outside the context of this court school. In
later life, though, the *privado* seems to have felt the lack of thorough
instruction and set out, at least for a time, to remedy his deficiencies. Badoero commented that

> He shows no fondness for letters; however, since the king has con-
> fided important matters to him, he has attempted to acquire instruc-
> tion, and has been at some pains to achieve this, but lately, whether
> because of the press of business, or because his *maestro* lacks talent,
> he has renounced it.[27]

According to the Venetian, Ruy Gómez was not a particularly versa-
tile linguist: "He speaks no language but Spanish, but he speaks it
to perfection, and understands a great deal of Italian."[28] This ac-

count gives a somewhat misleading impression, since Spanish was not his native tongue; in addition, he may have learned passable English in the mid-1550s.[29] Although we can catch a glimpse of him in 1563 taking down an ambassador's speech in French and then repeating it word-for-word in Spanish, a recognition of linguistic shortcomings perhaps lay behind Ruy Gómez's uncharacteristic reluctance to accept an illustrious position as a commissioner for peace talks with the French in 1555.[30]

Of course, his demurrer on this occasion—"I am not sufficiently experienced to be of use in this connexion, and I will see what I had better do in case it falls to me to be present"—might be seen as an instance of the modesty thought becoming in a courtier.[31] Modesty was prized primarily as a precaution against engendering jealousy, which was perceived as a great pitfall for the courtier. Castiglione judged that a man striving for recognition at court must avoid affectation and presumption and exercise great sensitivity in interpersonal relations in order to avoid exciting envy. Only rare individuals could consistently enjoy both success and popularity. Prowess and competence would not suffice to win respect and friendship for the courtier,

> for, truly we are all naturally more ready to censure errors than to praise things well done; and many men, from a kind of innate malice, and even when they clearly see the good, strive with all effort and care to discover some fault.[32]

As we have seen, in the years of his *privanza* the prince of Eboli was the focus of a raging storm of envy at the court of Philip II, and he calmed its worst outbursts in the early 1560s by exercising the sort of amiable self-effacement counseled by Castiglione. His efforts along these lines were well described by Luis Cabrera de Córdoba:

> [Ruy Gómez de Silva] made friends of enemies, granting them favors so that they should know his power: a hard and difficult action, generous, noble and Christian, but the difficulty enhances the virtue. He knew his rivals and defeated them courteously, shunning the occasions of open quarrels, doing good to their friends so that they might moderate their ill will. He restrained his retinue when he was moving through the Court.[33]

Ruy Gómez's technique for deflecting envy seems to have been one of passive amiability. Instead of engaging in undignified public wrangling with his adversaries, he tended to rely on charm and a rather deferential magnanimity to disarm them. He counseled forbearance: "It is very important for Courtiers, in order to keep friends and palliate enemies, to close their ears to slanderous tongues. Prince Ruygomez attested this from Experience."[34] This seeming generosity of spirit should not be taken too seriously, however. Ruy Gómez, with his privileged access to the king, had ample opportunity to undermine his enemies in private while turning toward them a sunny outward countenance. "Even though he covered it up in public," remarked one hostile observer, "in darkness he spread his poison where it seemed to him that it could cause injury."[35]

Of course, Ruy Gómez's supreme gift as a courtier was his ability to attract and retain the favor of Philip II, the fount of all blessings at the court. When the Englishman Arthur Atey described Ruy Gómez as "the most inwarde favourite that ever was with kinge," he was perhaps guilty of overstatement but not of hyperbole.[36] What was the secret of Eboli's status with Philip?

Proximity to the king was the key prerequisite of his favor. As *sumiller de corps* Ruy Gómez dressed and undressed Philip and, at least before the court returned to Spain, slept in the anteroom of his chamber.[37] Indeed, a contemporary witness described the *sumiller* as "he who sleeps in the King of Spain's room."[38] This household position, which he held for more than twenty years, provided him daily opportunities for private conversation with the king and kept him constantly within Philip's sight and attention. Coupled with the fact that Ruy Gómez de Silva had known Philip well since their youth, this access made him perhaps the most acute student of Philip's personality, desires, insecurities, likes and dislikes. Even the duke of Alba recognized this, in a remark he made after his rival's death to Eboli's protégé, Antonio Pérez. According to Pérez,

> one day in the King's private antechamber, the duke of Alba said to me these very words: "Señor Antonio, Señor Ruygomez with whom you are so taken was not one of the greatest Counsellors that there has been, but I acknowledge him, to you, as so great a master of that herein [in the *cámara* of the king], of the temper and disposition of Kings, that all the rest of us who pass through here have our heads where we think we are carrying our feet."[39]

Although the duke could not resist a snide preamble, this statement comprises a considerable testimonial to Ruy Gómez's courtly skills. A friendlier witness was the duke of Savoy, who told Jorge Manrique that, were he to send his son to Spain, he would entrust him only to Eboli, who might take him "for his own, instructing him to understand the will and pleasure of the king."[40]

How did Ruy Gómez behave in order to enjoy great influence over his master? Gregorio Marañón believed that Philip was pathologically timid and felt threatened by bold and decisive men like Alba and Don Juan de Austria; thus, he argued, the secret of Ruy Gómez's favor was "his murky personality" and willingness to subordinate himself to the king, coupled with a "mysterious gift" for divining and subtly manipulating his master's will and desires.[41] And indeed, a sort of suave obsequiousness is suggested in accounts of Ruy Gómez's interaction with the king. Consider, for example, Cabrera's description: he asserted that Ruy Gómez

> kept it [royal favor] because he attended on him [Philip II] without harassing him or obstructing him when he desired solitude, like a wise man observing with prudence the distribution of his time that the king had ordained. He [Ruy Gómez] held him [Philip II] in uniform respect in all his actions, and this deference increased with the favor and *merced* that he received. He performed his duties without trickery, with eager willingness and to the liking of his lord . . . winning first the reputation of an intelligent and prudent man with the unpretentious and opportune question and the brief and judicious answer, without relating tales nor rambling, speaking well of those whom the king loved. With creditable dissimulation, a quality both good and necessary, he did not hear more than he was meant to hear, at least when such discretion neither offended justice nor mocked the truth. What was said to him he kept secret, and if others said it to him he dissimulated and was the last to say it.[42]

Sigismondo Cavalli's description of Eboli's ingratiating touch with Philip is in some respects similar. According to the Venetian, Ruy Gómez

> has always manifested a miraculous dexterity and conduct, and accommodates himself very well to His Majesty's disposition, and in treating of affairs he always goes in to the king with the greatest respect, showing himself timid.[43]

The impression given is that Ruy Gómez, the soul of tact and discretion, blended imperceptibly into Philip's intimate surroundings, anticipating his lord's whims and moods, providing a safe sounding board and a steady source of reassurance and praise for the monarch, and exercising influence by subtle insinuation rather than blunt argument. Giovanni della Casa might have been thinking of Eboli when he wrote that

> I could name you many, whoe (being otherwise of litle account) have ben and be still, muche esteemed & made of, for their cherefull and plesaunt behaviour alone: which hath bin suche a helpe & advauncement unto them, that they have gotten greate preferments, leaving farre behinde them, such men as have bin endowed with those other noble and better vertues.[44]

In Marañón's analysis Philip chose to surround himself with just such comforting, rather than threatening, figures:

> there can be no doubt that the King preferred this type of suave courtier [Ruy Gómez de Silva, Antonio Pérez] to men of firm warlike character, like the Duke of Alba. . . . Such a preference is explained by its concordance with his own character, subtle, shrewd and pacific.[45]

In this view only his iron self-control and devotion to kingly duty as he understood it kept Philip II from giving over his government entirely to "yes men."[46] This struggle between personal comfort and a sense of responsibility accounts for the intermittency of Philip's reliance on men like Alba and also Granvelle, who was described by a contemporary as "by nature a little cantankerous and harsh"; he and his brother Chantonnay may "seem to want to flay you alive when they simply intend to scratch."[47]

Marañón's vision of Philip as timid, irresolute and uncomfortable with authoritative men is perhaps overstated, but it is undeniable that the king had a reclusive personality and preferred as intimate friends men whose personal origins and status tended to reinforce their dependence. During the course of Philip's long reign, few men spent a great deal of time in private with the king. Among those who did, Ruy Gómez de Silva and, later, Cristóbal de Moura were minor Portuguese nobles, Diego de Espinosa was a clergyman of low birth, as was Mateo Vázquez, and Antonio Pérez was, like Vázquez, a mere secretary and moreover the bastard son of a cleric. The Portuguese were outsiders, and Philip's liking for their company may indicate that in some sense he saw himself as likewise alienated from his surroundings. Alternatively, the king's mother was Portuguese, and his affinity for Ruy Gómez and Moura may have stemmed from a submerged sense of shared identity.[48] The others, Espinosa, Pérez and Vázquez, were even more clearly the king's creatures. His use and patronage of these men may indicate feelings of inadequacy and unworthiness that barred Philip from friendship with more imposing and independent figures; on the other hand, a king jealous of his authority could hardly safeguard it better than by delegating it to men who remained dependent on him for whatever status they enjoyed.

While his father ruled and during the early years of his own reign, Philip's choice of a favorite likely had less to do with calculations of statecraft and more to do with personal preference and insecurities. Ruy Gómez de Silva was first and foremost the friend of the young prince and the inexperienced king, a confidant who, in Castiglione's words, could

> lay aside grave matters for another time and place, and engage in conversation that will be amusing and pleasant to his lord, so as not to prevent him from gaining such relaxation [as he can] . . . for I do not see why princes should not have the same freedom to relax their spirits as we should wish for ourselves.[49]

Even when he attained the status of Philip's *privado*, entrusted with major governmental posts, Ruy Gómez de Silva remained primarily the king's friend and only secondarily a statesman. Scrutiny of his record does not lead to the conclusion that Ruy Gómez entirely shared the aims of the ideal courtier of Castiglione's imagination, who sets out

> to win for himself . . . the favor and mind of the prince whom he serves that he may be able to tell him, and always will tell him, the truth about everything he needs to know, without fear or risk of displeasing him; and that when he sees the mind of his prince inclined to a wrong action, he may dare to oppose him and in a gentle manner avail himself of the favor acquired by his good accomplishments, so as to dissuade him of every evil intent and bring him to the path of virtue.[50]

The career of Ruy Gómez de Silva reveals no major instances of strenuous principled opposition to the king's expressed will. Instead, his courtly actions and motivations seem to comport more closely to the views of Lorenzo Ducci (in *Arte Aulica*, 1601), as paraphrased by Sydney Anglo:

> For Ducci . . . the courtier submits his neck voluntarily to the yoke of servitude. But his end is, blatantly, "his own profit"; and all his service to a lord is only to achieve this. "It appeareth then that the ends or scopes that the courtier hath are three, that is his *proper interest*, and this is that which chiefly he endeavoureth; next, the *favour of the prince*, as the cause of the first end; and then, the *service of the prince*, as the efficient cause of that favour." [51]

Nevertheless, this is perhaps not as damning a condemnation as it might seem at first glance, since Ducci's apparently cynical analysis in fact represents a rather keen dissection of the common motivations of a client within a patronage system. In the exceedingly unequal power relationship between a king and a courtier of limited personal assets, like Ruy Gómez de Silva, it is implausible to expect the client to conceive of his primary role as one of opposing his patron's inclinations, when such opposition might jeopardize his own position. Thus, while perhaps hardly admirable, it is not for example surprising to find Ruy Gómez, in conversation with the nuncio in 1566 or 1567, first denouncing Alba's opposition to a papal proposal to form a league against the Turks and then asking the nuncio to keep his dissent secret, since he believed that Alba's view would prevail with the king.[52] His contemporaries knew the *privado*'s tendency to tell Philip only what he wanted to hear. Thus Gutierre López de Padilla urged Ruy Gómez to inform the king in no uncertain terms of the financial exhaustion of Castile and to make this point "without mumbling as though you had a mouthful of water." [53]

There is in fact no necessary contradiction between the courtly motivations adduced by Ducci and the achievement of the higher goal—of steering the prince along "the path of virtue"—espoused by Castiglione. Good advice was often a by-product of the courtier's pursuit of self-interest; the dynamics of the situation, however, usually dictated that self-interest would override any temptation to preach to a prince bent on pursuing an ill-considered course. The actual strategy of a practicing courtier, attempting both to sway his prince and to maintain his own position, is revealed in Antonio

Pérez's account of his discussions on this subject with Ruy Gómez de Silva.

Antonio Pérez's writings, although problematic, comprise the best extant source of insights into Eboli's vision and practice of courtiership.[54] No mean courtier himself, Pérez acclaimed Ruy Gómez de Silva as "that great Privado, that master of Privados and of the understanding of Kings" and as "the greatest master of this science that there has been in many centuries."[55] After Pérez's disgrace, he wrote extensively on the techniques and problems of the *privanza* and larded his letters and discourses with references to sayings and deeds of the prince of Eboli. "I quote the Prince Ruygomez so much," he wrote, "because he was my teacher [*maestro*], and the Aristotle of this philosophy."[56]

Pérez, in a discourse on the sources and preservation of *privanza*, argued that

> If it [favor] is based on the great judgment and value of the person [favored], here is the greatest danger, here are the shoals of human small-mindedness, here great circumspection is needed, and navigation with the sounding lead always in hand. Oh, that the Earth (I mean the Prince) in which the tree (I mean the *privado*) is planted may have great virtue, and the profundity to tolerate such trees. Because there is not a Prince—what am I saying, "a Prince"; there is not a man (this is a disease native to all)—who persists in tolerating greater knowledge and judgment [than his own]. But if the *privado* knows how to moderate the use of it, from this type of *privados* come the most durable ones.[57]

He supports this argument by reference to the practice and precepts of the prince of Eboli:

> I tell what he said to me, that . . . in the Counsels that he gave his Prince, and in speaking with him, he always bore in mind an important admonition, *To adjust his judgment to that of his Prince;* . . . that what works in swaying the will of a Prince is a bit of adulation (natural fare to the human temperament), since that homage confirms that they are Lords and powerful. And he added that he even strove to see that the happy outcomes of his Counsels should seem the success of good luck, and born of much care and vigilance in his service, in order that the Prince might acquire love for him, like those who, in gambling, seek players who are lucky more than [those] who have knowledge; because the former [luck] caused affection for the person and the latter, envy.[58]

In order to underscore this point, Ruy Gómez related to Antonio Pérez the story of Count Luys de Silvera, a favorite of the Portuguese King Manuel. The king asked Silvera's advice about a reply to an extremely well-drafted letter from the pope, and the two men contrived an outline of an answer. King Manuel asked the count to draft the reply; meanwhile, the king, who was proud of his own eloquence, would draw up an alternative letter. Silvera was reluctant to compete with his master, but at length he accepted the task. When they met the next day the king conceded that the count's draft was superior to his own and ordered it sent to the pope. Immediately after this meeting

> the Count left for his house and, even though it was midday, ordered two horses to follow his own, for his two sons, and without eating, he led them to the country, and said to them: "My sons, each of you seek your life, and I mine, as there is none to be lived here, since the King now knows that I know more than he."[59]

Clearly, in Ruy Gómez's view, advice had to be tempered to avoid challenging or threatening the royal ego or pretensions. The secret of his prolonged hold on Philip's affections was perhaps just this ability to provide an insecure young king with private admiration and to act as a foil accentuating the qualities of lordship, power and wisdom that Philip desperately sought to see in himself. The knack of private enchantment, rather than a pronounced aptitude for statecraft, was the key to Ruy Gómez's favor with Philip II. Antonio Pérez had to look no farther than the patron of his youth to find the model for his aphorism that *"Privados* are great and bewitching charmers."[60]

In the mid-1560s this courtly magic began to fail Ruy Gómez de Silva, or perhaps the magician tired of his act. From 1565 on a series of events testified to the slippage of Eboli's favor with Philip II. First, despite the fact that Ruy Gómez had long argued the desirability of high-level talks with Catherine de' Medici and clearly wanted to represent Philip at the Bayonne meetings that were arranged between the two powers, the king chose in spring 1565 to send Alba and excluded Eboli from the delegation. Ruy Gómez was humiliated by this rebuff, and his then-ally Juan Manrique de Lara attempted, to no avail, to delay preparations for the mission to gain time during which the king might change his mind.[61] Eboli even enlisted the French ambassador to plead his case with Philip, and he was doubtless rather taken aback by the king's lame excuse that "during this journey [to Bayonne], his son the prince must travel to Guadalupe, which he would not wish to entrust to anyone other than Ruy Gómez, and there may be danger if he is not always near him." In desperation, Ruy Gómez asked Saint-Sulpice to insist further with the king, telling the Frenchman that he had many enemies at court who strove to keep him down out of envy and because he was Portuguese by birth.[62] Additional pleas were unavailing, though, and Ruy Gómez stayed behind. Bayonne became a substantial triumph for Alba and provided clear evidence that the duke's star at court was again on the rise after the relative eclipse of 1563–1564.[63]

In the same period Eboli's old ally Francisco de Eraso was facing serious charges of peculation and misuse of his official authority, instigated by Don Juan de Figueroa, president of the Council of Castile and a longtime enemy of the secretary. Although the accusations were doubtless largely justified, the case was pressed with such bitter personal venom that Granvelle referred to it as "Figueroa's war on Eraso."[64] Despite the death of the president of Castile in the midst of the investigation, and notwithstanding Eboli's impassioned testimony on behalf of Eraso, the secretary was found guilty in early 1566. Philip II approved the verdict, which fined Eraso 12,600 ducats, stripped him of some of his offices and barred him for a year from the Council of Hacienda, where he had long acted as Ruy Gómez's chief lieutenant. Although some of the penalties were eventually commuted, Eraso was never to regain the dominance of conciliar affairs that had made him such a powerful ally of Ruy Gómez de Silva.[65]

In the meantime a new rival was rising to prominence at Philip's court. This was Diego de Espinosa, a priest of exceedingly humble origins who became inquisitor-general in 1564 and then succeeded Figueroa as president of the Council of Castile in 1565. Espinosa, who had a tremendous capacity for administrative routine, essentially replaced Eraso as the workhorse of the councils, and he seems also to have supplanted Eboli as the king's *hombre de confianza*. According to another counselor, the count of Chinchón, between 1565 and his disgrace and death in 1572 Espinosa was "the man in all Spain in whom the king places most confidence, and with whom he discusses most business, both concerning Spain and foreign affairs."[66] There was some retrospective speculation that Espinosa's rise was initially engineered by Ruy Gómez de Silva as a stratagem to dilute Alba's reviving influence, "but as it turned out," concludes Luciano Serrano, "his calculations were misguided, since Espinosa, once ensconced as President [of Castile] shrugged off all tutelage" and pursued an independent and ambitious course.[67] Espinosa's emergence as a dominant figure was demonstrated during the summer of 1566, when he persuaded the king, over Eboli's objections, to allow him to conduct the meetings of the council at his home in Madrid while the court was absent in the Segovia Woods.[68] Shortly thereafter, Ruy Gómez was reduced to attempting to learn through a third party what the king had written to Espinosa concerning a matter of interest to himself.[69] The president of Castile was beginning to stand between Ruy Gómez and the intimate confidences of his master.

These reversals for Eboli occurred against the backdrop of heated debate in the Council of State over how to deal with the mounting unrest in the Netherlands. Eboli was seen as an ally by the Netherlands nobles whom he had cultivated in the 1550s. Count Egmont stayed with Ruy Gómez during his 1565 visit to Madrid to urge a conciliatory settlement, and Montigny and Berghes wrote the king to ask that he send Eboli to govern the Low Countries.[70] At the crucial meeting of the Council of State on 29 October 1566, Eboli and Alba squared off in what was essentially a replay of their 1558 debate over the war with France. Ruy Gómez argued that the revolt was a relatively minor threat, too insignificant to require the king's presence in the Netherlands, especially when he was desperately needed in the peninsula. He suggested that the count of Feria be sent as governor to reconcile rather than punish the rebels. Alba, predictably, reacted violently to this suggestion and asserted that the king's honor and the preservation of his authority demanded his personal presence at the head of an army sent to the Netherlands to chasten rebellious subjects. The duke allowed that, alternatively, a general could be sent ahead to prepare the ground for a subsequent journey by Philip. At this meeting Eboli was deserted by Juan Man-rique de Lara, traditionally an ally in the council, who seconded Alba's proposals. Philip rejected Ruy Gómez's counsel in favor of the second plan proposed by the duke and his allies. A month later Alba accepted the command of the planned expedition.[71] In the in-tervening days the court buzzed with rumors that Eboli was to go to Flanders, one observer going so far as to assert that "Ruy Gómez governs absolutely."[72] Even Feria evidently thought the outcome un-certain until the public announcement of Alba's command, since in early December he was reportedly "so malcontent at not having been made general" that he fumed about abandoning the court en-tirely.[73] In the event, though, Ruy Gómez had clearly lost this debate, and "entirely preoccupied, could neither close his eyes in sleep nor bring rest to his mind."[74] Among Granvelle's circle it was thought that Eboli's intrigues with his friends among the Netherlands nobil-ity reflected disloyalty to the Crown and that Philip should "exam-ine who has been serving him until now, and . . . look to who will serve him from now on."[75] Even the prospect of the removal of his antagonist to the Netherlands provided Ruy Gómez little comfort, since in January 1567 Fourquevaulx reported to the French court that "the Duke of Alba has had such power with this king—as full power as he has thought to request."[76]

As if all this were not bad enough, since late summer 1564 Ruy Gómez de Silva had been saddled with the unenviable post of *may-ordomo mayor* to the increasingly disturbed crown prince, Don Car-los. He was granted full authority over the prince's governance, household and finances.[77] On the positive side, this post had tradi-tionally been regarded as one of great honor, and certainly its be-stowal was a mark of Philip's confidence that Ruy Gómez would take good care of his troubled heir. In fact, the king told the French ambassador that he would not entrust his son to any man in the world except Ruy Gómez.[78] Eboli seems also to have believed in 1564 that this appointment was the prelude to sending Don Carlos, under his supervision, to govern the Netherlands; he told Saint-Sulpice that

> the king his master had wished to entrust this duty to him on account of the trust that he had in him, and in order that he [Ruy Gómez] might be near his son until he married, since then the woman would

take care of him, and, if in the meantime the king his father were to
send Don Carlos to Flanders to pacify the Netherlands . . . he would
accompany the prince to attend to his household.[79]

But the drawbacks of the position outweighed its advantages. Don
Carlos greeted his new *mayordomo mayor* with open hostility, regarding him as a spy for his father. Subsequently the illness and frenzied
antics of his charge "interrupted Eboli's constant presence in the
king's intimate circle" and thus contributed to his growing estrangement from Philip.[80]

Some examples will illustrate the frustrations of Ruy Gómez's
post as *mayordomo mayor* to the prince. In the midst of his other
problems Ruy Gómez had to derail an insane plot hatched in the
summer of 1565 by the prince (now twenty years old) and two of
his aristocratic playmates. Don Carlos, at odds with his father,
wanted to escape Madrid for Aragon, where as the sworn heir he
could act as governor. From there he could fulfill his desire to go on
to Flanders. His companions urged the prince to take Ruy Gómez
de Silva along to Aragon, since the *privado*'s presence would convince the inhabitants of the localities he visited en route that the
journey had Philip's blessing. The three young men made their preparations, caching money and traveling costumes in the prince's
country lodge outside Madrid. They agreed that they would lure
Ruy Gómez to the lodge and inform him of the plan. If Eboli did
not agree to join them, they would kill him so he could not block
their departure. They duly confronted Ruy Gómez, who was able,
after a lengthy discussion, to dissuade Don Carlos from his half-
baked plan by dissecting the flaws in this adolescent fantasy.[81] Some
months later the prince doubtless embarrassed his minder when
he stormed into the *cortes* of Castile and threatened the assembled
procuradores that "he would strip them of all their power" should
they continue, as he put it, to meddle in his affairs.[82] Then, in 1567,
Ruy Gómez was caught between the king and the prince when the
latter asked him for a loan, to be concealed from Philip, to finance
his flight to the Netherlands or Portugal. Eboli went to the king, and
Don Carlos, his plans undone, was very angry with his *mayordomo*.
In fact, Ruy Gómez took second place only to Philip on a list of
enemies said to have been found among the prince's effects.[83]

In his post as *mayordomo mayor* to Don Carlos, Eboli was burdened with a thankless task; certainly by 1567, and probably much

earlier, he realized that his charge would never rule either the Netherlands or Spain itself.[84] He was condemned to manage as best he could the antics and tantrums of the prince, while Philip, at the end of his patience, was already in 1567 considering imprisoning his son.[85] A few years later, speaking of another bizarre prince, Sebastian of Portugal, Ruy Gómez would remark

> that it is necessary, in a manner of speaking, to guide him and deal with him with apples in hand, and not with reason or remonstrances, since he neither knows nor wishes to understand what is good or bad for him.[86]

This observation smacks of the rueful wisdom of experience. As *mayordomo mayor*, though, beyond the attempt to steer Don Carlos like a wayward pet, he could do nothing to stem the prince's degeneration and thus please the king; meanwhile, Ruy Gómez's image in Philip's mind likely became tainted by association with the personal tragedy of his son's mounting insanity.

Beginning in mid-decade observers of the court were aware of a deterioration in Ruy Gómez de Silva's relationship with Philip II. Visiting Madrid in late 1564, Brantôme speculated that Eboli no longer enjoyed his great favor with the king, noting that his continual pleas to be relieved of the care of Don Carlos went unheeded.[87] Meanwhile, the envy of the grandees, somewhat muted for the past few years, had reemerged to trouble Eboli. Giovanni Soranzo, in his report of 1565, noted that, while Ruy Gómez was well liked by those who had business at Madrid, because of his "very sweet and clement nature toward everyone," he was "much hated" by the Spaniards at court, "who cannot bear his great grandeur, primarily because he is a foreigner and of the Portuguese nation, most deeply loathed by them." Ironically, this envy seems to have been exacerbated by Philip's choice of Ruy Gómez as *mayordomo mayor* to Don Carlos, "a rank that all the grandees of Spain wanted and aspired to."[88] Another Venetian, Sigismondo Cavalli, reported later in the decade that, because of various altercations with Espinosa, Eboli had lost some of his favor with Philip II, "having come under suspicion by the king as a self-serving man." Noting what he believed to be Ruy Gómez's genuine amity toward Venice and his reputation as an honest broker of affairs at court, Cavalli concluded that "it would surely mean grievous harm were he to fall."[89]

A tangible measure of the growing estrangement between Ruy Gómez and his master the king is provided by the fact that, during the summer of 1567, Eboli and his family left their longtime lodgings in the palace and took up residence in a nearby house in the parish of Santa María that had belonged to Gonzalo Pérez. Ruy Gómez would never again live for an extended period under Philip's roof, except during Don Carlos's detention, when, as the prince's keeper, he resided in the prisoner's apartments abutting the palace.[90]

There is also perhaps some indication of a souring relationship between Philip and his old favorite in the growing number of unpleasant tasks entrusted to Ruy Gómez in these years. Most obviously, his role as minder and then warder of Don Carlos eminently qualified as dirty work. Another ugly chore fell to Ruy Gómez in May 1567. His old friend the marquis of Berghes was gravely ill at Madrid, and Philip sent him a secret instruction from the Escorial, directing him to visit the sick man. If he ascertained that Berghes's illness was terminal, Ruy Gómez should tell him that the king had granted his oft-repeated request for leave to return to the Low Countries; if, however, there was any chance that Berghes might recover, he should merely hold out hope of such permission in future. Furthermore, in the event of Berghes's death, Eboli was to write to Margaret of Parma, instructing her on his own authority—citing Philip's absence from the capital—to seize the dead man's estates in the Netherlands.[91] Ruy Gómez carried out this distasteful mission. Evidently he reckoned Berghes's affliction fatal, for he relayed Philip's safe-conduct to the marquis. Nevertheless, before Berghes died early on the morning of 21 May he expressed his great bitterness toward the king for delaying this permission and thus effectively killing him. Berghes's body was hardly cold when Ruy Gómez dispatched a courier to Brussels in the mid-afternoon of the 21st, relaying the news and the instruction to confiscate the marquis's estate. Margaret of Parma replied on 1 June, reporting to Ruy Gómez that, under the pretext of protecting Berghes's heirs and their property rights, she had dispatched soldiers to hold his property.[92]

This distasteful episode may be read as an instance of Philip compelling a demonstration of loyalty from Ruy Gómez, at the expense of honor, old friendship and Eboli's well-known and now discredited views on the proper handling of the Netherlands situation. The king's behavior carried a whiff of sadistic caprice, while Ruy

Gómez's compliance was nothing if not obsequious; certainly the relationship between master and favorite had deteriorated from the warm mutual regard of earlier days. In the wake of this episode Eboli seems to have seen the handwriting on the wall, and he wasted no time in denying his other former friends among the Netherlands nobility. For example, soon after Berghes's death he advised Gaspar de Robles (the seigneur de Billy) to burn the letters of recommendation that Egmont had written for him.[93] Some further evidence of Philip's assignment of unpleasant duties to Ruy Gómez is provided by the fact that Eboli wrote on the king's behalf to inform Margaret of Parma of her removal from office in October 1567. Although he cushioned the blow with—in Gachard's term—"paroles flatteuses" and extended a "golden parachute," Eboli's role here was clearly that of hatchet man.[94]

Diego de Espinosa's star continued to rise in this period, and the contrasting trajectory of his own favor must have become increasingly evident to Ruy Gómez. In the spring of 1568, while Eboli guarded the jailed heir to the throne, Espinosa was at Philip's instance invested as a cardinal. Both Gachard and Serrano interpreted this honor as both an exaltation of Espinosa and a calculated humbling of the other lords around Philip, including Alba and Eboli.[95] Through his ambassador in Rome Philip had lobbied for Espinosa's elevation since the fall of 1567; contemporaries believed that the king wanted this dignity for Espinosa so that he might leave the new cardinal as regent in Spain if he chose to go in person to the Netherlands.[96] Recognition of Espinosa as a mutual danger may have played some part in the public reconciliation undertaken by Ruy Gómez and Alba before the duke left for Brussels in the spring of 1567.[97]

When Espinosa received the biretta, in April 1568, Philip made a great public show of respect and deference. As a more concrete token of esteem the king gave Espinosa the lucrative see of Sigüenza, from which he reportedly realized 100 escudos a day. The year before, his nephew, also Diego de Espinosa—"who is dear to him and whom he looks always to advance"—had received an *hábito* of Santiago and other *mercedes* from the monarch. The cardinal seems to have acted as Philip's private chaplain, thus assuring himself solitary time with his master, particularly in 1568, a year of personal heartbreak during which the king presumably had great need of spiritual comfort. Meanwhile, the Council of Castile continued to meet in Espinosa's house.[98] Court observers in the late 1560s had no doubt that the cardinal was preeminent in Philip's affections and the most powerful adviser in the court. In 1569 Catherine de' Medici's ambassador urged her to cultivate Espinosa, "who can do whatever he wishes with this king." A year later the same envoy wrote that, despite Ruy Gómez's own candidacy for the post, Espinosa would prevail on the king to make his relative Don Antonio de la Cueva *mayordomo mayor* of the new queen: the cardinal of Sigüenza, Fourquevaulx asserted, "does and undoes what he pleases."[99] By 1571 Ruy Gómez had formed an alliance with the new favorite. He and Espinosa were described as "two heads in one hood," but it was the cardinal's head that carried Philip's warmest benediction.[100]

While the dwindling of his position at court posed a threat to Eboli's influence and to the steady flow of royal *mercedes*, he also faced growing uncertainty in his private life. His relations with Doña Ana, now the princess of Eboli, seem to have been tempestuous but not miserable, and certainly their marriage was fecund— ten children were born to them between 1558 and 1572, of whom six survived. The four eldest survivors, including three sons, were born between 1561 and 1566.[101] Obviously Ruy Gómez would have to make some provision for these children, and his ambitions for them were lofty. He had a considerable income, estimated at as much as 60,000 ducats a year in 1565, from his official posts, his *encomienda* and his annuities and other royal grants, but a major part of this was payable for life alone, and almost all was directly dependent on Philip's continued favor.[102] Given the ebbing of this favor, the financial future of Ruy Gómez de Silva, and especially that of his children, could not be regarded as secure.

The private fortune represented by Doña Ana's presumptive inheritance of the house of Mélito seemed increasingly uncertain as well. First, Ruy Gómez had gained accurate knowledge of the value of the Mélito estate during the period 1555–1560, when, by the terms of his marriage, he had been allowed to collect its revenues. During this period the estate returned a net income of rather less than 8,000 Neapolitan ducats per year, a far cry from its reputed annual yield of 20,000–30,000. According to a governmental report of the late 1550s the capital city, Mileto, was "extremely depopulated," while the count's "fortresses and houses are falling into ruins." The shortfall of income stemming from these conditions was compounded by the fact that many revenues were sequestered pending the outcome of protracted litigation. A history of corrupt and inefficient administration—one observer noted that "the lack of justice in Mélito is proverbial"—was also partly to blame. Although Ruy Gómez, with his special influence, had been able to expedite some of the lawsuits and had attempted to improve the management of the estate, his experience must have left doubts about the sufficiency of the Mélito inheritance as a financial foundation for his lineage.[103]

To make matters worse, the inheritance itself had become a dubious prospect. In 1557 severe public disagreement had erupted between Doña Ana's parents, the duke and duchess of Francavila (previously the count and countess of Mélito and subsequently the prince and princess of Mélito). The precipitant was the flagrant philandering of the duke, Ruy Gómez's father-in-law. Doña Ana sided with her mother and secured the aid of the regent, the Princess Juana, against her father. She thus incurred Francavila's lasting enmity. Ruy Gómez, in Spain attending to royal financial matters, was drawn into the dispute, and he unsuccessfully urged a settlement. The best he could do was to prevail upon Philip to summon the duke to his side in the Low Countries. Doña Ana's parents publicly separated in the aftermath of this episode and lived apart until 1564. Ruy Gómez assumed the responsibility of supporting his mother-in-law during these years. Relations between father and daughter, and increasingly between mother and daughter as well, remained stormy. Francavila was arrogant and unrepentant, while the duchess's "principal activity is to grumble and backbite without mercy for anyone." The situation was awkward for Ruy Gómez not least because he had to have political dealings with his father-in-law. Although their relations became so strained by the late 1560s that Francavila was acting as an Alba partisan, Ruy Gómez and his father-in-law seem to have patched up their relationship at least by 1573, the year of Eboli's death. The sources uniformly praise Ruy Gómez for his tactful handling of this three-cornered dispute. He seems to have taken the familial bond very seriously: "since I took them [the duke and duchess] for parents, it is necessary to carry them on my shoulders even though this burden causes me considerable travail." Nevertheless, the princess of Eboli remained estranged from her father, and her inheritance was doubtful because of it. Just how uncertain is evident from the fact that, upon the death of Doña Ana's mother in 1576, her father remarried immediately and left his widow pregnant when he died in 1578. The posthumous child was a stillborn daughter; had it been a live son, he would have preempted Doña Ana's succession.[104]

The precarious nature of the Mélito legacy was clear at least from the early 1560s. To compound the problems posed by familial antagonisms, there were other potential obstacles to Doña Ana's inheritance of the House of Mélito. These arose from the fact that conditions of the entail barred female succession to at least some of the properties. This led to extensive litigation when the estate was finally settled; other observers noted these problems, and it seems unlikely that Ruy Gómez was himself unaware of them.[105]

In the 1560s, then, Ruy Gómez de Silva saw his luck beginning to turn sour. His standing and fortune, public and private, were essentially dependent on the goodwill and the whims of other men, the king and his father-in-law. The mounting evidence of experience indicated that this goodwill was not reliable. Records of Ruy Gómez's thoughts and feelings in this period are scarce, but some indications can be found in the later writings of Antonio Pérez. Pérez's ruminations on the fortune and misfortune of *privados* were hardly disinterested, but he was a protégé of Ruy Gómez, and there is no reason to dismiss his assertion that Philip's Portuguese favorite confided in him and was his primary instructor in the courtly arts. Eboli's troubles seem to have turned his mind toward musings on the workings of Fortune. This was a characteristic preoccupation of the courtly thought of the Renaissance. Castiglione, for example, believed that the aspiring courtier should always retain in the back of his mind the image of the revolving wheel of fortune and should temper hubris with the consideration of "how often Fortune in midcourse, and sometimes near the end, dashes our fragile and futile designs and sometimes wrecks them before the port can even be seen from afar."[106] Antonio Pérez epigrammatized this conventional wisdom ("Fortune is to be feared when it is most fully in hand"[107]) and went on to apply it specifically to the realities of life at court:

Privados and others most securely favored by Dame Fortune ought to recall, in the midst of the banquets of her favors, just who She is: That She attacks the careless, and squeezes dry and drowns those who most firmly embrace her: that her hugs are those of a bloodthirsty and treacherous bear.[108]

Writing long after the death of Eboli and after his own fall from grace at court, Pérez reproduced a conversation that he had had with Ruy Gómez. This conversation, as distilled and doubtless embellished by Pérez, reveals a man disillusioned by court life and saddened by the waning of favor that he perceived as having been earned through a lifetime of loyal service. Pérez reported that

> On our private strolls, he [Ruy Gómez de Silva] came to say this to me: "Señor Antonio, think you that I would not flee away from here if I were able without incurring censure for ingratitude? You had better believe that I would do so, and would hold myself fortunate: but I cannot without peril of the censure I speak of. . . . It is happening to me, finally, which happens to women (the comparison was his) who have grown rich from their beauty: that, in order to be respected, they must return in old age what they acquired in youth; and, by the same token, I should continue on here so that they may not hold me ungrateful for the prosperity that has come to me in the King's service."[109]

The inveterate courtier seems finally in middle age to have lost his zest for the game. Of course, there is a stylish element of world-weary rhetoric here. "At court," the moralist bishop and courtesy-writer Antonio de Guevara remarked, "everyone curses the court, and then they all follow it."[110] Nevertheless, the bustle and tension of court life had to be wearing, especially as the years advanced. "Those who pass their time in palaces," wrote Diego de Hermosilla in 1573, "must have iron heads and copper stomachs."[111] Guevara went on to observe that courtiership was enjoyable only for favorites when they were riding high or for callow youths who did not feel the pain of its vicissitudes.[112] With his youth gone and his *privanza* dissolving, it is no wonder that court life began to lose its charm for Ruy Gómez de Silva.

According to Pérez, Ruy Gómez went on to speak, presumably from personal experience, about the cruelty of a reversal of fortune:

> Also that day, Prince Ruygomez came to say to me something singular, which pleased me greatly, among many other very fine things on

this subject, that when Fortune deserted those whom she had favored (it was for him a very characteristic pastime to occupy himself with this subject), and had passed them by, they felt more deeply slaps on the face than mortal blows. The reason may be the same as with spoiled children, who suffer more from the visible stigma of blows that show and the bruises they leave than from the pain of secret blows they receive.[113]

These reflections capture something of the bewildered humiliation that Ruy Gómez must have suffered in the mid-1560s, as it became obvious, not just to him but to his envious adversaries as well, that Philip's favor was receding.

Thomas de Chantonnay, Granvelle's elder brother, was musing in 1565 about a similar predicament. He warned his brother that

princes show good warm affections when they need to make use of men; but they don't hold them in such esteem when they come too cheaply, and if they become accustomed to having such men under their feet, they hold them in no account, and it seems to them that they can dispose of their bodies and their honor at a whim; and, if they become accustomed to doing without them, they forget them and find they no longer have need of them.[114]

He counseled Granvelle "not to put so much faith in the beautiful words of princes," but instead to make his own luck.

The past is gone; and from now on, it is time to look out for one's own honor, and to show one's face and teeth, because the times are such that the bold and those who make themselves difficult are well-treated, cherished, wooed, bought and held in awe, while those who are adaptable and self-sacrificing are ground underfoot.[115]

Chantonnay's counsel of aggressive self-promotion was perhaps appropriate for Granvelle, but less so for Ruy Gómez, whose stock at court had always been based more on suavity than on boldness. His style had never been "to show his teeth." Nonetheless, Eboli found his own way of combating the changeability of his fortunes. While he may have brooded on the cruel blows of fortune, Ruy Gómez was taking action to ensure some security for himself and his lineage. Beginning in 1562 he rapidly assembled a collection of properties in the New Castilian region of the Alcarria (between the Tajo and Tajuña rivers, east and southeast of Madrid), evidently with the notion of establishing himself as a substantial seigneur. The Alcarria did not have a great deal to recommend it in terms of rich lands or thriving towns, but it did offer some advantages. First, it was near the court, firmly established at Madrid since 1561; Ruy Gómez would thus be able to adopt some aspects of a seigneurial style of life without abandoning his crucial connection with the court. Moreover, a considerable number of properties were available in the Alcarria. Various towns and villages had been expropriated from the military orders and put up for sale by the Crown.[116] Others were held by more or less impecunious relatives of Doña Ana. The region was a traditional preserve of the various branches of the Mendozas and, because of familial connections, Eboli was doubtless well informed about opportunities to purchase jurisdictions there. Another reason why Eboli may have chosen to concentrate his acquisitions in the Alcarria is that he already had something of a foothold as a lord in the region. Since 1559 he had been, by Philip's appointment, the *alcaide* (castellan) of the castle of Zorita de los Canes on the Tajo.[117]

Whatever his reasons for choosing the Alcarria, analysis of the pattern of Eboli's purchases indicates that he was more interested in amassing a sizable estate rapidly than in constructing a particularly coherent economic or jurisdictional unit. He seems to have begun scouting potential purchases in 1561.[118] In 1562 he opened negotiations with Don Gaspar Gastón de la Cerda, Doña Ana's paternal uncle, to purchase his jurisdiction over the town of Pastrana and its neighboring villages. The deal was closed and a royal privilege obtained, but the seller died before the arrangements could be finalized. Eboli continued the negotiations with the new owner, his wife's cousin Don Iñigo de Mendoza (later first marquis of Almenara), but he did not succeed in purchasing this centerpiece of his future duchy until 1569. The purchase included the palace in Pastrana (valued in 1562 at 15,000 ducats), various monopolies and a portion of the town's *alcabalas.* Eboli secured the remainder of the *alcabalas* and *tercias* and assorted real property in Pastrana by purchase from another of his wife's uncles in the same year.[119]

During the period of negotiations over Pastrana, Ruy Gómez had purchased several other jurisdictions. In 1565 he bought the towns of Estremera and Valdaracete from the estate of Don Francisco de Mendoza, the son of the second marquis of Mondéjar and admiral of the galleys, who died on campaign in 1563.[120] Also in 1565 and 1566, Eboli purchased from the Crown the towns of La Zarza, Zorita de los Canes and Albalate, which had been "dismembered" from the lands of the military orders. He rounded out these holdings by purchasing *alcabalas* and *tercias* within the jurisdictions and buying the *alfoz* of Almonacid and the mills of Pangía and Verdugo on the Tajo.[121] At one point he expressed interest in the holdings of Don Bernardino de Cárdenas in Colmenar de Oreja, but nothing came of these initial inquiries.[122] Ruy Gómez also obtained a papal privilege of 1569 to found and patronize the Collegiate Church of Pastrana. In the same year he and Doña Ana invited Teresa de Avila to establish a Carmelite convent in Pastrana, which she did. Eboli secured hereditary patronage rights for the other religious foundations in Pastrana as well, and in 1571 he sponsored the institution of a short-lived college in the University of Alcalá under the rectorship of John of the Cross.[123]

In at least one instance Ruy Gómez's new vassals resisted incorporation into his growing estate. The people of Albalate, protesting the king's sale of their town, demonstrated in the *plaza*, and in August 1566 they sent a delegation to register their objections with Philip, then summering in the Segovia Woods. The king refused to see them, but the priest heading the delegation left a written petition. In it the citizens of Albalate asked Philip to nullify the sale of the town to Ruy Gómez, offering instead to purchase it themselves. In a letter to Escobedo, Ruy Gómez noted with relief that the townspeople could raise only 13,000–14,000 ducats, far short of the 34,000 ducats he had agreed to pay. Philip seems to have taken no notice of the counteroffer from Albalate, and he may never have seen it. Nevertheless Ruy Gómez, still wary that his purchase might be nullified, ordered his agents to forgo further amendments to the terms of sale, for fear that any innovations would attract the attention of the king and the Council of Castile. By November 1566 Eboli's purchase had been finalized, and he enjoyed a vacation in Albalate, praising the town's "refreshing air and peaceful aspect."[124]

Ruy Gómez's acquisitions in the Alcarria entailed considerable expense. The haste with which they had been negotiated had allowed little time for hard bargaining or careful appraisals, and Eboli complained in 1568 that he had been defrauded in some of his purchases.[125] In any case, Pastrana, Estremera and Valdaracete, the three major towns, alone cost more than 366,000 ducats. Despite an impressive list of salaries and his *juro* income of perhaps 20,000 ducats per year, these expenditures were well beyond the means of the prince of Eboli. The purchases were primarily financed through loans, mostly from major creditors of the Crown, such as the royal Treasurer-General Melchor de Herrera (subsequently marquis of Auñón), the Genoese financier Niccolò Grimaldo (known to contemporaries as "el rey") and "Antonio Fucar [Fugger] y sobrinos." At the time of his death in 1573 Ruy Gómez de Silva still owed about 70,000 ducats to Herrera and 35,000 to the Fuggers. Grimaldo was even more deeply involved. On behalf of Ruy Gómez he paid the purchase price of more than 160,000 ducats for Estremera and Valdaracete, and he advanced money to Eboli on a number of other occasions. The means by which he was repaid are complex. In a tangled transaction of 1566–1568 Grimaldo purchased Eboli and some other Italian properties from Ruy Gómez. These properties were not particularly valuable, but Grimaldo also obtained the socially legitimizing title of duke of Eboli, presumably through Ruy Gomez's influence with Philip II.[126]

The sale of Eboli accounted for 32,000 ducats of Ruy Gómez's debt to Grimaldo; the debt stood at 2,600 ducats when Ruy Gómez died.[127] It is not clear how the remainder (a balance of more than 125,000 ducats for the Estremera purchase alone) was settled. It is difficult to avoid the suspicion of improprieties involving the Crown finances, given Ruy Gómez's influence and Grimaldo's interests in that sphere. In this connection one unusual circumstance involving Grimaldo and Ruy Gómez bears examination. A year before the purchase of Estremera and Valdaracete, Eboli asked the French ambassador in Madrid to secure a license for him to transport 50,000 escudos from Spain to Naples across French territory. The Frenchman seems to have regarded this as a personal rather than an official request, and he recommended approval by his superiors as a means of maintaining good relations with Ruy Gómez. The license was duly granted in December 1564; two months later the French ambassador wrote a safe conduct for Grimaldo, who was transporting 23,000 escudos under the terms of Eboli's license.[128] This episode suggests the possibility of financial chicanery involving Ruy Gómez and Grimaldo. Was Ruy Gómez using his official position to help Grimaldo remove bullion from Spain? Corruption cannot be clearly documented in this case. Still, at the very least it seems indisputable that Ruy Gómez's position as a *contador* and an intimate of the king must have made him a desirable debtor from the point of view of men like Grimaldo, Herrera and the Fuggers.[129] Perhaps some whiff of financial impropriety in the assembly of Eboli's estates lay behind the king's suspicion, reported by Cavalli in 1570, that Ruy Gómez de Silva was "a self-serving man."[130] Certainly it is striking that less than a week after Eboli's purchase of Estremera and Valdaracete, financed by Grimaldo, the French ambassador noted that the king had just borrowed "a million in gold" from the same banker.[131]

Grimaldo and Herrera were intimately involved in other aspects of Ruy Gómez's finances in the 1560s and 1570s. Grimaldo was Eboli's creditor from at least 1562; in that year Ruy Gómez ordered his receiver in Naples to pay the balance of what he was owed from his period of control of the County of Mélito to the Genoese financier.[132] Eboli was uncomfortable as Grimaldo's debtor, remarking to Escobedo in 1564 that "as you say, it seems to me good advice that I should escape from his hands, since, however smooth they may seem, they are always sticky."[133] Nevertheless, he seems to have been unable to extricate himself, since in 1565 Grimaldo was collecting Eboli's dues as *contador mayor* from the treasury,[134] and of course Ruy Gómez would incur even greater debts to Grimaldo in the course of acquiring his estates.

While he was buying properties in the Alcarria, Ruy Gómez also purchased a number of large *juros* from the Crown, and Melchor de Herrera figured in several transactions involving these annuities. For example, in May 1568 Ruy Gómez purchased a *juro*, worth 2,453 ducats per year, by paying the initial price of 34,347 ducats (at the common rate of 14:1) to Herrera, acting as treasurer-general for the Crown. Subsequently, in 1577, it was revealed that, although Eboli held the royal privilege for the annuity, 85 percent of it actually belonged to Herrera.[135] This pattern was repeated with several other *juros*,[136] and two explanations come readily to mind. Perhaps Ruy Gómez signed over portions of the *juros* to Herrera in repayment of loans, although this begs the question of how Eboli came up with the substantial initial capital to purchase the annuities. On the other hand, it seems possible that these *juros* were fraudulent, with Herrera merely claiming to receive payment on the Crown's behalf in return for the lion's share of the annuity income. Leonardo Donato suspected Herrera of corruption, tolerated by Ruy Gómez and the Council of Hacienda, in the arrangement of major royal loans.[137] Juan Milio said of Ruy Gómez that he "never saw a loose halfpenny that he did not grab, so long as he could do so safely and easily."[138] Given their privileged positions within the financial bureaucracy, it is at least possible that Herrera and Eboli might have conspired to embezzle *juro* income.

The history of another of Ruy Gómez's *juros*, a 1572 gift from Philip worth 533⅓ ducats per year, may shed more light on the means by which Eboli's debt to Herrera was eventually repaid. This was a perpetual and heritable annuity, with a buy-out price of 20:1, and in 1579 Ruy Gómez's widow signified that she had sold it to Herrera at the established rate for 10,667 ducats. In the course of subsequent litigation, however, Herrera revealed that he had actually paid only 7,467 ducats for the *juro*; he explained the lower purchase price by resorting to an affidavit from Niccolò Grimaldo attesting that the annuity had been difficult to collect and that he had thus advised Doña Ana to sell at the lower rate of 14:1. What, if anything, Doña Ana realized from the sale remains unclear, since her sworn bill of sale of 1579 was obviously false, but there can be no doubt that Herrera made out well. He collected the annuity for two years before selling it to a third party in 1581 for 8,000 ducats.[139]

Again in the case of these *juro* transactions, the evidence allows no clear verdict of impropriety, and given the confusion of private interest and public trust so characteristic of the era, it may be that such a verdict would be at best anachronistic. Another observer, however, did imply that Ruy Gómez benefited from his inside knowledge of royal finance. Antonio Tiepolo, reporting to the Venetian senate in 1572, claimed that on the basis of gifts, *mercedes* and his close ties to wealthy elites throughout the empire, Ruy Gómez had assembled, "over a period of little more than twenty years," holdings worth 80,000 escudos per year. He added that "it is universally believed that each year, through the manipulation of exchange, [Ruy Gómez] realizes vast profits in gold."[140] Tiepolo doubtless overestimated Eboli's income, but his central point—that Ruy Gómez had become wealthy in the king's service—is incontrovertible.

The estate that Ruy Gómez assembled, beginning with his first negotiations for the purchase of Pastrana in 1562, comprised his attempt to escape the dual bind of aristocratic rancor and personal dependence on the king and his father-in-law. His failure to gain acceptance as an equal by the Castilian lords doubtless impelled his first efforts to join their seigneurial ranks, and the pace of his estate-building accelerated in mid-decade simultaneous with the erosion of his favor with the king. The purchases were made with an eye to attaining a Castilian title, and preferably a grandeeship. As early as 1567 Ruy Gómez de Silva was using the title of duke of Estremera, without any apparent legal basis or authorization.[141] Although his use of the ducal title was premature, his strategy paid off, and the estate became the basis of exalted social status and financial security for his descendants.

While he went about acquiring a landed patrimony, Ruy Gómez was also busy arranging for the futures of his growing children. First, in 1566 he contracted a magnificent match for his oldest child, Doña Ana de Silva y Mendoza, who had been born in 1561. The tiny girl was to marry the teenaged Don Alonso Pérez de Guzmán el Bueno, seventh duke of Medina Sidonia (born 1549). The marriage was arranged by Eboli and Doña Ana, acting for their daughter, while the duke was represented by his mother, the countess of Niebla, and his kinsmen, the count of Olivares and the marquis of Ayamonte. The capitulations, drafted in Madrid in June 1566, provided for an immediate betrothal by proxies, to be ratified soon by the duke in person and by the prospective bride when she reached her seventh birthday, the so-called age of reason. The little girl was present at the initial betrothal, and it is rather poignant to find her excused from signing the documents because "she said that she didn't know how to write." The binding *palabras de presente* were to be exchanged when Doña Ana was twelve, with the final nuptials and subsequent consummation deferred until the bride reached age thirteen, unless a papal dispensation to speed the process could be obtained. Both parties agreed to sizable deposits to guarantee performance—to be held, incidentally, by Niccolò Grimaldo—and Ruy Gómez agreed to provide his daughter with a dowry of 100,000 ducats, in cash, household luxuries and annuities, while Medina Sidonia would present his bride with an *arras* of 12,000 ducats. The match was effected as planned, with a dispensation allowing an early betrothal by *palabras de presente* in 1572. The marriage was finalized after Eboli's death in a lavish ceremony at Pastrana in 1574.[142]

The motives for this match are not far to seek. Ruy Gómez was eager to cement a close link with the high Castilian aristocracy, in order to gain allies in his time of need and social legitimation as part of his own drive to secure a Spanish title. Meanwhile, the house of Medina Sidonia perceived the need for protection at court from a royal initiative to recover alienated revenues and customs dues. Ruy Gómez, with his power in the financial bureaucracy and intimate knowledge of the workings of administration, could be a useful advocate for the interests of the house.[143] Medina Sidonia wasted no time calling in the favors bought by his hand. By September 1566 Eboli was complaining that the duke's affairs at court were so tangled that "I would give a goodly portion of my own fortune to be obliged to nothing more than serving his interests out of the goodness of my heart, without my own advantage being so closely bound up with his."[144]

In the late 1560s Ruy Gómez also tried to arrange a marriage for his eldest son, Don Rodrigo, with the daughter and heiress of Don Bernardino de Cárdenas, lord of Colmenar de Oreja. Cárdenas's holdings were quite valuable, reportedly returning around 30,000 ducats per year, and Ruy Gómez had long been interested in adding Colmenar to his estates. A match between Don Rodrigo and the heiress Doña Luisa was agreed in 1567, but Cárdenas's widow and mother backed out after Don Bernardino was killed at Lepanto in 1571. Eboli was persistent, and he managed to negotiate a new contract, this time affiancing a younger son, Don Ruy Gómez, to Doña Luisa. But this match fell through as well, perhaps because Eboli died before the binding betrothal was celebrated. Finally, after her husband's death, Doña Ana concluded a marriage for her favorite child, the second son, Don Diego, with the Cárdenas heiress. This was to be a brief and stormy marriage, ending in annulment and prolonged litigation.[145]

As his name would suggest, the third son of the prince and princess of Eboli, Don Pedro González de Mendoza, was destined for a position in the church. Evidently he was pledged to the Franciscans as a toddler. In 1570 the duke of Savoy offered to use his influence with the pope to secure for the lad a cardinal's hat. Ruy Gómez accepted gratefully, but this plan suffered a setback when Don Pedro González died in 1571. The youngest son of Ruy Gómez and Doña Ana, Don Fernando (born February 1570) was eventually renamed Pedro González de Mendoza after his deceased brother and went on to enjoy a long and distinguished clerical career.[146]

It remained to provide for the succession of Eboli's newly acquired estate. On 29 August 1572 Philip II granted a license to found a *mayorazgo* to Ruy Gómez de Silva and Doña Ana. The *mayorazgo,* formed for the benefit of their eldest son Don Rodrigo and his successors, was legally established on 11 November of the same year. In addition to the properties in the Alcarria, this entail bound a vast amount of *juro* income granted by Philip II to Ruy Gómez over the course of his career.[147] Fortune's gifts were thus rendered truly permanent, as the king's *mercedes* to his favorite were placed beyond the purview of royal second thoughts and became the principal patrimony of the *privado's* lineage. The final step in the astounding rise of Ruy Gómez de Silva came on 20 December 1572, when Philip elevated Pastrana to the status of an hereditary duchy.[148] Ruy Gómez became a Castilian duke and thus a grandee of Spain.[149]

Philip's gift of this *grandeza* constitutes proof that Ruy Gómez retained favor with the king after the crisis of the mid-1560s. Philip had to some extent distanced himself from Ruy Gómez after 1565, but he did not refuse to ease his old friend's transformation into an aristocrat. Coming from a monarch not noted for gratitude to his servants, this final great gift bespeaks deep and lasting feeling for the friend of his youth, and perhaps royal approval of the route Ruy Gómez had chosen in order to circumvent the social snobbery that had placed a ceiling on his rise in the court. This impression of lingering royal generosity is further confirmed by the fact that, on 30 April 1571, Philip II named Ruy Gómez *clavero* of the Order of Calatrava. The *clavería* carried with it one of the most lucrative *encomiendas* of the military orders. The *merced* was enhanced by the king's grant of Ruy Gómez's former *encomienda* (Herrera, in the Order of Alcántara) to seven-year-old Don Diego de Silva y Mendoza, Eboli's second son.[150] News of this favor angered allies of the duke of Alba, who believed that their man was not receiving due reward for his service in the Netherlands, while Ruy Gómez absorbed more than his share of royal largesse. "I should have been content had our victories been rewarded proportionally," wrote one Alba partisan. But, he added philosophically, "many things occur in the world that bring on laughter and weeping together."[151]

These lucrative gifts, however, were never accompanied by a

commensurate restoration of Ruy Gómez's credit and influence as an adviser to the king. Espinosa remained the chief of the key bureaus of government until his disgrace and sudden death in the fall of 1572,[152] and the days of secretarial government, with the king acting as his own chief minister and imposing his will with the written word (communicated through Antonio Pérez and then Mateo Vázquez) were about to dawn. From the late 1560s "the progressive involution of [Philip's] personality" was becoming evident. The hardening of his policies and the greater confidence and belligerence that characterized him in the 1570s and 1580s, date from the period of the Netherlands crisis of 1565–1566 and his personal tragedies of 1568. Philip's seeming withdrawal of confidence from his *privado* coincided with a more deep-seated withdrawal; from that period "he allowed himself to see less of the supplicants, of the courtiers, and even of the counselors." "Imprisoned with his papers," concludes the historian Antonio Domínguez Ortiz, Philip II was "isolated from men and from reality."[153]

From his earliest days Philip had always been aloof and uncomfortable in public. Ruy Gómez had provided first a private friend and then something of a public face for his monarch. During the second decade of his reign, however, the king found that he preferred to live essentially without confidants and without a physical public persona. His papers became his life, and the men who shuffled paper well, most notably Espinosa and Vázquez, became the only human contacts he truly needed. In this austere royal maturity Philip felt less need of a *privado,* and Ruy Gómez de Silva was gradually denied his long-standing intimacy with the king and the influence that it had conferred. Still, he never entirely lost power. In 1571 Ruy Gómez remained among the five men regarded as Philip's "consejo selecto."[154] When what was to be his final illness became evident, at the end of 1572, the Venetian envoys noted that

> this man is a very great minister in the court, and supremely well-informed, and this illness of his causes His Majesty much annoyance and much greater exertion in his affairs.[155]

And, as we have seen, the bonds of old friendship were never entirely severed; the *mercedes* granted Ruy Gómez in the early 1570s were tokens of the remnants of a great affection. Nevertheless, in the last years of his life Ruy Gómez was no longer by any measure "the most inwarde favourite that ever was with kinge,"[156] and he spent more and more time away from Philip and the court, playing the grand seigneur on his estates in the Alcarria.[157] He made frequent journeys to Albalate and Estremera, as well as to his ducal seat at Pastrana, and by 1568 was arranging to conduct business in flurries during brief stays at court.[158] Even his official correspondence increasingly betrayed an overriding concern with personal affairs and the business of his estates. For example, in 1568 Melchor de Herrera, negotiating the king's loans at Medina del Campo, was meanwhile hunting for perfume ingredients—civet musk and black amber—on behalf of Doña Ana. Jorge Manrique, on a diplomatic mission to northern Italy in 1570, appears to have spent a great deal of time hiring skilled artisans for Ruy Gómez's remodeling projects at Pastrana.[159]

Ruy Gómez de Silva was to live less than a year as the duke of Pastrana and thus did not have long to savor his new status of equality with the grand old houses of Castile. Nevertheless, the formation of the duchy and *mayorazgo* of Pastrana marked a great personal victory and a triumphant emergence from the grave crisis of his career. No longer an upstart or a dependent, this second son of an obscure Portuguese nobleman had cheated the turning wheel of fortune and established the permanent grandeur of his lineage on the treacherous basis of transitory favor. "Good fortune," observed one chronicler, "is a hard-mouthed horse: few can manage her or give a good account of themselves in her presence."[160] Looking back on his life, Ruy Gómez might well have agreed, and he could be forgiven if he thought himself a horseman of considerable prowess.

Conclusion
Ruy Gómez de Silva and Philip II

"Ay Monstros de la Fortuna, como de la Naturaleza."
Antonio Pérez

Ruy Gómez de Silva was a major figure of the greatest court in Europe in the second half of the sixteenth century. Still, he remains a shadowy figure to historians, due both to the sketchiness of the extant sources and to the nature of his role in the monarchy of Philip II. Throughout the records of the court and government of Philip II, the researcher finds traces of the presence of the prince of Eboli, but nearly always he stands slightly off stage, whispering in the darkened passageways of the court. Only occasionally are his deeds and words illuminated, as though in the flashes of a stroboscope; the pulses of bright light are random and haphazard, but taken in sequence they define for us the broad contours of a life and the trajectory of an extraordinary career.

From his youth Ruy Gómez de Silva was first and foremost a courtier. He was always a social climber, occasionally a statesman and, at the end, an aristocrat. He was a self-made man in the style of his time and place; that is, he knew how to manipulate his superiors into clearing an ascending path for him. Early on, his fortunes were cast with those of a young prince, and in many ways that prince, as he matured into a king, took the place of Fortune in Ruy Gómez's firmament. In youth and in manhood Ruy Gómez moved through the court in close orbit around Philip, steered and protected by the gravitational bonds of affection and favor. His station, his marriage, his wealth, his influence, all were blessings conferred by the benevolence of the prince. Understandably the maintenance of his intimacy with Philip became Ruy Gómez's principal study and occupation. The search for the political principles or the ideology that underlay the actions of Ruy Gómez de Silva is in essence a vain and misconceived quest. His politics were those of a courtier and a client; his guide in life, a compass aligned to the shifting magnetic pole of royal patronage rather than to the true north of conviction and principle.

But, late in life, even this born dependent forged and asserted his independence, and herein lies a significance that illuminates the nature and the evolution of absolutism in Habsburg Spain. First, the astonishing rise of Ruy Gómez de Silva demonstrates the power of the Crown. Philip's will was sufficient authority to make an obscure and impecunious foreigner dominant in his household and in the land. The prince's favor, rather than any inherent qualities of blood or wealth, made Ruy Gómez a fit match for the heiress to an established noble house. And in the last phase of his favorite's career the king, unquestioned, was able to transform a shabby scattering of small Castilian towns into a duchy and thus a grandeeship.

The rise of Ruy Gómez de Silva not only illustrates the extraordinary skill and assiduity of a lithe and sinuous courtier but also demonstrates the degree to which it was within the power of Philip II to bend and shape the political and social hierarchy of Castile. The last stage of Ruy Gómez's career, however, and the final form that his rise assumed reveal a curious reluctance on the part of the king to undermine the foundations of a power that was antithetical to his own. In his refusal to intervene to halt the grandees' persecution of his favorite, Philip in essence ratified the aristocrats' claims to an authority more legitimate than any the Crown could create. Subsequently the king turned away from reliance on his *privado* as an instrument of policy and adopted, in the remainder of his reign, a policy of governing through collaboration with aristocrats on the one hand and lowborn secretaries on the other. Finally, despite gradually having revoked Ruy Gómez's *privanza*, Philip could not entirely sever the bonds of long friendship, and he facilitated his creature's escape from dependence on the royal will.

A modern historian, in analyzing the rise of absolutism in the Kingdom of France, described one crucial component of the process:

> To secure its authority and meet its growing fiscal needs, the monarchy surrounded itself with a class of retainers owing direct allegiance to its authority, closely supervised but granted noble privileges in return for services rendered, and completely subservient. In this way

it brought about a transfer of power from the feudal nobility to a royal nobility, to which it delegated, under its immediate control, segments of public authority. . . . Thus was created a new nobility, which gradually replaced feudal remnants as they shrank to a purely decorative role.[1]

The implicit argument here, of course, is that the achievement of absolutism hinged upon the outcome of a power struggle between Crown and aristocracy. If one of the antagonists secured an increase in power or influence, the other was consequently and inevitably weakened. Under the terms of this analysis the Crown acted contrary to its own interests in entrusting governmental power to members of the landed nobility. Thus it was necessary for kings who aspired to enhance their own power to break with the tradition that gave the great nobles a preponderant voice in policymaking and administration. The Crown needed and had to create and utilize a class of servants who were simultaneously dependent upon the king and of sufficient stature to hold their own with the haughty *noblesse de race.*

This vision of conflict between Crown and aristocracy was not unknown in early modern Spain. Charles V, in his famous instruction, warned his son against entrusting governmental power to the grandees.[2] Antonio Pérez paraphrased this advice, arguing "that the major and supreme posts of Government and War should not be entrusted to anyone for very long, nor should they be entrusted to Grandees born, but instead to the one who distinguishes himself through services in arriving at that rank."[3]

Philip II, however, did not consistently follow this advice, and in the end missed an opportunity to enhance the power of the Crown and weaken the pretensions of the aristocracy. The *privanza* of Ruy Gómez de Silva was in some ways an early and tentative attempt to create a new type of governing elite. The king's will briefly raised Ruy Gómez to a status approximating that of a minister, somewhere between the servility of the secretaries who had controlled day-to-day administration since the era of the Catholic Kings and the proud independence of the aristocrats who claimed a voice in the formulation and execution of grand policy. At the outset of his reign, Philip entrusted great power to Ruy Gómez de Silva and richly rewarded him for his services with grants from the royal patrimony. But these marks of confidence and favor were not accepted by the old elite as the equivalents of the status of high birth, and the king, himself trapped in the mind-set of an aristocratic society, refused to press the point. In the end, even his chosen *privado* recognized that security for himself and his lineage resided not in reliance upon the Crown but among the antique elite of the land. With the king's acquiescence, Ruy Gómez took with him into the perpetual safe haven of an aristocratic entail the rewards that he had originally gained by placing his loyalty and his talents in the service of the monarch.

Bartolomé Bennassar has noted that, despite his father's advice, the Prudent King made much greater use of aristocrats in his government than Charles V ever had. Philip's governing apparatus as it matured comprised two groups—great lords, who filled the Council of State and the proconsular and military posts, and secretaries who saw to the operation of the administration.[4] The king's own secretarial bent, his unequaled devotion to detail and to preserving his own dignity and authority, acted to keep a government comprised of such social unequals in balance. The king's successors, less capable and less attentive to duty, were unable to maintain this balance, and the seventeenth century saw the reappearance in Spain of a problem described by Garrett Mattingly:

> The importance attached by their society to personal status and a personal nexus of relationships was certainly one obstacle impeding the development of the secretary's office. Unless he was a person of great force of character, and very confident of his master's support, the secretary found it difficult to deal with the magnates of the royal council. He was likely to be snubbed and by-passed and kept in ignorance of things it behoved him to know.[5]

Under weak kings the secretaries were socially disbarred from providing an effective defense of monarchical power against the pretensions of the aristocrats. This is exactly what happened in Spain under Philip III and Philip IV, as the once-proud government of the Habsburgs fell under the sway of a succession of grandee *validos* and their family cliques, while the secretaries were scornfully dismissed as "partos de la pluma" and relegated to drudge work as retainers of the aristocrats.[6]

Philip II left his successors a system of government unworkable in the absence of a very hardworking king. He had failed to grasp the importance of creating royal servants of sufficient stature to oppose the power hunger or resist the social condescension of the old aristocracy. As Antonio Pérez wrote in defense of the creation of *privados:*

> It is an excellent thing for kings to raise men up, and make them by their own hand. This is profitable to Princes for their old age, and for a minor successor, as these are both situations in which the discontented are daring.[7]

The *privanza* of Ruy Gómez de Silva had marked a first halting step in the direction of the creation of a service nobility of truly ministerial stature. Perhaps Ruy Gómez was not an ideal choice for this role—Alba was right to say that Eboli "was not one of the greatest Counselors that there has been"[8]—but nevertheless Philip erred when, from disinterest or disillusion with his *privado,* he abandoned the experiment entirely.

This is not to say that the king did not have his reasons. Much of the advice he received from his *privado,* not surprisingly, conflated the interest of monarch and state with the courtier's own self-interest. Toward the end of Eboli's life, one aspect of this truth was recognized rather cynically by Antonio Tiepolo. Ruy Gómez's celebrated opposition to belligerence stemmed from the fact that he had been

> enriched and aggrandized in peace, and thus could not cherish that which might retard his earnings, which could grow so much greater in time of peace.[9]

Even Espinosa, whose elevation had in some sense been an attempt to bolster the secretarial function with the prestige and *privanza* necessary to overawe mighty subjects, in the end disappointed Philip II. After the cardinal's disgrace and death, Philip regretted having entrusted so many of his affairs to Espinosa:

> Perhaps there were good reasons for it then. But experience has shown that it was not a good thing; and although it meant more leisure and less work for me, I do not think it should be allowed to continue.[10]

Philip II never again put such great reliance on a single minister of his own creation, and, when the time came to pass along his accumulated wisdom about ruling to his successor, the king cautioned the future Philip III to "make use of all, without submitting yourself to anyone . . . but rather hearing out many men and maintaining proper discretion with each."[11] The king believed that the close personal relationships of his youth and early manhood had clouded his monarchical judgment; in later life he preferred to know his servants and subjects from written reports, and even his lands were more familiar to him from research than from experience:

> He had full reports of all his provinces, cities, towns, sites, wildernesses, rivers, of their advantages civil and military, their finances, manufactures and tributes: and what he neither strode nor saw was represented to him in pictures.[12]

As we know, Philip III had neither the energy, nor the will, nor the capacity for solitude that had allowed or compelled his father to hold all the strands of his government in his own hands, and the monarchy may in the long term have suffered from the fact that, needing a minister and favorite, the young king elevated a man from the highest ranks of the aristocracy to the preeminence of the *valimiento.*

In the seventeenth century Habsburg absolutism crumbled, the victim in part of the Crown's abdication of power to the particularist and centrifugal forces of aristocratic resurgence. The comparison of the personal legacies of Philip II and Ruy Gómez de Silva illustrates this point nicely. While the monarchy headed by Philip's descendants floundered and eventually faltered in the pitiful spectacle of the court of Charles II, the house of Pastrana, buttressed by the reliable revenues that Philip had conferred on his *privado,* survived the feeble administration of the son and grandson of its founder. Rebuilt and strengthened by the fourth and fifth dukes and amalgamated with the house of Infantado, the house that Ruy Gómez built remained a great power in the land for a century after the demise of the Spanish Habsburgs.

Ruy Gómez de Silva was truly a "Monster of Fortune," a supreme opportunist with an unerring instinct for the main chance, who negotiated the pitfalls of the court with the inexplicable assurance and luck of a somnambulist. His career provides a stunning example of the courtly path to social mobility. Beyond this, the denouement of the career comprised a faint but ominous foreshadowing of the eventual fate of Habsburg absolutism. We shall never know whether the Prudent King ever pondered the disquieting fact that the uncannily fortunate destiny of Ruy Gómez de Silva, the quintessential king's man, beckoned the erstwhile *privado* at last into the secure harbor of aristocratic privilege. In the last analysis the career of Ruy Gómez de Silva illustrates the limits of the social mobility attainable through courtiership and thus reveals both the strength of the old social order and some of the weaknesses of Philip's conception and practice of royal absolutism.

Notes

PROLOGUE

1. Don Hernando de Toledo [son of the duke of Alba] to Juan de Albornoz, from Madrid, 27 July 1573, in Duquesa de Berwick y de Alba, ed., *Documentos escogidos del archivo de la Casa de Alba* (Madrid, 1891) [cited henceforth as DECA], p. 457.

2. Ibid.; Gregorio Marañón, *Antonio Pérez* (Madrid, 1951), vol. I, pp. 29, 174.

3. Luis de Salazar y Castro, *Historia genealógica de la Casa de Silva* (Madrid, 1685), vol. II, p. 507. The extraordinary honor of this visit was enhanced by the fact that the king was himself ill in the latter days of July 1573 (Juan de Zúñiga to Pedro Manuel, from Rome, 22 or 23 August 1573, *Colección de documentos inéditos para la historia de España* [Madrid, 1842–1895], vol. CII, p. 225; also Giovanni Soranzo, Leonardo Donà and Lorenzo Priuli to the Senate, from Madrid, 29 July 1573, in Mario Brunetti and Eligio Vitale, eds., *La corrispondenza da Madrid dell'ambasciatore Leonardo Donà (1570–1573)* [Venice and Rome, 1963], vol. II, p. 725). Philip had paid a similar deathbed visit to Juan de Figueroa in 1565; see Baron de Bolwiller to Granvelle, from Haguenau, 9 May 1565, in Charles Weiss, ed., *Papiers d'État du Cardinal de Granvelle*, vol. IX (Paris, 1852), p. 181.

4. Archivo Histórico Nacional, Madrid (AHN), Sección Osuna, legajo 2024, no. 13¹. Nos. 13² through 13⁴ comprise further copies of this will.

5. Ibid.; Manuel Santaolalla Llanas, *Pastrana: Apuntes de su historia, arte y tradiciones* (Pastrana, 1979), p. 35.

6. Antonio Pérez to Philip II, 29 July 1573, in Marañón, *Antonio Pérez*, vol. I, p. 29.

7. AHN Osuna, leg. 2024, no. 13¹. The persistent attendance of the royal secretaries at the deathbed may be accounted for by the fact that Escobedo and Pérez (and perhaps Losilla as well) were clients of the dying man. They may also have had a motive more vulturine than respect for their patron. Another secretary, Mateo Vázquez, had greatly enhanced his power at court by gaining and holding the papers of his patron, Cardinal Espinosa, upon the latter's death in September 1572. See A. W. Lovett, *Philip II and Mateo Vázquez de Leca* (Geneva, 1977).

8. Soranzo, Donà and Priuli to the Senate, from Madrid, 29 July 1573, in Brunetti and Vitale, *La corrispondenza*, vol. II, p. 725.

9. Antonio Pérez to Philip II, 29 July 1573, in Marañón, *Antonio Pérez*,

vol. I, p. 29; Soranzo, Donà and Priuli to the Senate, from Madrid, 12 August 1573, in Brunetti and Vitale, *La corrispondenza,* vol. II, p. 727.

10. Brunetti and Vitale, *La corrispondenza,* vol. II, p. 727; Hernando de Toledo to Juan de Albornoz, 30 July 1573, DECA, p. 458.

11. Marañón, *Antonio Pérez,* vol. I, p. 29.

12. Dr. Juan Milio to Juan de Albornoz, 14 August 1573, DECA, p. 460.

13. Ormaneto to the Cardinal of Como, 29 July 1573, excerpted in Silverio de Santa Teresa, ed., *Obras de Santa Teresa de Jesús,* vol. V (Burgos, 1918), p. 132 n. For another expression of loss, see M. de Leni to Monsignor Della Croce, from Turin, 12 August 1573, Archivo General de Simancas, Secretaría de Estado, leg. 1233, no. 109.

14. Salazar y Castro, *Casa de Silva,* vol. II, pp. 512–513.

15. Hernando de Toledo to Juan de Albornoz, 30 July 1573, DECA, p. 458; Fernando Alvarez de Toledo, Duque de Alba to Dr. Juan Milio, 2 September 1573, in Duque de Alba, ed., *Epistolario del III Duque de Alba, Don Fernando Alvarez de Toledo* (Madrid, 1952), vol. III, doc. 1.979, p. 519.

16. Dr. Juan Milio to Juan de Albornoz, 14 August 1573, DECA, p. 460. For another report of barely concealed glee among Alba's friends, see St.-Gouard to Charles IX, from Madrid, 23 August 1573, in Louis-Prosper Gachard, ed., *La Bibliothèque Nationale à Paris* (Brussels, 1877), vol. II, p. 431.

17. José Ortega y Gasset, *La rebelión de las masas* (Mexico City, 1976), p. 73.

CHAPTER ONE

1. William Maltby, *Alba: A Biography of Fernando Alvarez de Toledo, Third Duke of Alba, 1507–1582* (Berkeley, 1983), p. 330, n. 17. See also his comments on p. 86. Another scholar has remarked Ruy Gómez's "almost uncanny ability to hide his feelings and cover his tracks." M. J. Rodríguez-Salgado, *The Changing Face of Empire: Charles V, Philip II and Habsburg Authority, 1551–1559* (Cambridge, 1988), p. 16. Concerning the scarcity of correspondence, Paul David Lagomarsino suggests, without supplying evidence, that Ruy Gómez's papers may have been burned after his death on the king's orders ("Court Factions and the Formulation of Spanish Policy towards the Netherlands (1559–1567)," Ph.D. dissertation, University of Cambridge, 1973, p. 19).

2. Luis Cabrera de Córdoba, *Historia de Felipe II, rey de España* (Madrid, 1876–1877), vol. II, libro X, capítulo I, pp. 141–142.

3. A word should be added here about the name Ruy Gómez. Even though the family surname had once been Gómez de Silva, by the time of Ruy Gómez de Silva's birth, Ruy Gómez (often spelled as one word— Rruigomez or Ruigomes—in contemporary documents) had become in essence a forename. The name, as a first name, recurs over several generations of the Silva family, and it should be classified as one of the traditional names honoring prominent ancestors that were adopted by many noble houses. More familiar examples are *Iñigo López* or *Diego Hurtado* de Mendoza, or *Per Afán* de Ribera. (At a somewhat more humble social level, the Loyola clan

seems to have been inordinately fond of these compound names; see William W. Meissner, *Ignatius of Loyola* [New Haven, 1992], p. 13, for the names of the siblings of the Jesuit founder—himself *Iñigo López*.) Also, since I have gained my knowledge of Ruy Gómez's family from Spanish documents and treatises, I have chosen to use the Castilianized names that appear in the sources.

4. Luis de Salazar y Castro, *Historia genealógica de la Casa de Silva* (Madrid, 1685), vol. II, p. 456.

5. Ibid., p. 442.

6. Ibid., pp. 419–422; Cabrera de Córdoba, *Felipe II,* vol. IV, lib. VII, cap. V, p. 158.

7. Cabrera de Córdoba, *Felipe II,* vol. IV, lib. VII, cap. V, p. 158; Salazar y Castro, *Casa de Silva,* vol. II, pp. 425–434.

8. Salazar y Castro, *Casa de Silva,* vol. II, pp. 435–437.

9. Ibid., pp. 435, 437, 438–441.

10. Archivo Histórico Nacional, Madrid (AHN), Sección Ordenes Militares, Pruebas de Caballeros de Alcántara, expediente 1.430 (prueba of Don Diego de Silva y Mendoza).

11. Salazar y Castro, *Casa de Silva,* vol. II, p. 447; Cabrera de Córdoba, *Felipe II,* vol. IV, lib. VII, cap. V, p. 158. The Meneses and the Noronhas were among the greatest families of Portugal throughout the early modern period. The Meneses in particular had benefited from the irresponsible alienation of royal lands and revenues by the weak Afonso V (reigned 1438–1481). (See A. H. de Oliveira Marques, *History of Portugal* [New York, 1976], pp. 178–179, 284, 341.)

12. Salazar y Castro, *Casa de Silva,* vol. II, pp. 418, 448–456.

13. For examples, see Pedro Aguado Bleye, "Príncipe de Eboli," in *Diccionario de historia de España,* ed. by Germán Bleiberg (Madrid, 1981), vol. I, p. 1181; John H. Elliott, *Imperial Spain, 1469–1716* (Harmondsworth, 1970), p. 406.

14. Salazar y Castro, *Casa de Silva,* vol. II, p. 456. To my knowledge, there is no extant copy of Ruy Gómez's *fe de bautismo,* at least in the Spanish archives. I have not encountered any record of his birth or baptism in the papers of the ducal house, nor does such a testimony appear in the proof of Ruy Gómez's pedigree drawn up in 1540 for his admission as a knight of Calatrava (AHN Ordenes Militares, Pruebas de Caballeros de Calatrava, exped. 2472). This is unusual, but the document is incomplete and badly damaged.

15. Federico Badoero, "Relazione delle persone, governo e stati di Carlo V e di Filippo II (1557)," in Eugenio Albèri, ed., *Le relazioni degli ambasciatori veneti al Senato durante il secolo decimosesto,* ser. I, vol. III (Florence, 1853), p. 241. Confusion persists, however, since J. García Mercadal, in his Spanish version of this *relazione,* notes that an alternate copy gives Ruy Gómez's age as thirty-six. See J. García Mercadal, ed. and trans., *Viajes de extranjeros por España y Portugal* (Madrid, 1952), vol. I, p. 1115.

16. José Cornide, *Estado de Portugal en el año de 1800,* vol. II, in *Memorial*

histórico español, vol. XXVII (Madrid, 1894), pp. 146–147; Salazar y Castro, *Casa de Silva,* vol. II, p. 445.

17. Salazar y Castro, *Casa de Silva,* vol. II, p. 443.

18. AHN Ordenes Militares, Pruebas de Caballeros de Alcántara, exped. 1.430, testimony of Andrés Vaes.

19. Salazar y Castro, *Casa de Silva,* vol. II, p. 445.

20. AHN Ordenes Militares, Pruebas de Caballeros de Alcántara, exped. 1.431 (prueba of Don Diego de Silva y Portugal, 1613).

21. Salazar y Castro, *Casa de Silva,* vol. II, p. 442; AHN Ordenes Militares, Pruebas de Caballeros de Alcántara, exped. 1.430, testimony of Andrés Vaes.

22. Juan de Zúñiga to Charles V, 20 July 1523, abstract in José M. March, ed., *Niñez y juventud de Felipe II* (Madrid, 1941–1942), vol. I, ser. IV, no. 1, p. 90.

23. AHN Ordenes Militares, Pruebas de Caballeros de Alcántara, exped. 1.430, testimony of Andrés Vaes.

24. Ibid., testimony of Manuel de Mello Cotiño; Salazar y Castro, *Casa de Silva,* vol. II, pp. 456–457.

25. Salazar y Castro, *Casa de Silva,* vol. II, pp. 456–457; Cabrera de Córdoba, *Felipe II,* vol. IV, lib. VII, cap. V, p. 158; AHN Ordenes Militares, Pruebas de Caballeros de Alcántara, exped. 1.430, testimony of Andrés Vaes.

26. Ruy Gómez de Silva to Francisco de Eraso, from Madrid, 25 November 1552, Archivo General de Simancas (AGS), Secretaría de Estado (Estado), legajo 89, no. 123.

27. Salazar y Castro, *Casa de Silva,* vol. II, p. 457.

28. Cabrera de Córdoba, *Felipe II,* vol. IV, lib. VII, cap. V, p. 158; Badoero, "Relazione," p. 240. There is, however, no reason to credit Badoero's suggestion that Ruy Gómez's mother was Philip's wet nurse.

29. *Albalá* of Charles V, Madrid, 1 March 1535, in March, *Niñez y juventud,* vol. I, ser. VII, no. 3, pp. 282–283 (quotation at p. 282). The prince's governor was to receive a salary and *ayuda de costa* totaling 2000 ducats per year. Zúñiga commissioned the *Libro de la cámara real* of Gonzalo Fernández de Oviedo and doubtless consulted it while arranging Philip's household. See Juan Beneyto Pérez, *Historia de la administración española e hispanoamericana* (Madrid, 1958), p. 345.

30. Estefanía de Requesens [wife of Juan de Zúñiga] to Hipólita de Liori, Condesa de Palamós [her mother], 17 March 1535, in March, *Niñez y juventud,* vol. II, ser. XIII, no. 25, pp. 225–227. Presumably the lifelong friendship of Ruy Gómez and Luis de Requesens stemmed from their youthful association in this household.

31. My account of this incident and its aftermath is based on the following documents, printed by March in *Niñez y juventud:* Estefanía de Requesens to the Condesa de Palamós, from Madrid, 5 December 1535, in vol. II, ser. XIII, no. 53, p. 285; Report of Juan de Zúñiga, 1535 (day and month missing), in vol. II, ser. XVI, III:3, pp. 411–412; El Cardenal presidente (Ta-

vera) to Charles V, 1535 (day and month missing), in vol. II, ser. XVI, III:3, pp. 409–411; Juan de Zúñiga to Charles V, from Madrid, 11 February 1536, in vol. I, ser. VI, no. 11, p. 230. Direct quotations will be identified specifically.

32. The president is not identified in March's volume, but Tavera held this post in 1535. See Jules Gounon-Loubens, *Essais sur l'administration de la Castille au XVIe siècle* (Paris, 1860), p. 174; Hayward Keniston, *Francisco de los Cobos, Secretary of the Emperor Charles V* (Pittsburgh, 1960), p. 167.

33. Report of Juan de Zúñiga, in March, *Niñez y juventud*, vol. II, p. 411.

34. El Cardenal presidente to Charles V, ibid., vol. II, p. 410.

35. Ibid. The two young men were to be held in separate fortresses, "one in Zorita [de los Canes] and the other in another." Later in life, Ruy Gómez de Silva would have a happier connection with the fortress of Zorita. He was named its governor in 1559 by Philip II (AHN, Sección Osuna, leg. 2015, no. 1).

36. El Cardenal presidente to Charles V, in March, *Niñez y juventud*, vol. II, p. 411.

37. Report of Juan de Zúñiga (Charles V's marginal comment), ibid., vol. II, p. 412. The emperor's acquiescence in leniency contradicts Badoero's dramatic account of this incident. The Venetian ambassador, writing twenty-odd years after the fact, claimed that only the pleas of young Philip saved Ruy Gómez from execution by command of Charles V (Badoero, "Relazione," p. 240; for the same version, told even better, see William H. Prescott, *History of the Reign of Philip the Second, King of Spain,* vol. III [Boston, 1858], p. 399).

38. Salazar y Castro, *Casa de Silva,* vol. II, p. 458. He quotes from the *albalá* of Empress Isabel, countersigned by Juan Vázquez de Molina, Madrid, 24 December 1535. Again, Badoero's account, echoed by Prescott, of Philip's tearful intercession with his father to lift Ruy Gómez's exile seems unlikely, not least because Charles was absent from Spain in this period (Badoero, "Relazione," pp. 240–241; Prescott, *Philip the Second,* vol. III, pp. 399–400).

39. Estefanía de Requesens to the Condesa de Palamós, 5 December 1535, in March, *Niñez y juventud,* vol. II, ser. XIII, no. 53, p. 285. It may be that Zúñiga too had an interest in dismissing this matter rather lightly, since the other page involved may have been his relative (the *ayo*'s full name was Juan de Zúñiga y Avellaneda). *Niñez y juventud,* vol. I, ser. IV, intro., pp. 83–84.

40. On Zúñiga's character, ibid., vol. I, pp. 215–225. Perhaps as a result of his mother's efforts, Philip evinced a marked predisposition toward the Portuguese throughout his life. Both of his *privados,* and arguably the two men he trusted most, Ruy Gómez de Silva and Cristóbal de Moura, were Portuguese, a fact first remarked by Agustín Manuel de Vasconcelos (quoted in Salazar y Castro, *Casa de Silva,* vol. II, p. 518).

41. Salazar y Castro, *Casa de Silva,* vol. II, p. 458. Two months before, Ruy Gómez had been among a select group of the servants of the empress who

had accompanied her funeral cortege to Granada (March, *Niñez y juventud*, vol. II, editor's intro. to ser. XIV, pp. 355–357). It was at the end of this journey that Francisco de Borja, marquis of Lombay and the leader of the funeral retinue, experienced the epiphany that caused him to rededicate his life to religion (March, *Niñez y juventud*, vol. II, pp. 454–455).

42. "Memoria de las carretas y azemilas," etc., ibid., vol. II, ser. XVI, II:2, pp. 405–408. The document is undated. March makes no estimate, but it must date from the period 1540–1543, since it refers to Siliceo as the bishop of Cartagena (he was named to that diocese upon the death, in March 1540, of the incumbent), and since it makes no mention of the princess or her household (Philip was married in November 1543).

43. AGS, Guerra y Marina, leg. 23, nos. 92–93.

44. "Relación del casamiento del Príncipe Don Felipe con Doña María de Portugal," in March, *Niñez y juventud*, vol. II, ser. XI, no. 14, p. 87.

45. "Torneo celebrado en Valladolid con ocasión de la Boda del Príncipe Don Felipe con la Infanta Doña María de Portugal (1544)," in Amalio Huarte, ed., *Relaciones de los reinados de Carlos V y Felipe II* (Madrid, 1941), pp. 87–88.

46. Ibid., p. 94.

47. Salazar y Castro, *Casa de Silva*, vol. II, p. 458.

48. Ibid.; Juan Cristóbal Calvete de Estrella, *El felicissimo viaje del muy alto y muy poderoso principe don Phelippe* (1552) (Madrid, 1930), vol. I, pp. 1–2; Cabrera de Córdoba, *Felipe II*, vol. I, lib. I, cap. II, p. 11.

49. Salazar y Castro, *Casa de Silva*, vol. II, p. 458. The original grant had covered the period 1546–1555; Ruy Gómez was now to have ⅛ of the mines' yield for 1531–1545 as well. This income had apparently been held in escrow pending the outcome of a legal dispute between the Crown and the heirs of its previous owner.

50. Ibid., p. 459; Calvete de Estrella, *El felicissimo viaje*, vol. I, pp. 2–5; Francisco López de Gómara, *Annals of the Emperor Charles V*, trans. R. B. Merriman (Oxford, 1912), p. 257; Maltby, *Alba*, pp. 66–70; Elliott, *Imperial Spain*, p. 160. In "Habsburg Ceremony in Spain: The Reality of the Myth," *Historical Reflections/Réflexions Historiques* 15:1 (1988), Helen Nader refutes the tenacious notion that the introduction of Burgundian ceremonial sparked a xenophobic reaction in Castile.

51. Antonio Ballesteros y Beretta, *Historia de España y su influencia en la historia universal* (Barcelona, 1927), vol. IV, part II, p. 518. Ballesteros's account condenses that of Antonio Rodríguez Villa, *Etiquetas de la Casa de Austria* (Madrid, 1913?), pp. 62–64.

52. Calvete de Estrella, *El felicissimo viaje*, vol. I, p. 19; Salazar y Castro, *Casa de Silva*, vol. II, p. 459.

53. Salazar y Castro, *Casa de Silva*, vol. II, pp. 459, 464.

54. Ibid., p. 517, for quote from Garibay; Cabrera de Córdoba, *Felipe II*, vol. IV, lib. VII, cap. V, p. 158.

55. Prescott, *Reign of Philip the Second* (Philadelphia, 1904), vol. IV, p. 351.

56. William, Prince of Orange, *The Apologie of Prince William of Orange*

against the Proclamation of the King of Spaine, ed. by H. Wansink after the English edition of 1581 (Leiden, 1969), p. 45.

57. Martin Hume dismissed the notion of a marriage but stated, without offering proof, that "subsequently for some years marital relations certainly existed between them [Philip and Isabel Osorio]." Similarly, A. W. Lovett asserts, again on uncertain evidence, that Philip did indeed have an affair with Isabel Osorio "either just before, or just after, the death of Mary of Portugal." See Hume, *Philip II of Spain* (1897) (New York, 1969), p. 27; Lovett, *Early Habsburg Spain, 1517–1598* (Oxford, 1986), p. 119. Be this as it may, nothing has surfaced to either confirm or refute William the Silent's charges against Ruy Gómez de Silva.

58. Badoero, "Relazione," p. 241.

59. For Lerma, see Ciríaco Pérez Bustamante, *Felipe III: Semblanza de un monarca y perfiles de una privanza* (Madrid, 1950), pp. 38–41; for Olivares, Gregorio Marañón, *El Conde-Duque de Olivares,* 15th ed. (Madrid, 1980), p. 41. According to these authors, Lerma and Olivares won points with their young protégés by providing them with money to supplement their rather lean allowances. Ruy Gómez lacked the private financial resources of these men, so it seems unlikely that he was often in a position to advance funds to Philip.

60. Marañón attempted to refute these charges, but his righteous indignation is not altogether convincing (*Conde-Duque de Olivares,* pp. 40–41); more recently, R. A. Stradling concluded that "it must be held probable that Olivares was privy to Philip's sexual adventures" (*Philip IV and the Government of Spain, 1621–1665* [Cambridge, 1988], p. 53; for his discussion of this subject, see pp. 20, 51–54).

61. Agustín G. de Amezúa y Mayo, *Isabel de Valois, Reina de España (1546–1568)* (Madrid, 1949), vol. I, pp. 427, 430 (citing Saint-Sulpice to Charles IX, 7 October 1564).

62. Charles V to Prince Philip, letter of instructions, 4 May 1543, in Francisco de Laiglesia y Auset, *Estudios históricos (1515–1555)* (Madrid, 1918), vol. I, p. 75. This instruction is also reproduced in March, *Niñez y juventud,* vol. II, ser. IX, no. I (quoted passage at pp. 18–19).

63. March, *Niñez y juventud,* vol. II, ser. IX *passim.*

64. Cabrera de Córdoba, *Felipe II,* vol. II, lib. X, cap. I, p. 140.

65. Gustav Ungerer, ed., *A Spaniard in Elizabethan England: The Correspondence of Antonio Pérez's Exile* (London, 1974–1976), vol. II, p. 335.

66. Elliott, *Imperial Spain,* p. 208. López de Gómara gives 1545 as the year of Zúñiga's death (*Annals of the Emperor,* pp. 121–122).

67. López de Gómara, *Annals of the Emperor,* pp. 121–122.

68. Maltby, *Alba,* p. 70.

69. See Chapter 5.

70. María of Portugal died in childbirth in 1545.

71. Charles V to Prince Philip, 6 May 1543, in March, *Niñez y juventud,* vol. II, ser. IX, no. II, p. 27.

72. In the documents and histories consulted in preparing this study, I

have never seen Ruy Gómez accorded this title except by Venetian ambassadors.

73. Salazar y Castro, *Casa de Silva,* vol. II, p. 465; Gregorio Marañón, *Antonio Pérez* (Madrid, 1951), vol. I, p. 169, n. 6.

74. The most detailed account of this journey is, of course, Calvete de Estrella, *El felicissimo viaje.* There is also a useful summary, focused on Ruy Gómez's role in these events, in Salazar y Castro, *Casa de Silva,* vol. II, pp. 459–462.

75. Calvete de Estrella, *El felicissimo viaje,* vol. I, pp. 14–19.

76. Ibid., vol. I, p. 21.

77. For Ruy Gómez's participation in various festivities in Italy and the Low Countries, see ibid., vol. I, pp. 82–88, 142, 189–204, 306–311; vol. II, 13–15, 396–400, 404–409. For the *juego de cañas,* Milan, 6 January 1549, see ibid., vol. I, pp. 87–88. For the *damas tudescas,* see ibid., vol. I, p. 310.

78. Ibid., pp. 396–400.

79. Salazar y Castro, *Casa de Silva,* vol. II, p. 462.

80. Ibid., pp. 464–465.

81. A rather confusing entry in AGS Estado, leg. 89, no. 195, seems to give the value of Argamasilla in 1552 as 500,000 *maravedís,* or 1,333 ducats. In the *Actas* of the general chapter of Calatrava for 1600/1602, one of the order's encomiendas is listed as "Obrería y Argamasilla." Assuming that this is the right encomienda and that it corresponds to the 1523 listing for "La encomienda de la Obra" and to the 1573 designation of "La Obrería," Argamasilla was worth 830 ducats per year in 1523 and 2,256 ducats per year in 1573. See Hermann Kellenbenz, "El valor de las rentas de las encomiendas de la Orden de Calatrava en 1523 y en 1573," *Anuario de historia económica y social* 1 (1968), pp. 588, 595, 597. See also Antonio Domínguez Ortiz, *La sociedad española en el siglo XVII* (Madrid, 1964), vol. I, pp. 199–200.

82. AHN Ordenes Militares, Pruebas de Caballeros de Calatrava, expeds. 1074*bis* and 2742. The allowance paid a caballero was probably in the neighborhood of 80 ducats per year (Kellenbenz, "El valor," p. 584).

83. Salazar y Castro, *Casa de Silva,* vol. II, pp. 464–465.

84. Kellenbenz, "El valor," p. 595.

85. Salazar y Castro, *Casa de Silva,* vol. II, p. 463.

86. Antonio Domínguez Ortiz, *El antiguo régimen: los Reyes Católicos y los Austrias* (Madrid, 1973), p. 115, observes that *hábitos* were greatly prized by lesser noblemen even though they "did not produce income," since the possession of one "afforded public testimony that its holder was of noble and pure blood."

87. Ruy Gómez de Silva to Francisco de Eraso, from Madrid, 25 November 1552, AGS Estado, leg. 89, no. 123; see also AGS Estado, leg. 508, no. 58.

88. AGS Estado, leg. 89, no. 196.

89. Don Diego Hurtado de Mendoza to Ruy Gómez de Silva, March 1550, in R. Foulché-Delbosc, ed., "Cartas de Don Diego Hurtado de Mendoza," *Archivo de investigaciones históricas,* II (1911), pp. 273–274. Neither the exact object nor the outcome of these negotiations is clear from this letter,

but Ruy Gómez had evidently asked Mendoza's aid in securing a papal dispensation, which the latter thought could be obtained more cheaply should the present pope die of his dropsy. Mendoza's comments indicate that the negotiations had been delayed and that Ruy Gómez feared that the family of the prospective bride would back away from the match, but I have been unable to find any other letters that shed light on this affair.

90. Salazar y Castro, *Casa de Silva*, vol. II, p. 465.

91. Such evidence as there is indicates that further children of this marriage were rendered unlikely because of the personal animosity between the count and the countess, rather than impossible because of sterility. This issue will be taken up below.

92. Maltby, *Alba*, p. 71.

93. Salazar y Castro, *Casa de Silva*, vol. II, p. 465; Gaspar Muro, *Vida de la Princesa de Eboli* (Mexico City, 1883), ch. II, pp. 114–115, 118. The numbering of the pages in this edition is hopelessly muddled; for example, the same page numbers recur in ch. III.

94. Ibid., ch. II, p. 118.

95. "Lo que se asienta, e capitula entre el Principe nro S⁰ʳ y conde y condesa de Melito, sobre el Cassamiento que se ha tratado entre Ruy Gomez de Silva sumilier de Corps de Su Alteza y Dᵃ Ana de Mendoza hija delos dhos condes," Madrid, 18 April 1553, AHN Osuna, leg. 2029, no. 13¹. There is another copy of this document in AGS, Guerra y Marina, leg. 50, no. 171.

CHAPTER TWO

1. Diego Gutiérrez Coronel, *Historia genealógica de la casa de Mendoza* (1772), ed. by Angel González Palencia (Madrid, 1946), pp. 373–379; John H. Elliott, *Imperial Spain, 1469–1716* (Harmondsworth, 1970), p. 100; Gregorio Marañón, *Antonio Pérez* (Madrid, 1951), vol. I, p. 167; Gaspar Muro, *Vida de la Princesa de Eboli* (Mexico City, 1883), ch. I, pp. 62–64, 97.

2. Genealogy drawn up by Gerónimo de Ponte, quondam notary of the Chancillería de Granada, 1 January 1565, Archivo Histórico Nacional, Madrid (AHN), Sección Osuna, legajo 2224², no. 3¹; Gutiérrez Coronel, *Casa de Mendoza*, pp. 378–379. Gutiérrez Coronel speculates that although well born, Doña Mencia did not possess "el mejor recato."

3. "Copia simple de la legitimación . . . ," AHN Osuna, leg. 3350.

4. Gutiérrez Coronel, *Casa de Mendoza*, pp. 381–384; José M. March, ed., *Niñez y juventud de Felipe II* (Madrid, 1941–1942), vol. I, ser. VI, p. 239, n. 23, and Inventory at death, March, *Niñez y juventud*, vol. II, ser. XV, p. 366.

5. "Escriptura de mayoradgo que otorgaron los yllˢ señores don diego hurtado de mendoza Conde de melyto e la señora doña Ana de la cerda su muger," AHN, Sección Consejos Suprimidos, leg. 36,474. The *tercias* were a portion of the ecclesiastical tithes, usually ⅔, that had been granted to the Crown. Thus the portion of the *tercias* included in this *mayorazgo* was equivalent to ²⁄₂₇ (about 7.5 percent) of the tithes of Guadalajara and its district.

6. AHN Osuna, leg. 2224^2, no. 3^1, and leg. 2077, nos. 10^2 and 10^3; Gutiér-rez Coronel, *Casa de Mendoza,* pp. 387–390; Muro, *Vida,* ch. I, pp. 102–105; Juan de Mariana, *Historia general de España* (Valencia, 1794), vol. II, p. 532; Felipe Picatoste, *Estudios sobre la grandeza y decadencia de España* (Madrid, 1887), tomo II, *Los españoles en Italia,* libro II, capítulo III, parte III, pp. 69–78; Marañón, *Antonio Pérez,* vol. I, p. 167; Giuseppe Galasso, *Economia e società nella Calabria del cinquecento* (Naples, 1967), p. 1. The Sanseverini continued to press their claim to the county of Mélito; they did not achieve reinstate-ment, but in exchange they were allowed to raise the rate of the silk gabelle they collected. See Galasso, *Economia e società,* pp. 4, 32.

7. See the titles, confirmed by Charles in 1516, catalogued in Jesús Er-nesto Martínez Ferrando, *Privilegios otorgados por el Emperador Carlos V en el Reino de Nápoles. (Sicilia aquende el Faro)* (Barcelona, 1943), p. 138.

8. Gutiérrez Coronel, *Casa de Mendoza,* pp. 387, 390; Joan Reglà Campis-tol, *Els virreis de Catalunya. Els segles XVI i XVII* (Barcelona, 1961), pp. 90–92. Reglà emphasizes that Mélito was "lloctinent de tota la Corona d'Aragó," the last to hold this post before the introduction of viceroys for each king-dom. For a critical assessment of his handling of the *Germanías,* see A. W. Lovett, *Early Habsburg Spain, 1517–1598* (Oxford, 1986), pp. 36–37.

9. Gutiérrez Coronel, *Casa de Mendoza,* pp. 194–195, 391; Marañón, *Anto-nio Pérez,* vol. I, p. 169.

10. Gutiérrez Coronel, *Casa de Mendoza,* pp. 391–396.

11. AHN Osuna, leg. 2080, no. 13^3; "Escriptura de mayoradgo . . . " (22 April 1529), AHN Consejos, leg. 36,474.

12. "Escriptura de mayoradgo" (22 April 1529), AHN Consejos, leg. 36,474. Galasso describes the Italian lands in terms of modern administra-tive units, in *Economia e società,* p. 31. The first counts of Mélito subsequently acquired additional properties, among which only a small annuity drawn on the royal revenues from the Atienza salt mines was added to the *ma-yorazgo.* Some of these properties were bestowed on their younger children; almost all of them were sources of litigation and disputes for future genera-tions of the family.

13. Juan de Samano to Francisco de Eraso, 7 May 1553, *Colección de docu-mentos inéditos para la historia de España* (Madrid, 1842–1895) (cited hence-forth as CODOIN), vol. LVI, p. 555.

14. Gutiérrez Coronel, *Casa de Mendoza,* p. 390. The second count's inher-itance of his father's lands, as opposed to his titles, was disputed, as will be seen. This Diego Hurtado de Mendoza should not be confused with the diplomat and writer of the same name (1503–1575), who was a cadet of the house of Mondéjar.

15. Ibid., pp. 396–397, 526–528.

16. Juan de Samano to Francisco de Eraso, 7 May 1553, CODOIN, vol. LVI, p. 555.

17. Marañón, *Antonio Pérez,* vol. I, p. 168.

18. See Muro, *Vida,* ch. II, p. 107. Despite the shared *apellido* of Silva, there was no blood relation between Ruy Gómez and Ana's maternal ances-

tors. See Erika Spivakovsky, "La Princesa de Eboli," *Chronica Nova,* no. 9 (1974), p. 8.

19. Muro, *Vida,* ch. II, p. 110; Marañón, *Antonio Pérez,* vol. I, p. 169; Spivakovsky, "Princesa de Eboli," p. 13.

20. Reglà, *Els virreis,* p. 102, states that the second count of Mélito was born "around 1515."

21. Guillermo Hernández Peñalosa, *El derecho en Indias y en su metrópoli* (Bogotá, 1969), pp. 246–247. The history of the house of Pastrana provides several examples of marriages arranged for very young children.

22. Juan de Samano to Francisco de Eraso, 7 May 1553, CODOIN, vol. LVI, p. 555.

23. Gutiérrez Coronel, *Casa de Mendoza,* pp. 393, 395.

24. "Lo que se assienta, e capitula entre el Principe nro S^{or} y conde y condesa de Melito, sobre el cassamiento que se ha tratado entre Ruy Gomez de Silva sumilier de Corps de Su Alteza y Dª Ana de Mendoza hija delos dhos condes," AHN Osuna, leg. 2029, nos. 13$^{1-2}$.

25. Luis de Salazar y Castro, *Historia genealógica de la Casa de Silva* (Madrid, 1685), vol. II, p. 465.

26. Hernández Peñalosa, *El derecho,* pp. 246–247; for a discussion of contemporary attitudes, in France, about the validity of marriages contracted by virtue of *paroles de présent,* see David Hunt, *Parents and Children in History* (New York, 1972), pp. 60–62. Heath Dillard, dealing with an earlier period, provides the best available account of Castilian marriage customs and procedures, in Chapter 2 of her *Daughters of the Reconquest* (Cambridge, 1984). See p. 60 for *palabras de presente.*

27. AHN Osuna, leg. 2029, nos. 13$^{1-2}$. See Dillard, *Daughters of the Reconquest,* p. 63, for an account of wedding ceremonies.

28. AHN Osuna, leg. 2029, nos. 13$^{1-2}$.

29. The *arras* was a sum promised by the groom to his bride to provide for her support should he predecease her; as such it was the functional equivalent of the English jointure, although unlike the latter it was usually paid in a lump sum rather than as an annuity and was often delivered to the bride at the time of the marriage rather than upon the husband's death. Dillard provides a good discussion (*Daughters of the Reconquest,* pp. 47–48) and makes the point that the groom's provision of the *arras* constituted "a necessary condition of betrothal."

30. In most cases, a widow was entitled to reinstatement of the amount of her marriage portion, with some interest, as well as to payment of her *arras.*

31. AHN Osuna, leg. 2029, nos. 13$^{1-2}$.

32. Juan de Samano to Francisco de Eraso, 7 May 1553, CODOIN, vol. LVI, p. 555; Salazar y Castro, *Casa de Silva,* vol. II, p. 465; Gutiérrez Coronel, *Casa de Mendoza,* pp. 565–566.

33. Samano to Eraso, 7 May 1553, CODOIN, vol. LVI, p. 555. According to López de Gómara, Philip also "bestowed great gifts" on another of his household gentlemen, Juan de Benavides, who was married in the same

year to the heiress of the marquis of Cortés (Francisco López de Gómara, *Annals of the Emperor Charles V* [Oxford, 1912], p. 265). See also Ruy Gómez de Silva to Francisco de Eraso, no date (but from internal evidence, early 1554), Archivo General de Simancas (AGS), Secretaría de Estado (Estado), leg. 808, no. 134, for Ruy Gómez's request, on Philip's behalf, that Eraso should expedite the grant of the *tenencia* of Viana—evidently part of the marriage settlement—to Benavides.

34. "Diferentes papeles pertenecientes al Estado de Melito," AHN Osuna, leg. 2708, includes a summary of this lawsuit.

35. Gutiérrez Coronel, *Casa de Mendoza*, p. 195.

36. Cédula of Philip, King of Naples, Brussels, 9 Oct. 1555, AHN Osuna, leg. 2077, no. 28; Martínez Ferrando, *Privilegios*, nos. 1240 and 1242, p. 139.

37. Cédula of Charles V, Ratisbon, 30 June 1532, AHN Osuna, leg. 2080, no. 2; see also Galasso, *Economia e società*.

38. See the royal confirmations of these arrangements, Madrid, 21 August and 25 September 1539, summarized in Martínez Ferrando, *Privilegios*, nos. 668 and 669, pp. 76–77; Luis de Salazar y Castro, *Historia genealógica de la Casa de Lara, justificada con instrumentos, y escritores de inviolable fe* (Madrid, 1696), vol. I, p. 636; Gutiérrez Coronel, *Casa de Mendoza*, p. 399.

39. AHN Osuna, leg. 2080, nos. 12, 13^1.

40. AHN Osuna, leg. 2708.

41. AHN Osuna, leg. 2082^2, no. 2.

42. AHN Osuna, leg. 2080, nos. 6^1, 12, 13^1.

43. AHN Osuna, leg. 2708.

44. Ibid.

45. From the very outset of the wedding negotiations, Ruy Gómez strove to influence favorably Mélito's business at the emperor's court. See Ruy Gómez de Silva to Francisco de Eraso, from Madrid, 5 April 1552, AGS Estado, leg. 89, no. 129: "Esta q[ue] escrivo sera p[ar]a enderezar esta otra de su alteza y suplicar a v.m. por mi parte q[ue] en el negocio q[ue] lescrive del conde de melito ayude loq[ue] pudiere porq[ue] su cristiandad y la hidalgia [*sic*] y condiciones conq[ue] en aquel cargo quiere servir a su mag^d lo merecen allende de las partes q[ue] para ello tiene."

46. AHN Osuna, leg. 2029, no. 13^1.

47. Spivakovsky, "Princesa de Eboli," p. 9.

48. For this suggestion, I am indebted to an anonymous reader for the University of California Press.

49. Cédula of Prince Philip, countersigned by Juan Vázquez, Madrid, 3 June 1553, CODOIN, vol. LVI, pp. 557–558. A tenth of the groom's property was the long-standing limit on the size of *arras*; see Dillard, *Daughters of the Reconquest*, p. 47.

50. See M. J. Rodríguez-Salgado, *The Changing Face of Empire* (Cambridge, 1988), pp. 126–127.

51. See Chapter 1, n. 92.

52. Spivakovsky, "Princesa de Eboli," pp. 8–9.

53. Diego Hurtado de Mendoza, Duke of Francavila, to Ruy Gómez de Silva, from Valladolid, 13 September 1557, CODOIN, vol. XCVII, p. 291.

54. Ibid.; see also Spivakovsky, "Princesa de Eboli," p. 18.

55. Joan Reglà Campistol, *Felip II i Catalunya* (Barcelona, 1956), p. 17.

56. AHN Osuna, leg. 2077, nos. 10⁵, 22¹⁻³; the grant of the title of Algecilla and the properties that comprised the marquisate are treated in Gutiérrez Coronel, *Casa de Mendoza,* p. 396. I have been unable to determine the precise date of the grant, but Mélito was styling himself "Marques de Algezilla" by 13 March 1555 (see AHN Osuna, leg. 2077, no. 6). Some news regarding new titles for Mélito already circulated at the imperial court late in 1554; see (Diego de Vargas?) to Ruy Gómez de Silva, from Brussels, 14 December 1554, AGS Estado, leg. 508, no. 242: "Sup[li]co a v.m. me avise del titulo q[ue] pone el Rey p[rincip]e n[uest]ro señor al sʳ Conde de Melito por que en lo q[ue] de aca se le screviere no discrepemos." Mélito seems to have been accorded the treatment due a grandee from about the time of his appointment to Aragon; Philip's letter of 11 May 1554 (AGS Estado, leg. 808, no. 24) addresses him as "conde primo."

57. Francavila's tenure as viceroy is most thoroughly examined in Reglà, *Felip II i Catalunya,* esp. pp. 17–18. The Zaragoza incident and its outcome are also discussed in Luis Cabrera de Córdoba, *Historia de Felipe II, rey de España* (Madrid, 1876–1877), vol. I, lib. I, cap. IX, p. 44; A. Llorente, "La primera crísis de hacienda en tiempo de Felipe II," *Revista de España* (Madrid), I (1868), pp. 327–328; Rodríguez-Salgado, *Changing Face of Empire,* pp. 289–290; Fernand Braudel, *The Mediterranean and the Mediterranean World in the Age of Philip II* (New York, 1976), vol. II, p. 959; John Lynch, *Spain under the Habsburgs* (New York, 1984), vol. I, p. 209. See below for his adoption of the title of Francavila.

58. Helmut Georg Koenigsberger, *The Practice of Empire* (Ithaca, 1969), p. 60; Reglà, *Felip II i Catalunya,* p. 18.

59. Reglà, *Felip II i Catalunya,* p. 19.

60. Spivakovsky, "Princesa de Eboli," p. 14.

61. Leonardo Donato, "Relación de las cosas de España, leída al senado veneciano por Leonardo Donato, embajador de aquella república," printed (despite its title, in Italian) as an appendix to Cabrera de Córdoba, *Felipe II,* vol. IV, pp. 403–480. The quotes are from page 417. Francavila's ineffectiveness in the Council of Italy is also remarked in Koenigsberger, *Practice of Empire,* p. 70. On the other hand, in *Felip II i Catalunya* Reglà argues that Francavila was a competent and innovative viceroy in Catalonia; he insists that he learned a great deal, at least about the constitutionalist mind-set of the subjects of the eastern kingdoms, from his experience as viceroy in Aragon. Although Francavila's activities as an administrator lie outside the scope of this study, I will add that the correspondence I have seen reveals him as obstinate, volatile and not particularly industrious or well informed. I thus retain doubts about Reglà's assessment. On a minor point, both Koenigsberger and Reglà mention that Francavila left the presidency of Italy

when he was named viceroy in Catalonia, without stipulating that the former post was discharged by an acting president (Quiroga) and resumed by Francavila when he left Barcelona in 1571. See Luciano Serrano, ed., *Correspondencia diplómatica entre España y la Santa Sede durante el pontificado de S. Pio V* (Madrid, 1914), vol. IV, p. 221 (Castagna to Alessandrino, from Madrid, 12 March 1571).

62. Quoted by Manuel Rivero Rodríguez, "La fundación del Consejo de Italia: Corte, grupos de poder y periferia (1536–1559)," in *Instituciones y élites de poder en la Monarquía Hispana durante el siglo XVI,* ed. by J. Martínez Millán (Madrid, 1992), p. 216.

63. See AHN Osuna, legs. 2077 (esp. no. 6) and 2078, and the "Relacion de loq contienen en suma los assensus Regios y escripturas q passaron antes el duque mi s^{or} y el Principe Ruygomez," AHN Osuna, leg. 2708, "Diferentes papeles pertenecientes al Estado de Melito. . . ." This transaction is very well documented.

64. "Philippus/Copia de una provision para que se consiguen al Principe Ruy Gomez 60U [60,000] ducados en quenta de lo que a de aver en el principado de Melito," AHN Osuna, leg. 2077, no. 28.

65. "Escriptura de donacion, cesion e trespasacion," Valladolid, 7 April 1554, AHN Osuna, leg. 2029, no. 15.

66. Ibid.

67. The donations were made on 14 March and 7 April 1554; the viceregal appointment was announced on 22 April (Reglà, *Felip II i Catalunya,* p. 17).

68. AHN Osuna, leg. 2029, no. 15.

69. See William Maltby, *Alba: A Biography of Fernando Alvarez de Toledo, Third Duke of Alba, 1507–1582* (Berkeley, 1983), p. 75, and the evidence of this relationship presented in this work, below.

70. Ruy Gómez de Silva to Francisco de Eraso, from Valladolid, 21 August 1553, CODOIN, vol. LVI, p. 559.

71. Ruy Gómez de Silva to Francisco de Eraso, no date, AGS Estado, leg. 808, no. 134. This letter was likely written in early 1554, since it opens with the news of the death of Princess Juana's husband (January 1554, according to Rodríguez-Salgado, *Changing Face of Empire,* p. 5).

72. AHN Osuna, leg. 2029, no. 14. For Philip's original *cédula,* countersigned by Francisco de Ledesma, Valladolid, 22 February 1554, see AGS, Guerra y Marina, leg. 50, no. 172.

73. AGS, Guerra y Marina, leg. 50, no. 172; AHN Osuna, leg. 2242, no. 5^2.

74. AGS, Contaduría de Mercedes, leg. 491, nos. 13–14; *Mayorazgo* of Pastrana, AHN Osuna, leg. 2326, no. 9^1, clause XXX.

75. AHN Osuna, leg. 2029, no. 14.

CHAPTER THREE

1. Andrés Muñoz, *Sumaria y verdadera relación del buen viaje que el . . . Príncipe . . . don Felipe hizo a Inglaterra* (Zaragoza, 1554), reprinted in Pascual

de Gayangos, ed., *Viaje de Felipe Segundo á Inglaterra, por Andrés Muñoz (impreso en Zaragoza en 1554), y relaciones varias relativas al mismo suceso* (Madrid, 1877), p. 34. Despite some confusion of terminology on this point, I refer to the *infante* in this passage, following Gachard, who records Don Carlos's joy at first being called *príncipe* in March 1556, after his father's accession as king (Louis-Prosper Gachard, *Don Carlos y Felipe II* (San Lorenzo de el Escorial, 1984), p. 46).

2. "As a Portuguese and His Highness's servant," Ruy Gómez had been involved from the outset of the negotiations for this match, agreeing to host a reception for the ambassador sent from Portugal to propose it; see Ruy Gómez de Silva to Francisco de Eraso, from Toro, 2 January 1552, Archivo General de Simancas (AGS), Secretaría de Estado (Estado), legajo 89, no. 125. For Ruy Gómez's mission to Portugal and its outcome, see the following documents in *Calendar of Letters, Despatches and State Papers relating to the Negotiations between England and Spain, Preserved in the Archives at Vienna, Simancas, Besancon, Brussels, Madrid and Lille* (cited henceforth as *CalStP–S*), ed. by Royall Tyler, vol. XI, *Edward VI and Mary, 1553* (London, 1916): Charles V (at Brussels) to Philip (at Valladolid), 30 July 1553 (pp. 126–127); same to same, 12 August 1553 (pp. 162–163); Philip to Charles V, 22 August 1553 (pp. 177–178); Simon Renard (London) to Antoine Perrenot de Granvelle, Bishop of Arras (Brussels), 7 August 1553 (pp. 153–154); Charles V to Luis Sarmiento de Mendoza (Lisbon), 21 November(?) 1553 (pp. 377–378). For an account of the negotiations, see M. J. Rodríguez-Salgado, *The Changing Face of Empire* (Cambridge, 1988), pp. 78–79.

3. The negotiations for the marriage can be followed closely in AGS Estado, legs. 807 and 808 (an interesting memorandum on unresolved points of the match is preserved at AGS Estado, leg. 807, no. 23), and in *CalStP–S*, vol. XI, and vol. XII (*Mary, Jan.-July, 1554* (London, 1949). The vehemence of Philip's objections are evident in a curious "writing *ad cautelam*" drawn up in Valladolid on 4 January 1554, in which the prince stated that "because by his own free will he had never agreed and never would agree to the articles [of the marriage contract], although he was about to grant the power to enable [various officials in England] . . . to ratify and swear to observe them, and he himself would agree to and swear by them, using the customary legal forms to render the oath binding, he protested before me, the secretary, and the other witnesses mentioned below, against the articles and everything contained therein . . . " (*CalStP–S*, vol. XII, pp. 4–6). For the belief that Philip was procrastinating, see Tyler's preface to *CalStP–S*, vol. XI, pp. x–xii, and the calendared documents cited there. For the journey to England and the events that transpired in the first weeks there, see Gayangos, *Viaje de Felipe Segundo*; Juan de Varaona [Barahona], "Viaje de Felipe II á Inglaterra en 1554 cuando fué á casar con la Reina Doña María," *Colección de documentos inéditos para la historia de España* (Madrid, 1842–1895) (cited henceforth as CODOIN), vol. I, pp. 564–574; Martin A. S. Hume, "The Visit of Philip II," *English Historical Review* 7 (1892), pp. 253–280; Mariano González-Amao, "La boda inglesa de Felipe II," *Historia 16* 9:97 (May 1984),

pp. 34–42. Disagreements over the date of Philip's departure have been convincingly settled (in favor of 13 July 1554) by Carl Bratli, *Felipe II, rey de España* (1909) (Madrid, 1927), p. 176, n. 229.

4. For the accompanying household, see the list in Muñoz, *Viaje*, pp. 31f. The aristocrats in the entourage are listed in a document of 20 July 1554 that is reproduced in *CalStP–S*, vol. XII, p. 317, and the *ayudas* are discussed in Muñoz, *Viaje*, pp. 1, 4–5. I have found no record of the *ayuda* paid to Ruy Gómez de Silva, but an approximate figure for the grants made to prominent courtiers can be inferred from the fact that Philip offered a lump sum of 20,000 ducats, plus an annuity of 2,000 ducats for two or three years, to Don Fernando Francisco Dávalos, marquis of Pescara. Pescara seems to have regarded even this sum as insufficient, and he may have received more. Draft memo of Philip for Ruy Gómez de Silva, 2 August 1555, *CalStP–S*, vol. XIII, *Philip and Mary, Jul. 1554–Nov. 1558* (London, 1954), pp. 239–240.

5. On the size of the entourage, see Philip to Simon Renard, 8 February 1554, CODOIN, vol. III, pp. 478–480; Philip to Charles V, 9 February 1554, *CalStP–S*, vol. XII, pp. 90–92. The quotation is from Philip's minute of 16 February 1554, CODOIN, vol. III, p. 488. Philip's following in England must have been considerably smaller than this prior estimate, since according to Badoero Philip's establishment in the Low Countries in about 1557 amounted to around 1,500 persons. Federico Badoero, "Relazione delle persone, governo e stati di Carlo V e di Filippo II," in Eugenio Albèri, ed., *Le relazioni degli ambasciatori veneti al Senato durante il secolo decimosesto*, ser. I, vol. III (Florence, 1853), p. 236.

6. Don Juan Hurtado de Mendoza to Arras, 19 March 1554, *CalStP–S*, vol. XII, pp. 161–162. Similarly, Charles V instructed Alba that under no circumstances should the soldiers accompanying Philip's fleet be allowed to set foot in England. Charles V to the Duke of Alba, from Brussels, 1 April 1554, AGS Estado, leg. 508.

7. Ruy Gómez de Silva to Eraso, from Winchester, 26 July 1554, CODOIN, vol. III, pp. 526–528 (quotation at p. 527); Don Juan de Figueroa to Charles V, from Winchester, 26 July 1554, ibid., pp. 519–525 (see p. 523).

8. *CalStP–S*, vol. XIII, doc. 11, p. 9.

9. Ibid., p. 12.

10. See the report of Don Juan de Figueroa (sent by the emperor to announce his gift in England) in CODOIN, vol. III, pp. 519–525. Figueroa's account (p. 524) implies that possession of Milan had been made over to Philip some time before but that the transfer had been kept secret. In fact, Philip was invested with the duchy in 1546, but Martin Hume argues that this investiture was "nominal" and that the real transfer took place at the wedding. Martin A. S. Hume, *Philip II of Spain* (1897) (New York, 1969), p. 62; see also Bratli, *Felipe II*, p. 77. For the announcement of the gift at the wedding ceremony (at Winchester, 25 July 1554), see also Varaona, "Viaje de Felipe II á Inglaterra en 1554," CODOIN, vol. I, p. 570; the English heralds' account in John G. Nichols, ed., *The Chronicle of Queen Jane, and of Two*

Years of Queen Mary (London, 1850), app. XI, p. 168; and Francisco López de Gómara, *Annals of the Emperor Charles V* (Oxford, 1912), p. 151.

11. Ruy Gómez de Silva to Eraso, from Winchester, 29 July 1554, CODOIN, vol. III, pp. 528–530 (quotation at p. 530). The original of this letter is at AGS Estado, leg. 808, no. 148.

12. *CalStP–S*, vol. XIII, doc. 11, p. 11.

13. Ruy Gómez de Silva to Eraso, from Winchester, 29 July 1554, CODOIN, vol. III, p. 530.

14. Privy Council register, 15 August 1554, in Nichols, *Chronicle of Queen Jane,* app. IX, pp. 135–136.

15. Simon Renard to Charles V, from Twickenham, 3 September 1554, *CalStP–S*, vol. XIII, doc. 56, p. 45.

16. "An account of what has befallen in the realm of England since Prince Philip landed there, written by a gentleman who accompanied the Prince to England . . . ," 17 August 1554, ibid., doc. 37, pp. 30–34 (quotation at pp. 33–34). For some specific departures, see Privy Council register, 13 August 1554, in Nichols, *Chronicle of Queen Jane,* app. IX, p. 135. See also D. M. Loades, *The Reign of Mary Tudor* (London, 1979), pp. 212–213, 222.

17. On the growing confusion of lines of authority between the two courts, however, see Diego de Vargas to Ruy Gómez de Silva, from Brussels, 30 November 1554, AGS Estado, leg. 508, no. 236.

18. Many of the state papers concerning Philip's sojourn in England and the Netherlands, 1554–1559, were lost at sea during the return voyage to Spain in 1559. Some of the surviving documents—most of them held at Simancas—have been printed in the British calendars, CODOIN, and other collections.

19. For a detailed account of the Habsburg politics of the 1550s, see Rodríguez-Salgado, *The Changing Face of Empire*. My account differs on several points from hers, in part because of the narrower focus of my interest in these issues and also because of my somewhat divergent view of Philip's personality and its evolution in these years.

20. Charles V to the Duke of Alba, from Brussels, 1 April 1554, AGS Estado, leg. 508.

21. Ibid.; translation from *CalStP–S*, vol. XII, p. 185.

22. Badoero, "Relazione," p. 279.

23. Charles V to Philip, "Carta autógrafa e instrucción secreta de 6 de mayo de 1543," in José M. March, ed., *Niñez y juventud de Felipe II* (Madrid, 1941–1942), vol. II, p. 27.

24. For an early (1544–1545) example of Philip's exasperation with Alba, see Hayward Keniston, *Francisco de los Cobos, Secretary of the Emperor Charles V* (Pittsburgh, 1960), p. 270.

25. Antonio Ossorio, *Vida y hazañas de Don Fernando Alvarez de Toledo, Duque de Alba* (1669) (Madrid, 1945), p. 470.

26. Rodríguez-Salgado attempts, not entirely convincingly, to revise the traditional vision of Philip's deference to his father. See *The Changing Face of Empire,* esp. pp. 7–9, 76.

27. On Perrenot's relations with Philip, see Maurice van Durme, *El Cardenal Granvela (1517–1586)* (Barcelona, 1957), pp. 109–110, 395–396 and *passim*; Paul David Lagomarsino, "Court Factions and the Formulation of Spanish Policy Towards the Netherlands (1559–1567)," Ph.D. dissertation, University of Cambridge, 1973, pp. 17–18; Rodríguez-Salgado, *The Changing Face of Empire*, p. 13 (including remarks about flattery). For Philip's first meeting with Arras and contemporary praise of Perrenot's abilities, see Juan Cristóbal Calvete de Estrella, *El felicissimo viaje del muy alto y muy poderoso principe don Phelippe* (1552) (Madrid, 1930), vol. I, p. 166. Arras's propensity for making enemies is discussed in Geoffrey Parker, *The Dutch Revolt* (Ithaca, 1977), p. 45.

28. The best account of this conflict is in Lagomarsino, "Court Factions," esp. ch. 3.

29. *CalStP–S*, vol. XI, pp. xxi and 222–225; Rodríguez-Salgado, *The Changing Face of Empire*, p. 75. For a gloomy report on Charles's health in this period, see "Relacion de las cartas del s^{or} Fer^{do} de vi y xvii de octubre 1553," AGS Estado, leg. 508, no. 32.

30. Arras to Charles V, 3 September 1554, *CalStP–S*, vol. XIII, doc. 55, p. 44. For a superb account of the feud between Perrenot and Renard, see Lucien Febvre, *Philippe II et la Franche-Comté* (Paris, 1970), ch. V, sections III and IV, pp. 83–88, and ch. VI, pp. 91–106.

31. Among many others, see Lagomarsino, "Court Factions," pp. 21ff.; *CalStP–S*, vol. XIII, p. vi; and the evidence of the correspondence between the two men cited in this work.

32. See Louis-Prosper Gachard, ed., *Correspondance de Philippe II sur les affaires des Pays-Bas, 1558–1577*, vol. I (Brussels, 1848), p. lviii and n. 1. For criticism of the bishop's "ingratitude" for extravagant royal favor, see Ruy Gómez de Silva to Francisco de Eraso, from Madrid, 20 May 1552, AGS Estado, leg. 89, no. 131.

33. For the alliance in the early 1550s of Arras and Alba, along with the secretary Gonzalo Pérez, see Lagomarsino, "Court Factions," pp. 17–18. The shifting nature of the relations of all of these protagonists up to 1567 is cogently described in subsequent sections of Lagomarsino's dissertation.

34. For Arras's anxiety over the succession, see van Durme, *El Cardenal Granvela*, esp. p. 192. See also Royall Tyler, *The Emperor Charles the Fifth* (London, 1956), p. 167. For further discussion of the misgivings of the emperor's Netherlandish and Burgundian advisers, see Febvre, *Philippe II et la Franche-Comté*, pp. 84, 86, 95, 99; Manuel Fernández Alvarez, *Charles V, Elected Emperor and Hereditary Ruler* (London, 1975), pp. 167–168. Ethnic resentment was hardly a one-way street; witness Ruy Gómez de Silva to Eraso, from London, 23 August 1554, AGS Estado, leg. 808, no. 141, in which he complains that problems with the English marriage can be attributed to the fact that the negotiations were entrusted to Arras and Renard rather than to Spaniards.

35. Badoero, "Relazione," p. 239.

36. Ruy Gómez de Silva to Eraso, from Winchester, 29 July 1554, *CalStP–S*, vol. XIII, doc. 7, p. 6.

37. Ruy Gómez de Silva to Eraso, from Richmond, 12 August 1554, CODOIN, vol. III, p. 531; original (from "Rreximon") at AGS Estado, leg. 808, no. 143.

38. Ibid. Regarding Philip's relations with Mary, some confusion has been caused by Carl Bratli's misreading of Badoero (or, to be precise, of Gachard's paraphrase of the *relazione*); the Venetian's reference to mutual loathing between Philip and Queen Mary concerns Mary of Hungary, not Mary Tudor. See Bratli, *Felipe II*, p. 83 and n. 235, p. 177; Badoero, "Relazione," pp. 208–209; Louis-Prosper Gachard, ed., *Relations des ambassadeurs vénitiens sur Charles-Quint et Philippe II* (Brussels, 1855), pp. 16–17.

39. Ruy Gómez de Silva to Eraso, from London, 2 October 1554, *CalStP–S*, vol. XIII, doc. 71, p. 60.

40. Rodríguez-Salgado, *The Changing Face of Empire*, p. 127.

41. Diego de Vargas to Ruy Gómez de Silva, from Brussels, 30 November 1554, AGS Estado, leg. 508, no. 236.

42. In a letter to Charles V, 3 September 1554, Arras wrote "And now that your Majesty has resolved to retire . . . " (*CalStP–S*, vol. XIII, doc. 55, p. 44).

43. Rodríguez-Salgado, *The Changing Face of Empire*, p. 127.

44. See also Loades, *Reign of Mary Tudor*, pp. 123–124, 211–212; Rodríguez-Salgado, *The Changing Face of Empire*, p. 90.

45. See van Durme, *El Cardenal Granvela*, p. 192.

46. See Ruy Gómez de Silva to Eraso, 12 August 1554, *CalStP–S*, vol. XIII, doc. 30, p. 26.

47. Francisco de Eraso to Ruy Gómez de Silva, from Antwerp, 29 November 1554, AGS Estado, leg. 808, no. 133; printed in CODOIN, vol. III, pp. 532–536 (quotations from pp. 533–534).

48. Rodríguez-Salgado, *The Changing Face of Empire*, p. 73, suggests that Eraso had started to shift his allegiance to Philip as early as 1552.

49. Eraso to Ruy Gómez de Silva, from Antwerp, 29 November 1554, AGS Estado, leg. 808, no. 133.

50. Ibid.

51. They were in regular correspondence at least from early 1552; see, for example, some of that year's letters from Ruy Gómez to Eraso in AGS Estado, leg. 89, nos. 120–123, 125, 129–131.

52. "E superbissimo, collerico e rustico molto . . . " (Badoero, "Relazione," p. 248).

53. *Ambassades de Noailles,* reproduced in Nichols, *Chronicle of Queen Jane,* p. 138. The degree of their intimacy was in some ways rather revolting. See, for example, the memorandum "News from Various Quarters," prepared for Charles V, Brussels, June, 1555: "Ruy Gómez writes to me in a letter dated 4 June that the King had had a pain in the bowels, as he frequently does . . . " (*CalStP–S*, vol. XIII, doc. 209, p. 214). Over a decade later Ruy

Gómez was still broadcasting privy details of the king's physical ailments; see Ruy Gómez de Silva to Juan de Escobedo, from Pellejeros, 2 October 1566, AGS, Consejo y Juntas de Hacienda (CJH), leg. 50, no. 264.

54. See Charles V to Ruy Gómez de Silva, from Bethune, September 1554, AGS Estado, leg. 508, no. 203, where the emperor praises Ruy Gómez for his assistance, reported by Eraso, to Philip.

55. Ruy Gómez de Silva to Francisco de Eraso, no date (early 1554?), AGS Estado, leg. 808, no. 134.

56. Keniston, *Francisco de los Cobos,* p. 337; Lagomarsino, "Court Factions," p. 22; Badoero, "Relazione," p. 248. Eraso was accused and convicted in the mid-1560s of massive corruption involving government funds. See Badoero for indications that Eraso's peculations had begun with state contracts negotiated for Charles V.

57. Badoero, "Relazione," p. 248.

58. John M. Headley, *The Emperor and his Chancellor* (Cambridge, 1983), p. 143.

59. Lagomarsino, "Court Factions," pp. 22–23. In the mid-1560s Figueroa was to be Eraso's chief accuser and prosecutor for corruption. See, for example, Cardinal Granvelle to Viglius, from Besançon, 26 December 1564, in Charles Weiss, ed., *Papiers d'État du Cardinal de Granvelle,* vol. VIII (Paris, 1850), p. 570, referring to "la guerre que Figueroa fait à Erasso." From the early days of his collaboration with Eraso, Ruy Gómez played upon the secretary's dislike of Gonzalo Pérez, regaling him with tales of the sloth and presumption of his rival. See Ruy Gómez de Silva to Francisco de Eraso, from Aranjuez, 13 October 1552, AGS Estado, leg. 89, no. 122; same to same, from Madrid, 25 November 1552, AGS Estado, leg. 89, no. 123.

60. Ruy Gómez de Silva to Eraso, 12 August 1554, *CalStP–S,* vol. XIII, doc. 30, p. 26.

61. Ruy Gómez de Silva to Francisco de Eraso, from Hampton Court ("antoncurt"), 22 September 1554, AGS Estado, leg. 808, no. 139.

62. Ruy Gómez de Silva to Francisco de Eraso, from Garcillán (near Segovia), 7 May 1552, AGS Estado, leg. 89, no. 130. Somewhat similarly, the French diplomat Lansac de Saint-Gelais described the *sumiller de corps* as "celuy qui couche en la chambre du roy d'Espagne" (Lansac de Saint-Gelais to the Cardinal of Lorraine, June 1559, in Louis Paris, ed., *Négociations, lettres et pièces diverses relatives au regne de François II* (Paris, 1841), p. 177).

63. An extract of the letter of 7 December appears in *CalStP–S,* vol. XIII, p. 117. For earlier imperial misgivings about the visit, see Philip to Eraso, November 1554, ibid., p. 93.

64. For further indications of this, see (Diego de Vargas?) to Ruy Gómez de Silva, from Brussels, 12 December 1554, AGS Estado, leg. 508, no. 241, with the news that the emperor had decided to remit the accumulated *consultas de particulares* from Naples and Milan to Philip for resolution; Charles's instructions to Eraso, 1 September 1554, *CalStP–S,* vol. XIII, p. 39; Rodríguez-Salgado, *The Changing Face of Empire,* p. 90.

65. See the report of Philip's complaints in Diego de Vargas to Ruy

Gómez de Silva, from Brussels, 30 November 1554, AGS Estado, leg. 508, nos. 236–235 (a single letter, numbered out of sequence in the *legajo*). In *CalStP–S*, vol. XIII, pp. 110–112, Ruy Gómez's correspondent is identified as Eraso. This cannot be so, since the writer refers to Eraso in the third person and also because he praises the bishop of Arras, absolving him from any blame for Philip's displeasure. Eraso would hardly have been so charitable to his longtime enemy in a letter to a confidant. Moreover, the cover notation on the original letter suggests what I believe to be the proper attribution to Vargas.

66. Ruy Gómez de Silva to Francisco de Eraso, from London, 2 October 1554, AGS Estado, leg. 808, no. 138, reports the news of the pregnancy and contains a hint of early doubt about its viability.

67. See AGS, Patronato Real, leg. 44, no. 11[(ii)]; the following documents in *CalStP–S*, vol. XIII: Arras to Simon Renard, 5 January 1555, doc. 136, p. 131; Mary [Tudor] to Charles V, 18 January 1555, doc. 140, p. 135; Arras to Renard, 1 March 1555, doc. 155, pp. 143–144; Renard to Ferdinand, King of the Romans, July 1555, doc. 226, p. 236; draft letter, Eraso to Juan Vázquez de Molina, 20 August 1555, doc. 234, p. 243. See also Loades, *Reign of Mary Tudor*, p. 217; Rodríguez-Salgado, *The Changing Face of Empire*, p. 110. Arras's reliance on Ruy Gómez de Silva is evident from his letter of 1 March. Further evidence of recognition at the imperial court of Ruy Gómez's influence as a conduit to Philip is provided by Diego de Vargas to Ruy Gómez de Silva, from Brussels, 6 November 1554, AGS Estado, leg. 508, no. 221, and same to same, 1 August 1555, AGS Estado, leg. 508, no. 182.

68. News of this decision seems to have been brought to the imperial court by Ruy Gómez in February, 1555 (see Arras to Renard, 1 March 1555, *CalStP–S*, vol. XIII, doc. 155, pp. 143–144), but the duke did not leave England for the Continent until April and only departed Brussels for Italy in June ("From the Imperial Court on 14 April [1555], from the Ambassador in England," ibid., doc. 173, p. 161; Rodríguez-Salgado, *The Changing Face of Empire*, p. 141).

69. William Maltby, *Alba: A Biography of Fernando Alvarez de Toledo, Third Duke of Alba, 1507–1582* (Berkeley, 1983), pp. 86ff. For a more thorough and convincing account of these events, see Rodríguez-Salgado, *The Changing Face of Empire*, pp. 104–110.

70. For Maltby's depiction of the unwilling but duty-bound Alba, see his *Alba*, pp. 87–88.

71. Charles V, Instructions for Eraso, 1 October 1554, *CalStP–S*, vol. XIII, p. 59; Giovan Tommaso Langosco di Stroppiana to Arras, 6 October 1554, ibid., p. 63; Rodríguez-Salgado, *The Changing Face of Empire*, pp. 104–105.

72. Simon Renard to Charles V, 13 October 1554, *CalStP–S*, vol. XIII, p. 66; Renard to Arras, 13 October 1554, ibid., p. 69; Stroppiana to Arras, 22 October 1554, ibid., p. 75; Emmanuel Philibert, Duke of Savoy, to Charles V, December 1554, ibid., pp. 122–123; Arras to Charles V, 18 December 1554, ibid., p. 123; Antonio Maria de Savoia to Arras, 25 December 1554, ibid., p. 127.

73. Arras to Charles V, 18 December 1554, ibid., p. 124.

74. Stroppiana to Arras, 22 October 1554, ibid., p. 75; Ruy Gómez de Silva to Eraso, 23 November 1554, ibid., pp. 103–104; same to same, from London, 11 December 1554, AGS Estado, leg. 808, no. 131.

75. Arras to Renard, 1 March 1555, *CalStP–S*, vol. XIII, p. 143; Rodríguez-Salgado, *The Changing Face of Empire*, p. 107.

76. For Gonzaga's reaction, see AGS, Patronato Real, leg. 44, no. 11; Renard to Charles V, 13 March 1555, *CalStP–S*, vol. XIII, p. 146.

77. Anxiety over this competition is evident in Arras's letter to Charles V of 18 December 1554, *CalStP–S*, vol. XIII, pp. 123–124.

78. AGS, Patronato Real, leg. 44, no. 11[(ii)]; Eraso to Juan Vázquez de Molina, 12 April 1555, *CalStP–S*, vol. XIII, p. 159. Arras claimed credit for pacifying Savoy in his letter to Renard of 1 March 1555 (*CalStP–S*, vol. XIII, p. 143).

79. See AGS, Patronato Real, leg. 44, no. 11[(i-ii, v)]—11[(i)] dated Antwerp, 8 April 1555; also, Eraso to Juan Vázquez de Molina, 12 April 1555, *CalStP–S*, vol. XIII, p. 159. After describing the rather generous monetary settlement and the honors offered to Gonzaga, Eraso continues: "But he [Gonzaga] swept all this aside, insisting on the post of Lord Chamberlain (Mayordomo mayor) saying that nothing else was compatible with his honour and that he must not be inferior to anyone." See also Rodríguez-Salgado, *The Changing Face of Empire*, pp. 105–107.

80. Ruy Gómez de Silva to Eraso, 15 April 1555, *CalStP–S*, vol. XIII, p. 162.

81. Ibid., p. 163.

82. Ibid.

83. Ibid.

84. Eraso seems to have worked for Alba's appointment as well. See Rodríguez-Salgado, *The Changing Face of Empire*, p. 105.

85. Ramón Carande noted Alba's suspicions on this score in his account of the duke's finances in Italy (*Carlos V y sus banqueros* (Barcelona, 1983), vol. II, pp. 261ff.), and Lagomarsino makes this charge ("Court Factions," p. 334), while Maltby greatly elaborates the argument (*Alba*, pp. 88–89 and notes, p. 333). Lagomarsino and Maltby are concerned to demonstrate a precedent for similar obstruction of Alba's administration in the Netherlands in the late 1560s. Their evidence for the later period is more convincing, although this notion as well may require revision in light of the strenuous efforts to supply the duke reported in Melchor de Herrera to Ruy Gómez de Silva, from Medina del Campo, 10 September 1568, AGS CJH, leg. 90, no. 12. Maltby carries partisanship on this issue to considerable lengths, suggesting at one point that the provisioning of Alba's invasion of Portugal in 1580 was successful largely because "there was now no Ruy Gómez or Eraso to undermine him" (pp. 286–287, quote at p. 287). One might more plausibly argue that the Portuguese expedition benefited from the relative ease of marshaling resources within the peninsula during a period of comparative financial stability.

86. Rodríguez-Salgado, *The Changing Face of Empire,* pp. 140–141, refutes Maltby. Among a multitude of sources on the faltering finances of those years, see her book and Carande, *Carlos V y sus banqueros,* vol. II, ch. 4. Alba's financial situation in Italy is discussed on pp. 261–273. On p. 263 Carande remarks that Eraso served the duke as a scapegoat for the problems frustrating him: "era Eraso el blanco predilecto de los tiros del duque."

87. Ruy Gómez de Silva to Francisco de Eraso, from London, 5 December 1554, AGS Estado, leg. 808, no. 132; same to same, 21 December 1554, ibid., no. 130.

88. See Hume, *Philip II of Spain,* pp. 63–64, for a typical statement of this belief.

89. Maltby, *Alba,* pp. 70–71.

90. A few identifiable Mendozas—the count of Saldaña, Don Francisco de Mendoza (son of the marquis of Mondéjar) and Don Bernardino de Mendoza, himself an Alba partisan—were among the retinue and household taken to England, while Alba was accompanied by his wife and two sons, and his brother-in-law the *caballerizo mayor* Don Antonio de Toledo, to mention only the members of his immediate family. Furthermore, in his position as *mayordomo mayor,* Alba had presumably filled many household posts with his friends and clients. See *CalStP–S,* vol. XII, p. 317, for a list of the aristocratic retinue, and Muñoz, *Viaje de Felipe II,* p. 31, for an approximation of the personnel of the accompanying household. Feria became a friend and ally of Ruy Gómez de Silva in later years, and they may have grown close while in England, but there is no direct evidence to support this supposition.

91. The term is used by Loades to describe Mary Tudor's favorites (*Reign of Mary Tudor,* p. 84).

92. For examples, see Alba to Ruy Gómez de Silva, 3 May 1555, Duque de Alba, ed., *Epistolario del III Duque de Alba, Don Fernando Alvarez de Toledo* (Madrid, 1952), vol. I, p. 85; same to same, 6 May 1555 (a chatty note concerning Ruy Gómez's younger brother), ibid., p. 93; same to same, 23 July 1555, ibid., p. 268.

93. Carande, *Carlos V y sus banqueros,* vol. II, p. 262.

94. See, for example, the cordial missive Ruy Gómez de Silva to Alba, 30 March 1556, Duquesa de Berwick y de Alba, ed., *Documentos escogidos del archivo de la Casa de Alba* (Madrid, 1891), pp. 73–75.

95. Ruy Gómez de Silva to Eraso, 6 June 1555, *CalStP–S,* vol. XIII, doc. 207, p. 213. Royall Tyler notes that Ruy Gómez had recently received a letter from the marquis of Mondéjar complaining that "that dog Alva has bitten me, too" (ibid.). This may support a suspicion that Ruy Gómez had been mounting a campaign of backbiting against the duke. Certainly he criticized Alba in letters to Eraso even before the journey to England; see, for example, Ruy Gómez de Silva to Francisco de Eraso, 18 May 1554, AGS Estado, leg. 808, no. 152.

96. Maltby, *Alba,* p. 85. No sources are cited to support this assertion.

97. See D. M. Loades, "Philip II and the Government of England," in

Law and Government under the Tudors, ed. by Claire Cross, David Loades and J. J. Scarisbrick (Cambridge, 1988), pp. 177–194. He argues that Philip, handicapped by linguistic shortcomings and ignorance of English law and government, took little interest in the kingdom's affairs; moreover, he concludes that Mary, her pronouncements and subsequent tradition notwithstanding, was jealous of her own prerogatives and did little to empower Philip within England. William Paget, the only English counselor closely allied with Philip, was for the most part out of favor with Mary and thus little help to the king. See ibid., pp. 182–184; James Bassett to Paget, 14 November 1556, in Barrett L. Beer and Sybil M. Jack, eds., "The Letters of William, Lord Paget of Beaudesert, 1547–1563," *Camden Miscellany*, vol. XXV (London, 1974), p. 140. Rodríguez-Salgado, however, sees evidence of Philip's effective influence in English government and of the potential for more (*The Changing Face of Empire*, pp. 94–100).

98. Alone among the Spaniards, Feria married an Englishwoman and stayed on as Philip's ambassador. Joycelyne G. Russell, *Peacemaking in the Renaissance* (London, 1986), p. 148, suggests that Ruy Gómez de Silva acquired some English, but the evidence is scanty.

99. The allegation of Ruy Gómez's ignorance appears in Loades, "Philip II and the Government of England," p. 188. For his relations with the English lords, see Gustav Ungerer, *A Spaniard in Elizabethan England: The Correspondence of Antonio Pérez's Exile* (London, 1974–1976), vol. I, p. 33. See also Don Pedro de Córdoba to Ferdinand, King of the Romans, 10 December 1554, *CalStP–S*, vol. XIII, doc. 127, p. 119. For an English description of the typical Spanish tournament entertainment, the *juego de cañas* held 25 November 1554, see John Gough Nichols, ed., *The Diary of Henry Machyn* (London, 1848), p. 76.

100. Arras to Ruy Gómez de Silva, 23 August 1555, *CalStP–S*, vol. XIII, doc. 235, p. 246.

101. In 1554 Philip had named Ruy Gómez Groom of the Stole in his English household, in addition to his Castilian post of *sumiller de corps*. See Diego Gutiérrez Coronel, *Historia genealógica de la casa de Mendoza* (Madrid, 1946), p. 565.

102. Arras to Ruy Gómez de Silva, 23 August 1555, *CalStP–S*, vol. XIII, doc. 235, p. 246; Philip's draft instructions to Ruy Gómez de Silva, late August 1555, ibid., docs. 240–241, pp. 247–248; Ruy Gómez de Silva to Eraso, 4 September 1555, ibid., doc. 243, p. 249.

103. Good accounts of the abdication process are provided by A. W. Lovett, *Early Habsburg Spain, 1517–1598* (Oxford, 1986), p. 59; van Durme, *El Cardenal Granvela*, pp. 190–192; Roger Bigelow Merriman, *The Rise of the Spanish Empire in the Old World and in the New*, vol. III, *The Emperor* (New York, 1918), pp. 394–397; and Rodríguez-Salgado, *The Changing Face of Empire*, pp. 126–132. The circumstances of the transfer of 16 January 1556 are reported by Luis Cabrera de Córdoba, *Historia de Felipe II, rey de España* (Madrid, 1876–1877), vol. I, libro I, capítulo VII, p. 36, and Merriman, *Rise of the Spanish Empire*, vol. III, p. 396. Rodríguez-Salgado's account emphasizes

conflict in the abdication process between Philip and his father over the emperor's attempts "to retain power without responsibility" (*The Changing Face of Empire*, p. 128). She also argues, contradicting van Durme and Merriman, that Charles retained control of the county of Burgundy until his death (*The Changing Face of Empire*, p. 131).

104. For the revival of the council, see Lagomarsino, "Court Factions," p. 31, and M. J. Rodríguez-Salgado, "The Court of Philip II of Spain," in *Princes, Patronage, and the Nobility: The Court at the Beginning of the Modern Age, c.1450–1650*, ed. by Ronald G. Asch and Adolf M. Birke (Oxford, 1991), pp. 222–223; for its desuetude under Charles V, see John H. Elliott, *Imperial Spain, 1469–1716* (Harmondsworth, 1970), p. 173.

105. Cabrera de Córdoba, *Felipe II*, vol. I, lib. I, cap. VII, p. 37; Luis de Salazar y Castro, *Historia genealógica de la casa de Silva* (Madrid, 1685), vol. II, p. 471. The twelve councilors of state were Ruy Gómez de Silva, Alba, Feria, Arras, Ferrante Gonzaga, the duke of Savoy, Andrea Doria, Don Juan Manrique de Lara, Don Antonio de Toledo, the count of Chinchón (Don Pedro de Cabrera y Bobadilla), Don Bernardino de Mendoza (brother of the second marquis of Mondéjar) and Gutierre López de Padilla. Don Juan de Figueroa was soon added to the list. López de Gómara, *Annals*, p. 271, provides a shorter and different list (excluding Alba, Feria, Savoy, Doria, Chinchón and López de Padilla, but adding Juan de Vega and Don Luis de Avila).

106. Cabrera de Córdoba, *Felipe II*, vol. I, lib. I, cap. VIII, p. 41. For a strong recommendation, supporting Cabrera's judgment of this relationship, see Ruy Gómez de Silva to Francisco de Eraso, from Richmond, 12 August 1554, AGS Estado, leg. 808, no. 145. For acknowledgment of Ruy Gómez's patronage, see Gutierre López de Padilla to Ruy Gómez de Silva, from Valladolid, 8 December 1557, AGS CJH, leg. 32, no. 123. López de Padilla accompanied Philip to England, and he sometimes appears as a figure of fun in the correspondence between Ruy Gómez de Silva and Eraso. For example, in a letter of 8 June 1555 Ruy Gómez wrote, regarding the uncertainties of Mary Tudor's pregnancy, that "they say that the calculations got mixed up when they saw her with a girth greater than that of Gutierre López" (*CalStP–S*, vol. XIII, doc. 212, p. 222). In 1557, however, Juan de Escobedo warned Ruy Gómez that López de Padilla was a false friend and backstabber (Escobedo to Ruy Gómez de Silva, from Valladolid, 16 October 1557, AGS CJH, leg. 32, no. 121).

107. Van Durme, *El Cardenal Granvela*, p. 199; Badoero, "Relazione," p. 240.

108. Badoero, "Relazione," p. 248; Cabrera de Córdoba, *Felipe II*, vol. I, lib. I, cap. VII, pp. 38–39.

109. Badoero, "Relazione," p. 248; José Antonio Escudero, *Los secretarios de estado y del despacho (1474–1724)* (Madrid, 1969), vol. I, p. 107.

110. Lagomarsino, "Court Factions," p. 32. Antonio Rodríguez Villa, *Etiquetas de la Casa de Austria* (Madrid, 1913?), p. 62, estimates (without specifying the date) the compensation of the *sumiller* as 480 *maravedís* per diem,

plus an annual salary of 175,200 *maravedís*, plus a variety of allowances for tableware, wood and foodstuffs.

111. Badoero to the Doge and Senate of Venice, 24 February 1556, in *Calendar of State Papers and Manuscripts, relating to English Affairs, Existing in the Archives and Collections of Venice, and in other Libraries of Northern Italy* (cited henceforth as *CalStP–V*), ed. by Rawdon Brown and G. Cavendish Bentinck, vol. VI, pt. I (1555–1556) (London, 1877), doc. 410, pp. 356–357.

112. Archivo Histórico Nacional, Madrid (AHN), Sección Osuna, leg. 2078, nos. 4[1] and 12[7], and leg. 2077, no. 10[6]. See Chapter 2 for the 3,000-ducat debt.

113. Badoero to the Doge and Senate, 24 February 1556, *CalStP–V*, vol. VI, pt. I, doc. 410, p. 357. Note that the Venetian refers to Ruy Gómez de Silva as "don." No Spaniard accorded him this courtesy title.

114. Salazar y Castro, *Casa de Silva*, vol. II, p. 472; Gutiérrez Coronel, *Casa de Mendoza*, vol. II, p. 565.

115. See the title of office in AGS, Escribanía Mayor de Rentas, Quitaciones de Corte (EMR–QC), leg. 39, fols. 618ff. See also Cabrera de Córdoba, *Felipe II*, vol. I, lib. I, cap. VIII, p. 41; Salazar y Castro, *Casa de Silva*, vol. II, p. 472; Gutiérrez Coronel, *Casa de Mendoza*, vol. II, p. 565; Modesto Ulloa, *La hacienda real de Castilla en el reinado de Felipe II* (Madrid, 1986), p. 101.

116. Ulloa, *La hacienda real*, p. 101. For an example of the specific *derechos* pertaining to this office in 1564–1565, see AGS EMR–QC, leg. 39, fol. 687.

117. Van Durme, *El Cardenal Granvela*, pp. 193, 199.

118. Badoero to the Doge and Senate, 6 December 1555, *CalStP–V*, vol. VI, pt. I, p. 271.

119. See Lagomarsino's comments, "Court Factions," p. 13, and Chapter 5 of the present work.

CHAPTER FOUR

1. Federico Badoero, "Relazione delle persone, governo e stati di Carlo V e di Filippo II" (1557), in Eugenio Albèri, ed., *Le relazioni degli ambasciatori veneti al Senato durante il secolo decimosesto*, ser. I, vol. III (Florence, 1853), p. 240.

2. For corroborative comment on this phenomenon, see Jules Gounon-Loubens, *Essais sur l'administration de la Castille au XVIe siècle* (Paris, 1860), p. 148, and G. R. Elton, "Constitutional Development and Political Thought in Western Europe," in *The New Cambridge Modern History*, vol. II, *The Reformation, 1520–1559*, ed. by G. R. Elton (Cambridge, 1976), pp. 446–447.

3. On the institution of the *valimiento*, see the excellent monograph of Francisco Tomás y Valiente, *Los validos en la monarquía española del siglo XVII* (1963) (Madrid, 1982); for Philip III's empowerment of Lerma, see pp. 6–7, 157.

4. These observations are drawn from the *relazioni* of Marino Cavalli (1551), Badoero (1557) and Michele Suriano (1559), in J. García Mercadal, ed. and trans., *Viajes de extranjeros por España y Portugal* (Madrid, 1952), vol. I, pp. 1056, 1112–1113, 1142–1143, respectively.

5. Cavalli, ibid., p. 1056; Badoero, "Relazione," pp. 235–236; Roger Bigelow Merriman, *The Rise of the Spanish Empire in the Old World and in the New,* vol. IV, *Philip the Prudent* (New York, 1918), p. 28.

6. Geoffrey Parker, *Philip II* (Boston, 1978), p. 23. M. J. Rodríguez-Salgado, in *The Changing Face of Empire* (Cambridge, 1988), sees Philip as less awed by and deferential to his father, and certainly she demonstrates conflict between them on a variety of issues. Still, despite this evidence of rebellion and ambivalence, the older image of Philip as an obedient and somewhat intimidated son laboring to fill the shoes of a masterful father remains compelling.

7. Parker, *Philip II,* pp. 17–20; Martin A. S. Hume, *Philip II of Spain* (1897) (London, 1906), pp. 49–50, 77; Rafael Altamira y Crevea, *Ensayo sobre Felipe II hombre de estado* (Mexico City, 1950), pp. 30–31; Merriman, *Rise of the Spanish Empire,* vol. IV, p. 24; Leonardo Donato, "Relazione di Spagna," in Eugenio Albèri, ed., *Le relazione degli ambasciatori veneti al Senato durante il secolo decimosesto,* ser. I, vol. VI (Florence, 1862), p. 464.

8. See Marino Cavalli's penetrating comparison of Charles V, who was blessed with an ability to accommodate to all manner of customs and get along with a wide variety of people, and Philip, whom he saw as rigid, aloof and awkward in his public dealings (Cavalli, "Relación," in *Viajes,* vol. I, p. 1056).

9. Parker, *Philip II,* p. 24.

10. Quoted in ibid., p. 35 (Parker's source is unclear). R. A. Stradling, *Philip IV and the Government of Spain, 1621–1665* (Cambridge, 1988), p. 34, quoting Cánovas del Castillo, uses the term *rey papelista,* the likely original of Parker's "king of paper."

11. Merriman, *Rise of the Spanish Empire,* vol. IV, p. 20; Badoero, "Relazione," p. 236.

12. Ruy Gómez de Silva to Juan de Escobedo, from Aranjuez(?), 10 April 1563, Archivo General de Simancas (AGS), Consejo y Juntas de Hacienda (CJH), legajo 50, no. 238.

13. For a variety of citations on this point, see Fernand Braudel, *The Mediterranean and the Mediterranean World in the Age of Philip II* (New York, 1976), vol. II, p. 949. That Philip, upon inheriting his patrimony, hoped to return soon to Spain is agreed by most authors; see, for instance, Merriman, *Rise of the Spanish Empire,* vol. IV, pp. 3–5.

14. These events are clearly narrated in the opening pages of Merriman's volume on *Philip the Prudent* in *Rise of the Spanish Empire.* See also Ludwig von Pastor, *The History of the Popes,* vol. XIV (London, 1924), chs. V–VI, and Antonio Domínguez Ortiz, *The Golden Age of Spain, 1516–1659* (New York, 1971), pp. 64–65. Some reasons for papal rancor toward Philip II and the house of Austria are summarized in Badoero, "Relazione," pp. 306–308. See also Braudel, *The Mediterranean,* vol. II, pp. 937–940 (for the Ruy Gómez–Montmorency talks, p. 940), and Peter Partner, *Renaissance Rome, 1500–1559: A Portrait of a Society* (Berkeley, 1976), pp. 42–45.

15. Jean de Vandenesse, "Diario de los viajes de Felipe II," in J. García

Mercadal, ed. and trans., *Viajes de extranjeros por España y Portugal* (Madrid, 1952), vol. I, p. 1070; Royall Tyler, "Preface," *Calendar of Letters, Despatches and State Papers relating to the Negotiations between England and Spain, Preserved in the Archives at Vienna, Simancas, Besancon, Brussels, Madrid and Lille* (cited henceforth as *CalStP–S*), ed. by Royall Tyler, vol. XIII, *Philip and Mary, Jul. 1554–Nov. 1558* (London, 1954), pp. vii and xx.

16. Instruction of Philip II to Ruy Gómez de Silva, Brussels, 2 February 1557 ("Lo que vos, Ruygomez de Silva, conde de Melito, del mi consejo destado, haveys de hazer y proveer en el viaje que ys [*sic*] a España por nuestro mandado y commission"), AGS, Secretaría de Estado (Estado), leg. 515, nos. 92, 92⁽²⁾, 92⁽³⁾. This document is printed in Baron Kervyn de Lettenhove, ed., *Relations politiques des Pays-Bas et de l'Angleterre, sous le règne de Philippe II*, vol. I (Brussels, 1882), pp. 54ff., and for convenience this transcription will be cited. David Loades, among others, has noted that Paget was "very much Philip's man" in England (D. M. Loades, "Philip II and the Government of England," in *Law and Government under the Tudors*, ed. by Claire Cross, David Loades and J. J. Scarisbrick (Cambridge, 1988), pp. 183–184).

17. Ruy Gómez was still in the Netherlands on 4 February ("A Ruygomez sobre lo de la pimienta y gengibre," Brussels, 4 February 1557, AGS Estado, leg. 515, no. 104). Date of arrival at Valladolid from Louis-Prosper Gachard, *Retraite et mort de Charles-Quint au Monastère de Yuste*, vol. II (Brussels, 1855), p. 162. Ruy Gómez de Silva to Arras, from "Gramuchu" [Greenwich], 16 February 1557, précis in Baltasar Cuartero y Huerta and Antonio de Vargas-Zúñiga y Montero de Espinosa, eds., *Indice de la Colección de Don Luis de Salazar y Castro*, vol. V (Madrid, 1951), no. 9.136, p. 358 (announces Ruy Gómez's departure from England). For the ship provided to carry Ruy Gómez de Silva to Spain, see the Instruction of Philip II to Ruy Gómez de Silva, 2 February 1557, in Kervyn de Lettenhove, *Relations politiques des Pays-Bas*, vol. I, p. 55.

18. AGS Estado, leg. 515, no. 104, as well as Rodríguez-Salgado, *The Changing Face of Empire*, p. 223, note Gutierre López's participation in this mission.

19. AGS, Escribanía Mayor de Rentas, Quitaciones de Corte, leg. 39, nos. 618ff.

20. For a recent account, focusing on the problems of war finance, see Rodríguez-Salgado, *The Changing Face of Empire*, esp. chs. 4–6. The basic authorities on Crown finance in this period remain Ramón Carande, *Carlos V y sus banqueros* (Barcelona, 1977), esp. vol. II, ch. 4, and Modesto Ulloa, *La hacienda real de Castilla en el reinado de Felipe II* (Madrid, 1986), esp. ch. 4.

21. Carande, *Carlos V y sus banqueros*, vol. II, p. 289.

22. *Juros* were perpetual or term annuities, situated on the ordinary revenues of Castile and granted by the Crown in repayment of loans or as rewards for services. By 1556, at least two-thirds of the ordinary revenues were promised to the holders of *juros*. For a good brief discussion, see Henry Kamen, *Vocabulario básico de la historia moderna: España y América*

1450–1750 (Barcelona, 1986), pp. 124–127; see also Alvaro Castillo Pintado, "Los juros de Castilla. Apogeo y fin de un instrumento de crédito," *Hispania* 23 (1963), pp. 45–70.

23. The report of December 1554, drafted by Francisco de Almaguer, is discussed in Carande, *Carlos V y sus banqueros,* vol. II, pp. 260–261, and in Ulloa, *La hacienda real,* pp. 133–134, and is reproduced in full in Francisco de Laiglesia y Auset, *Estudios históricos (1515–1555)* (Madrid, 1918), vol. II, app. V. For advance commitment of income, see Rodríguez-Salgado, *The Changing Face of Empire,* p. 223.

24. See Rodríguez-Salgado, *The Changing Face of Empire,* pp. 232–251, for the best and most recent account of the complex and inconclusive financial maneuvers of this period. For a more traditional explanation that in light of Rodríguez-Salgado's work probably overstates the implementation and effects of the suspension of payments or "forced conversion" of 1557, see Ulloa, *La hacienda real,* pp. 138–143; he considers the expropriation of American treasure at pp. 151–158 and the papal revocations at p. 134. For the latter, see also A. Llorente, "La primera crísis de hacienda en tiempo de Felipe II," *Revista de España* (Madrid) I (1868), pp. 349–352, and Rodríguez-Salgado, *The Changing Face of Empire,* pp. 228–229. For Philip's reliance on Castile, see, in addition to these works, John Lynch, *Spain under the Habsburgs* (New York, 1984), vol. I, pp. 179–180.

25. Instruction of Philip II to Ruy Gómez de Silva, 2 February 1557, in Kervyn de Lettenhove, *Relations politiques des Pays-Bas,* vol. I, p. 55.

26. "Especialmente lo del dinero, en que no haveys de perder ora ni puncto de tiempo, por que en esto va mas que en todo" (ibid., p. 58).

27. Ibid., pp. 55–56.

28. Ibid., p. 58.

29. Ibid., pp. 56, 58. Provisions also had to be procured for the galleys carrying bullion to Alba; "you will tell the Princess" to order the speedy production of 5,000 quintals of hardtack in Barcelona and Rosas, for this purpose.

30. Ibid., p. 59.

31. Llorente, "La primera crísis," p. 349; Philip II to Arras, from London, 14 June 1557, *CalStP–S,* vol. XIII, doc. 310, p. 297; Braudel, *The Mediterranean,* vol. II, pp. 935–936.

32. Luis Cabrera de Córdoba, *Historia de Felipe II, rey de España* (Madrid, 1876), vol. I, libro IV, capítulo II, p. 169.

33. Again in 1559, while the king considered a replacement as president of Castile for the deceased Vega, Ruy Gómez received a letter from his ally the count of Feria boosting Figueroa for the post. "I am greatly saddened by the death of Juan de Vega . . . because I fear that they will place in the post he has vacated someone unsuitable. . . . God protect us from Gasquilla [Diego de la Gasca, member of the Council of Castile since 1552?], and from the Bishop of Jaen—Tavera—and also from Mondejar" (Feria to Ruy Gómez de Silva, from London, 16 February 1559, AGS CJH, leg. 34, no. 476). A peculiar message to send to the court champion of the Mendozas!

34. Cabrera de Córdoba, *Felipe II,* vol. I, lib. IV, cap. II, pp. 167, 169–170. Cabrera argues that Philip was concerned about relations between his sister and his son in early 1557; certainly there were rumors some years later about Juana's designs on Don Carlos. See, for example, Paolo Tiepolo to the Doge and Senate of Venice, from Toledo, 22 December 1559, *Calendar of State Papers and Manuscripts, relating to English Affairs, Existing in the Archives and Collections of Venice, and in other Libraries of Northern Italy* (cited henceforth as *CalStP–V*), ed. by Rawdon Brown and G. Cavendish Bentinck, vol. VII (London, 1890), doc. 120, pp. 139–140. Cf. Louis-Prosper Gachard, *Don Carlos y Felipe II* (San Lorenzo de el Escorial, 1984), pp. 48–49.

35. Llorente, "La primera crísis," pp. 335–342, 350; Braudel, *The Mediterranean,* vol. II, p. 957.

36. Llorente, "La primera crísis," pp. 350, 354 (quotation from p. 350); Rodríguez-Salgado, *The Changing Face of Empire,* pp. 226–227.

37. Cabrera de Córdoba, *Felipe II,* vol. I, lib. IV, cap. II, pp. 167–168; Llorente, "La primera crísis," pp. 354–355.

38. For the background to the dispute, see José M. March, ed., *Niñez y juventud de Felipe II* (Madrid, 1941–1942), vol. II, pp. 28, 37, and Luis de Salazar y Castro, *Historia genealógica de la Casa de Silva* (Madrid, 1685), vol. II, pp. 464–465. For Ruy Gómez's initial appointment as *adelantado mayor,* Salazar y Castro, *Casa de Silva,* vol. II, pp. 464–465; Diego Gutiérrez Coronel, *Historia genealógica de la casa de Mendoza* (Madrid, 1946), p. 565. Luciano Serrano provides an admirably brief and clear account of the controversy in *Correspondencia diplómatica entre España y la Santa Sede durante el pontificado de S. Pio V* (Madrid, 1914), vol. I, p. 259, n. 1. The 1557 confirmation of the appointment is reported in Salazar y Castro, *Casa de Silva,* vol. II, p. 473; Cabrera de Córdoba, *Felipe II,* vol. I, lib. IV, cap. II, p. 168; Llorente, "La primera crísis," p. 355. The Mélito stake in the properties of the *adelantamiento* is revealed in Gutiérrez Coronel, *Casa de Mendoza,* pp. 367–371.

39. Cabrera de Córdoba, *Felipe II,* vol. I, lib. IV, cap. II, p. 168; Salazar y Castro, *Casa de Silva,* vol. II, p. 473.

40. Salazar y Castro, *Casa de Silva,* vol. II, pp. 465, 474; March, *Niñez y juventud,* vol. II, pp. 28, 37; Serrano, *Correspondencia diplómatica,* vol. I, p. 259, n. 1. Juan de Mariana, *Historia general de España, compuesta, emendada y añadida por el padre Juan de Mariana de la compañia de Jesus, con el sumario y tablas* (Valencia, 1794), vol. II, p. 707, reports, in seeming contradiction to Serrano's contention that it eventually fell to Alba, that the *adelantamiento* was restored to the see of Toledo in 1608; we should probably assume that litigation continued after 1608.

41. " . . . le tenguo por ruines pulguillas." Count of Feria to Ruy Gómez de Silva, from London, 20 January 1559, AGS CJH, leg. 34, no. 475.

42. Llorente, "La primera crísis," pp. 355–359; Erika Spivakovsky, "La Princesa de Eboli," *Chronica Nova* 9 (1974), p. 10; Rodríguez-Salgado, *The Changing Face of Empire,* pp. 226–227.

43. Instruction of Philip II to Ruy Gómez de Silva, 2 February 1557, Kervyn de Lettenhove, *Relations politiques des Pays-Bas,* vol. I, p. 59 ("Y dada

orden en todas estas cosas, y especialmente en lo del dinero y la gente, os bolvereys con la mas brevedad que pudieredes"); Spivakovsky, "La Princesa de Eboli," p. 10; Llorente, "La primera crísis," p. 359; Rodríguez-Salgado, *The Changing Face of Empire,* pp. 208, 238.

44. For this estimate, see Gutierre López de Padilla to Ruy Gómez de Silva, November? 1557, AGS CJH, leg. 32, no. 122. But cf. Carlos Javier de Carlos Morales, "Grupos de poder en el Consejo de Hacienda en Castilla: 1551–1566," in *Instituciones y élites de poder en la Monarquía Hispana durante el siglo XVI,* ed. by J. Martínez Millán (Madrid, 1992), p. 123, where he asserts that Ruy Gómez brought the somewhat incredible sum of 1,650,000 ducats north with him in the summer of 1557.

45. The remittances are described in Llorente, "La primera crísis," pp. 360–361; Rodríguez-Salgado's figures, for the most part smaller and omitting remittances to Italy, may be found in *The Changing Face of Empire,* ch. 6, tables 10 and 11. Of the final remittance, López de Padilla wrote (to Ruy Gómez de Silva, from Valladolid, 8 December 1557, AGS CJH, leg. 32, no. 123): "Los DCCC U dᵒs. que al rrey se an de embiar estan ya todos en Medina de Pomar [north of Burgos] . . . Aqui se a dado toda la priesa possible a pero melendez para que se despachase."

46. Cabrera de Córdoba, *Felipe II,* vol. I, lib. IV, cap. III, p. 172. Rodríguez-Salgado characterizes the effort to fund the campaigns of 1557 and 1558 as a "chaotic mixture of conflict, deception and bullying" but admits that "it worked" and was "sufficient to fund two vast campaigns that established [Philip's] reputation and reduced French power" (*The Changing Face of Empire,* p. 245).

47. Michiel Surian (Michele Suriano) to the Doge and Senate of Venice, from Brussels, 13 November 1557, *CalStP–V,* vol. VI, pt. III (1557–1558) (London, 1884), doc. 1080, p. 1366.

48. The death of Bernardino de Mendoza (27 August 1557) is reported in Vandenesse, "Diario de los viajes de Felipe II," p. 1071; that of López de Padilla, in AGS CJH, leg. 47, no. 191, and in Llorente, "La primera crísis," p. 348. Mendoza's nasty character and financial acumen are revealed in one of the brilliant sketches of Federico Badoero ("Relazione," pp. 244–245).

49. Michele Suriano, "Relazione di Filippo II, re di Spagna" (1559), in Eugenio Albèri, ed., *Le relazioni degli ambasciatori veneti al Senato durante il secolo decimosesto,* ser. I, vol. III (Florence, 1853), p. 367.

50. For the alchemy scheme, ibid., and Marcantonio da Mula, "Relazione di Filippo II, re di Spagna" (1559), in Eugenio Albèri, ed., *Le relazioni degli ambasciatori veneti al Senato durante il secolo decimosesto,* ser. I, vol. III (Florence, 1853), p. 397. On Calderón's treachery, see Surian (Suriano) to the Doge and Senate of Venice, from Brussels, 16 April 1558 (*CalStP–V,* vol. VI, pt. III, doc. 1214, p. 1485), in which the Venetian reports the receipt of information from Calderón regarding Ruy Gómez's private negotiations with Anne de Montmorency. Calderón's name and title were enciphered in this letter, the usual Venetian practice for the protection of their agents. Calderón may also have been the source for Venetian knowledge of the

contents of Ruy Gómez's private correspondence a year later. See Paolo Tiepolo to the Doge and Senate of Venice, from Brussels, 4 March 1559, *CalStP–V,* vol. VII, doc. 34, pp. 41–42.

51. Cabrera de Córdoba, *Felipe II,* vol. I, lib. IV, cap. II, p. 167.

52. For the opening of negotiations with Caraffa, see Bernardo Navagero (Venetian ambassador in Rome) to the Doge and Senate, 15 January 1558, *CalStP–V,* vol. VI, pt. III, doc. 1143, pp. 1427–1428. The commissioners for the general peace were named in a *cédula* of Philip II, 11 October 1558, calendared by Julián Paz, *Documentos relativos a España existentes en los Archivos nacionales de París* (Madrid, 1934), p. 158, item no. 745. See also Alphonse de Ruble, *Le Traité de Câteau-Cambrésis* (Paris, 1889), pp. 3–4, and Joycelyne G. Russell, *Peacemaking in the Renaissance* (London, 1986), pp. 140–141.

53. On Granvelle's role, see Russell, *Peacemaking,* pp. 147–148. For Ruy Gómez's shuttling, see *CalStP–V,* vol. VII, Venetian reports for February and March 1559, and Thomas Gresham to Cecil, from Antwerp, 21 March 1559, *Calendar of State Papers, Foreign Series, of the Reign of Elizabeth, 1558–1559* (cited henceforth as *CalStP–F, 1558–1559*), ed. by Joseph Stevenson (London, 1863), doc. 437, p. 183.

54. Throckmorton to Cecil, from Paris, 6 June 1559, *CalStP–F, 1558–1559,* doc. 823, p. 302; Cabrera de Córdoba, *Felipe II,* vol. I, lib. V, cap. I, p. 261 (embassy to carry the jewels to Isabel). Philip, of course, had once again been widowed, this time by the death of Mary Tudor on 17 November 1558. On the memorial ceremony for the emperor, see Jean de Vandenesse, "Diario de los viajes de Felipe II," pp. 1075–1091, esp. p. 1080.

55. Jean de Vandenesse, "Diario de los viajes de Felipe II," p. 1094; Throckmorton to the Council, from Paris, 8 July 1559, *CalStP–F, 1558–1559,* doc. 950, p. 364; Salazar y Castro, *Casa de Silva,* vol. II, p. 478; Ruble, *Câteau-Cambrésis,* pp. 229–243. For a good discussion of Philip's motives regarding the Treaty of Cateau-Cambrésis, see Peter Pierson, *Philip II of Spain* (London, 1975), pp. 34–36.

56. Throckmorton to Cecil, from Paris, 13 July 1559, *CalStP–F, 1558–1559,* doc. 985, pp. 377–378; Ruble, *Câteau-Cambrésis,* pp. 242–243.

57. Giovanni Michiel to the Doge and Senate of Venice, from Paris, 18 July 1559, *CalStP–V,* vol. VII, doc. 87, p. 111; Throckmorton to Queen Elizabeth, from Paris, 27 July 1559, *CalStP–F, 1558–1559,* doc. 1075, p. 417; Ruy Gómez de Silva to Don Francisco de Mendoza y Bobadilla, Cardinal Archbishop of Burgos, from Valladolid, 15 August 1559, *Colección de documentos inéditos para la historia de España* (Madrid, 1842–1895) (cited henceforth as CODOIN), vol. III, pp. 420–421 ("Yo ha ocho dias que llegue . . . ").

58. Cabrera de Córdoba, *Felipe II,* vol. I, lib. V, cap. II, p. 268; Challoner to Queen Elizabeth, from Ghent, 3 August 1559, *CalStP–F, 1558–1559,* doc. 1114, pp. 438–439.

59. Challoner to Queen Elizabeth, from Ghent, 3 August 1559, *CalStP–F, 1558–1559,* doc. 1114, p. 440.

60. This privilege, granted at Brussels, 1 July 1559, countersigned by Juan Saganta and sealed with the great seal of "el Reyno de la Citerior

Sicilia," is reproduced in full by Salazar y Castro (*Casa de Silva,* vol. II, pp. 479–481). The quotation translated here is from pp. 479–480.

61. See Chapter 3.

62. Salazar y Castro, *Casa de Silva,* vol. II, pp. 480–481.

63. Gaspar Muro, *Vida de la Princesa de Eboli* (Mexico City, 1883), ch. II, p. 100.

64. For the royal donation of these properties, Salazar y Castro, *Casa de Silva,* vol. II, p. 482; for census of 1648, Giovanni Battista Pacichelli, *Il Regno di Napoli in prospettiva* (1702–1703) (Bologna, 1975), vol. I, p. 336; for revenues, Archivo Histórico Nacional, Madrid (AHN), Sección Osuna, leg. 2078, nos. 4^1 and 12^7, and leg. 2077, no. 10^6 (Eboli); AHN Osuna, leg. 2080, no. 1 (further grant of 236 ducats per year in Eboli, 1 July 1559); AGS, Visitas de Italia, leg. 348, no. 14 (Diano); AGS, Visitas de Italia, leg. 348, no. 14, and AHN Osuna, leg. 2708, "Racon de los papeles que hallado [*sic*] entre los papeles antiguos q[ue] estan en los Archivos tocantes a quentas con Nicolao de Grimaldo" (Lago Picholo); for the *servicios* of Eboli and Diano, Lope de Mardones to Ruy Gómez de Silva, from Naples, 17 May 1564, AGS CJH, leg. 56, no. 290, and *università* d'Eboli to Ruy Gómez de Silva, 18 April 1564, AGS CJH, leg. 56, no. 297.

65. For a good discussion of the Council of State in the early 1560s and of the ascendancy of Ruy Gómez de Silva and Eraso, see Paul David Lagomarsino, "Court Factions and the Formulation of Spanish Policy Towards the Netherlands (1559–1567)," Ph.D. dissertation, University of Cambridge, 1973, pp. 31–34.

66. Antonio Tiepolo, "Relazione," (1567) in Eugenio Albèri, ed., *Le relazioni degli ambasciatori veneti al Senato durante il secolo decimosesto,* ser. I, vol. V (Florence, 1861), p. 147. For Eboli's dominant position in the financial bureaucracy, see the *relazione* of Paolo Tiepolo (1563), ibid., p. 65, and Gounon-Loubens, *Essais sur l'administration,* pp. 283–284. For the rather loose organization of financial decisionmaking in these years, see Carlos Morales, "Grupos de poder," pp. 128–129.

67. By this time Philip's indefatigable obsession with paperwork seems to have become firmly established; also in the early 1560s, he began his practice of spending large parts of the year at the various rural lodges and palaces in the vicinity of Madrid, accompanied usually by a very small entourage. (On these points, see, for example, Pierson, *Philip II of Spain,* pp. 64, 119–121.) Many historians have commented on Philip's attempts to insulate himself in the mystery of kingship; among the most cogent remarks are those of Hume, *Philip II of Spain,* pp. 76–77.

68. See, for example, Badoero, "Relazione," pp. 241–242, for a description of how Philip and Ruy Gómez collaborated in the work of government.

69. J. de Saint-Sulpice to Charles IX, 1 June 1562, in Edmond Cabié, ed., *Ambassade en Espagne de Jean Ebrard* (Paris, 1903), p. 19.

70. Gonzalo Pérez to the Duke of Sessa, from Monzón, 31 December 1563, in *Pio IV y Felipe Segundo,* ed. by "F. del V." and "S. K." (Madrid, 1891), pp. 157–158.

71. Granvelle to Bolwiller, from Salins, 26 July 1564, in Charles Weiss, ed., *Papiers d'État du Cardinal de Granvelle*, vol. VIII (Paris, 1850), p. 174.

72. Thomas de Chantonnay to Ruy Gómez de Silva, from Paris, 28 April 1563, AGS CJH, leg. 50, no. 125. For some of Chantonnay's specific requests for *mercedes*, see same to same, from Blois, 24 February 1563, ibid., no. 124.

73. Ruy Gómez de Silva to Don Gabriel de la Cueva, Duke of Alburquerque, from Madrid, 27 July 1565, AGS Estado, leg. 1219, no. 16.

74. Ibid.

75. See, for example, Ruy Gómez de Silva to Juan de Escobedo, 7 April 1563, AGS CJH, leg. 50, no. 257, and Ruy Gómez de Silva to Duke of Alburquerque, from Madrid, October(?) 1570, AGS Estado, leg. 1227, no. 196. For some rather sketchy biographical information on Broccardo, see *Dizionario biografico degli italiani*, vol. XIV (Rome, 1972), pp. 393–394.

76. Quotation from Ruy Gómez de Silva to Juan de Escobedo, 7 April 1563, AGS CJH, leg. 50, no. 257. Salazar y Castro, *Casa de Silva*, vol. II, p. 487, reports that Broccardo was instrumental in securing from the pope a grant of 20,000 *escudos* for Ruy Gómez in 1561.

77. Sigismondo Cavalli, "Relazione," in Eugenio Albèri, ed., *Le relazioni degli ambasciatori veneti al Senato durante il secolo decimosesto*, ser. I, vol. V (Florence, 1861), p. 181.

78. Leonardo Donà and Lorenzo Priuli to the Venetian Senate, from Madrid, 29 January 1573, in Mario Brunetti and Eligio Vitale, eds., *La Corrispondenza da Madrid dell'ambasciatore Leonardo Donà (1570–1573)* (Venice, 1963), vol. II, p. 639.

79. Ruy Gómez de Silva to Juan de Escobedo, from Pellejeros, 5 August 1566, AGS CJH, leg. 74, no. 6.

80. Ruy Gómez de Silva to Francisco de Eraso, from Madrid, 25 November 1552, AGS Estado, leg. 89, no. 123.

81. Philip II to Granvelle, from Monzón, 23 January 1564, in Weiss, *Papiers d'État*, vol. VII, p. 335.

82. "Relacion de los sueldos y entretenimientos y ventajas hechas por el Duq de Sessa a diversas pers^as excesviam^te," AGS Estado, leg. 1229, no. 150.

83. Countess of Concentaina to Ruy Gómez de Silva, from Valencia, 31 May 1562, AGS CJH, leg. 46, no. 64*bis*.

84. Ruy Gómez de Silva to Juan de Escobedo, no date (about 1563–1565), AGS CJH, leg. 50, no. 266.

85. Catherine de' Medici to Sébastien de l'Aubespine, from Fontainebleau, 3 March 1560 (1561 N.S.), in Louis Paris, ed., *Négociations, lettres et pièces diverses relatives au regne de François II* (Paris, 1841), p. 819.

86. Duke of Savoy to Ruy Gómez de Silva, from Turin, 8 November 1570, AGS Estado, leg. 1229, no. 95.

87. Quoted in Gaspar Muro, *Vida de la Princesa de Eboli*, ch. II, p. 98.

88. This was the estimate of Badoero, in his "Relazione," p. 241. Some variants of the manuscript give the figure of 36,000 escudos (see García Mercadal, *Viajes*, vol. I, p. 1115, n. 1). The lower number more closely corresponds to the amount that can be archivally confirmed. Before 1566 the

escudo was a coin valued at 350 *maravedís,* or ¹⁴⁄₁₅ths of a ducat (see Lynch, *Spain under the Habsburgs,* vol. I, p. 369).

89. See Chapter 2.

90. For the consummation of the marriage and Doña Ana's pregnancy in 1557, see Duke of Francavila to Ruy Gómez de Silva, from Valladolid, 13 September 1557, CODOIN, vol. XCVII, pp. 291–292, and other letters in the same volume. Juan Vázquez de Molina, "para Erasso y ruygomez a 5 de abril 1558," AGS Estado, leg. 129, no. 160, reports the birth of the couple's first child—the unfortunate Diego—on 3 April 1558. For all the children, see Salazar y Castro, *Casa de Silva,* vol. II, and Muro, *Vida de la Princesa de Eboli,* ch. II, pp. 122–123, n. 29. Some of the baptismal certificates can be found in the Archivo Histórico Nacional, in Madrid. For example, the certificate for the Don Diego born in 1564 is in AHN, Sección Consejos Suprimidos (Escribanía Ayala: Pleitos), leg. 36,253, P. 117. Thomas de Chantonnay to Ruy Gómez de Silva, from Paris, 15 December 1562, AGS CJH, leg. 46, no. 45, offers congratulations on the birth of Don Rodrigo.

91. Boethius, *The Consolation of Philosophy* (New York, 1962), Bk. II, Prose 1, p. 22.

INTRODUCTION TO PART TWO

1. See the suggestive analysis of Georges Durand, "What is Absolutism?" in *Louis XIV and Absolutism,* ed. by Ragnhild Hatton (Columbus, 1976), pp. 18–36. On the immutability of aristocratic privilege, see Manuel Fernández Alvarez, *La sociedad española en el siglo de oro* (Madrid, 1983), p. 13.

CHAPTER FIVE

1. Leopold von Ranke, *The Ottoman and the Spanish Empires in the Sixteenth and Seventeenth Centuries* (1843) (New York, 1975), pp. 41–42.

2. Gregorio Marañón, *Antonio Pérez* (Madrid, 1951), vol. I, pp. 31–32 (composition of the factions) and pp. 126–127 (their ideologies).

3. John H. Elliott, *Imperial Spain, 1469–1716* (New York, 1964), pp. 254–256.

4. Elliott's phrase; ibid., p. 254.

5. Helen Nader, *The Mendoza Family in the Spanish Renaissance, 1350 to 1550* (New Brunswick, 1979), p. 125.

6. Ibid., pp. 168–173.

7. Paul David Lagomarsino, "Court Factions and the Formulation of Spanish Policy Towards the Netherlands (1559–1567)," Ph.D. dissertation, University of Cambridge, 1973. For a brief summation, see pp. 325–326.

8. William Maltby, *Alba: A Biography of Fernando Alvarez de Toledo, Third Duke of Alba, 1507–1582* (Berkeley, 1983), pp. 70–76.

9. José Martínez Millán, "Elites de poder en tiempos de Felipe II (1539–1572)," *Hispania* 49:171 (1989), pp. 111–149, quotation at p. 113.

10. Maltby's reliance on Erika Spivakovsky, "La Princesa de Eboli," *Chronica Nova* 9 (1974), pp. 5–48, is evident in his *Alba,* p. 71 and n. 18.

11. John B. Owens, "Despotism, Absolutism, and the Law in Renaissance Spain: Toledo versus the Counts of Belalcázar (1445–1574)," Ph.D. dissertation, University of Wisconsin, 1972, pp. 246–247 and 266, n. 99.

12. Maltby, *Alba*, p. 73.

13. Don Juan de Figueroa to Charles V, from Richmond, 15 August 1557, *Calendar of Letters, Despatches and State Papers relating to the Negotiations between England and Spain, Preserved in the Archives at Vienna, Simancas, Besancon, Brussels, Madrid and Lille* (cited henceforth as *CalStP–S*), ed. by Royall Tyler, vol. XIII, *Philip and Mary, July 1554–November 1558* (London, 1954), doc. 338, pp. 315–316; Juan de Galarza to Francisco de Ledesma, from St. Quentin, 11 September 1557, ibid., doc. 341, p. 318; Luis Cabrera de Córdoba, *Historia de Felipe II, rey de España* (Madrid, 1876–1877), vol. I, libro IV, capítulo XIII, p. 202.

14. For a truly exhaustive list, see Cabrera de Córdoba, *Felipe II*, vol. I, lib. IV, cap. XXIV, pp. 241–242.

15. Federico Badoero, "Relazione delle persone, governo e stati di Carlo V e di Filippo II (1557)," in Luigi Firpo, ed., *Relazioni di ambasciatori veneti al senato*, vol. VIII, *Spagna, 1497–1598* (Turin, 1981), p. 157.

16. Ibid., p. 160.

17. See, for example, the following dispatches of Michiel Surian (Michele Suriano) from Brussels to the Doge and Senate of Venice in *Calendar of State Papers and Manuscripts, relating to English Affairs, Existing in the Archives and Collections of Venice, and in other Libraries of Northern Italy* (cited henceforth as *CalStP–V*), ed. by Rawdon Brown and G. Cavendish Bentinck (London, 1873–1890): 5 March 1558 (vol. VI, pt. III, doc. 1178, pp. 1459–1460); 20 March 1558 (ibid., doc. 1201, p. 1475); 24 March 1558 (ibid., doc. 1203, pp. 1476–1477); 16 April 1558 (ibid., doc. 1214, p. 1485); 21 April 1558 (ibid., doc. 1215, p. 1485). See also Lord Cobham to Queen Elizabeth, from Brussels, 13 December 1558, in *Calendar of State Papers, Foreign Series, of the Reign of Elizabeth, 1558–1559* (cited henceforth as *CalStP–F, 1558–1559*), ed. by Joseph Stevenson (London, 1863), doc. 82, p. 30, reporting that "Rigomes" had approached the bishop of Ely to urge a rapid conclusion of peace.

18. English Commissioners [Howard, Ely, Wotton] to Queen Elizabeth, from Cateau-Cambrésis, 2 March 1559, *CalStP–F, 1558–1559*, doc. 373, p. 156.

19. Concerning Ruy Gómez's popularity among the Netherlands nobility, which largely stemmed from the impression he made in his years in residence there, see Adela Repetto Alvarez, "Acerca de un posible Segundo Gobierno de Margarita de Parma y el Cardenal de Granvela en los Estados de Flandes," *Hispania* 32:121 (1972), pp. 401–402, 474.

20. For a collection of contemporary testimony to Philip's preference for Spanish advisors, see José Antonio Escudero, *Los secretarios de estado y del despacho (1474–1724)* (Madrid, 1969), vol. I, p. 214.

21. Cabrera de Córdoba, *Felipe II*, vol. I, lib. IV, cap. XIII, p. 202. This *merced* for Feria may have come at the expense of Ruy Gómez's ally Gutierre López de Padilla; the affair is murky, but see Count of Feria to Ruy Gómez

de Silva, from London, 16 February 1559, Archivo General de Simancas (AGS), Consejo y Juntas de Hacienda (CJH), legajo 34, no. 476.

22. Michiel Surian (Michele Suriano) to the Doge and Senate of Venice, from Brussels, 28 November 1557, *CalStP–V*, vol. VI, pt. III, doc. 1093, p. 1380. By 1559 Feria clearly regarded Ruy Gómez as his patron at court; see Count of Feria to Ruy Gómez de Silva, from London, 20 January 1559, AGS CJH, leg. 34, no. 475, and same to same, 16 February 1559, ibid., no. 476. Ruy Gómez continued to cultivate his alliance with Feria for years afterward; in 1562 the French ambassador at Madrid reported that Eboli was endeavoring "to secure some bone to gnaw for the Count of Feria, who, for the folly of his marriage and past expenses, finds himself so poor and burdened here that he has no hope except to gain one of the governing posts that the king will be forced to distribute in the next months." S. de l'Aubespine to Catherine de' Medici, from Madrid, 3 January 1562, in Louis-Prosper Gachard, ed., *La Bibliothèque Nationale à Paris* (Brussels, 1877), vol. II, p. 127.

23. Badoero, "Relazione," pp. 157–158.

24. Ibid., p. 158.

25. Ibid., p. 193. ("[Alba] presume gran cose, ed è colmo d'ambizione e superbia, inclinato all'adulazione ed invido molto.")

26. Surian (Suriano) remarked that "Il duca d'Alva ha visto e maneggiato molte guerre, e per la pratica che ha, discorre meglio di ogni altro che io abbia conosciuto in quella corte." The Venetian, however, went on to express some doubts about Alba's military skills, as opposed to his discourse on war. Alba, he wrote, spends too much on his campaigns and is prudent to the point of timidity (Michele Suriano, "Relazione di Filippo II re di Spagna [1559]," in Luigi Firpo, ed., *Relazioni di ambasciatori veneti al senato*, vol. VIII, *Spagna, 1497–1598* [Turin, 1981], pp. 286–287). Badoero, "Relazione," p. 192, was less diplomatic, asserting that "in war, he has shown in all circumstances a great timidity and so little intelligence that the Emperor never entrusted him with a command far from his person." Similar comments had been voiced by Lorenzo Contarini in 1548 (quoted in J. García Mercadal, ed. and trans., *Viajes de extranjeros por España y Portugal* (Madrid, 1952), vol. I, p. 1122).

27. For a vivid sketch of the duke's "parched and bilious disposition" and for this pasquinade, see Badoero, "Relazione," pp. 192–193.

28. And certainly his generalship attracted praise as well—see, for example, Juan de Mariana, *Historia general de España* (Valencia, 1794), vol. II, p. 698, who argued that Alba "emerged victorious from all the wars he fought, which were a great many."

29. Maltby, *Alba*, p. 2.

30. Marañón, *Antonio Pérez*, vol. I, p. 155.

31. Ruy Gómez de Silva to Francisco de Eraso, from Madrid, 5 April 1552, AGS, Secretaría de Estado (Estado), leg. 89, no. 129.

32. Michiel Surian (Michele Suriano) to the Doge and Senate of Venice, from Brussels, 28 November 1557, *CalStP–V*, vol. VI, pt. III, doc. 1093, p. 1380.

33. Ibid.

34. Michiel Surian (Michele Suriano) to the Doge and Senate of Venice, from Brussels, 23 January 1558, *CalStP–V*, vol. VI, pt. III, doc. 1149, pp. 1436–1437.

35. Same to same, 26 January 1558, ibid., doc. 1152, p. 1438; Maltby, *Alba*, p. 109.

36. Cabrera de Córdoba, *Felipe II*, vol. I, lib. IV, cap. XIX, pp. 216–217; Luis de Salazar y Castro, *Historia genealógica de la Casa de Silva* (Madrid, 1685), vol. II, pp. 475–476; Ludwig von Pastor, *The History of the Popes*, vol. XIV (London, 1924), p. 212.

37. For Alba's dealings with Paul IV, see Michiel Surian (Michele Suriano) to the Doge and Senate of Venice, from Brussels, 28 November 1557, *CalStP–V*, vol. VI, pt. III, doc. 1093, p. 1380; same to same, 4 January 1558, ibid., doc. 1125, pp. 1412–1413; same to same, 26 January 1558, ibid., doc. 1152, pp. 1438–1439.

38. Same to same, 28 November 1557, ibid., doc. 1093, p. 1380; same to same, 4 January 1558, ibid., doc. 1125, pp. 1412–1413; Pastor, *History of the Popes*, vol. XIV, p. 212.

39. For the bids of Alba and Ruy Gómez de Silva, see Michiel Surian (Michele Suriano) to the Doge and Senate of Venice, 26 January 1558, *CalStP–V*, vol. VI, pt. III, doc. 1152, pp. 1438–1439; Cabrera de Córdoba, *Felipe II*, vol. I, lib. IV, cap. XIX, p. 216; and Salazar y Castro, *Casa de Silva*, vol. II, pp. 475–476. For Ruy Gómez de Silva's negotiations with Cardinal Caraffa, see Bernardo Navagero to the Doge and Senate of Venice, from Rome, 15 January 1558, *CalStP–V*, vol. VI, pt. III, doc. 1143, pp. 1427–1428; and same to same, 15 January 1558, *CalStP–V*, vol. VI, pt. III, doc. 1144, p. 1429.

40. Cabrera de Córdoba, *Felipe II*, vol. I, lib. IV, cap. XIX, p. 216.

41. Ibid.

42. Ibid., pp. 216–217; Giovanni Michiel to the Doge and Senate, from Moret [France], 26 March 1558, *CalStP–V*, vol. VI, pt. III, doc. 1206, p. 1479; Pastor, *History of the Popes*, vol. XIV, pp. 212–213; and Antonio Ossorio, *Vida y hazañas de Don Fernando Alvarez de Toledo, Duque de Alba* (1669) (Madrid, 1945), p. 310.

43. Giovanni Michiel to the Doge and Senate of Venice, from Moret, 26 March 1558, *CalStP–V*, vol. VI, pt. III, doc. 1206, p. 1478.

44. Ossorio, *Vida y hazañas*, pp. 313–316; Gutierre López de Padilla to Ruy Gómez de Silva, from Valladolid, 8 December 1557, AGS CJH, leg. 32, no. 123.

45. Ossorio, *Vida y hazañas*, pp. 313–316, quotation from p. 314. Incidentally, it is unlikely that Philip actually attended this debate in the Council of State; Ossorio's report of his silence is probably an embroidery.

46. Michiel Surian (Michele Suriano) to the Doge and Senate of Venice, from Brussels, 5 March 1558, *CalStP–V*, vol. VI, pt. III, doc. 1178, p. 1459.

47. These attitudes were well summarized by Sir Roger Williams: "The captains animate the King to wars to maintain their wealth and greatness." *The Actions of the Low Countries* (1618) (Ithaca, 1964), p. 9.

48. Ranke, *The Ottoman and the Spanish Empires*, p. 42.

49. For the appointments and Alba's displeasure, see Michiel Surian (Michele Suriano) to the Doge and Senate of Venice, from Brussels, 27 April 1558, *CalStP–V*, vol. VI, pt. III, doc. 1217, p. 1488. For Manrique's tenure as lieutenant in Naples, replacing Alba's son, see E. Fernández de Navarrete, ed., *Libro donde se trata de los virreyes lugartenientes del reino de Nápoles, Colección de documentos inéditos para la historia de España* (Madrid, 1842–1895) (cited henceforth as CODOIN), vol. XXIII, pp. 148–149, 162–164. Having arrived in May 1558, Manrique was replaced in October by the new viceroy, Cardinal Bartolomé de la Cueva. The offending reports from Rome are in *CalStP–S*, vol. XIII: Juan Manrique de Lara to Charles V, from Rome, 24 May 1555, doc. 195, pp. 180–181; same to same, 25 May 1555, doc. 197, pp. 183–187; and Instructions from the Cardinal Chamberlain and Don Juan Manrique de Lara to Giovan Francesco Lottini, 25(?) May 1555, doc. 198, pp. 187–188. For the cardinal's attempts to exonerate himself and put Manrique de Lara in a bad light, see Cardinal of Santiago to Charles V, from Rome, 25 May 1555, doc. 196, pp. 181–183.

50. "Memoir drafted by the Bishop of Limoges [de l'Aubespine] and sent to the Cardinal of Lorraine," from Toledo, 26 September 1560, in Louis Paris, ed., *Négociations, lettres et pièces diverses relatives au regne de François II, tirées du portefeuille de Sébastien de l'Aubespine, évêque de Limoges* (Paris, 1841), p. 561.

51. For the rather fickle allegiance of Manrique de Lara to Ruy Gómez de Silva, see Lagomarsino, "Court Factions," pp. 33, 230, and Maltby, *Alba*, p. 124. There is evidence of an earlier effort by Ruy Gómez to advance Manrique's career in Ruy Gómez de Silva to Francisco de Eraso, from Hampton Court, 22 September 1554, AGS Estado, leg. 508, no. 139. That Ruy Gómez supported Sessa in further patronage bids is revealed in Gonzalo Pérez to the Duke of Sessa, from Monzón, 31 December 1563, in *Pio IV y Felipe Segundo. Primeros diez meses de la embajada de Don Luis de Requesens en Roma, 1563–1564*, ed. by "F. del V." and "S. K." (Madrid, 1891), pp. 157–158.

52. Michiel Surian (Michele Suriano) to the Doge and Senate of Venice, from Brussels, 27 April 1558, *CalStP–V*, vol. VI, pt. III, doc. 1217, p. 1488.

53. For the composition and balance of power of the Council of State in 1559, see Cabrera de Córdoba, *Felipe II*, vol. I, lib. V, cap. II, p. 266; and Challoner to Queen Elizabeth, from Ghent, 29 July 1559, *CalStP–F, 1558–1559*, doc. 1091, p. 427.

54. Ossorio, *Vida y hazañas*, p. 319.

55. (Le Baron) Alphonse de Ruble, *Le Traité de Câteau-Cambrésis* (Paris, 1889), p. 233.

56. *Archivo documental español*, vol. I, *Negociaciones con Francia (1559–1560)*, p. 31.

57. Throckmorton to Cecil, from Dover, 15 May 1559, *CalStP–F, 1558–1559*, doc. 683, p. 254; same to same, from Paris(?), 6 June 1559, ibid., doc. 823, p. 302; Paolo Tiepolo to the Doge and Senate of Venice, from Brussels, 11 June 1559, *CalStP–V*, vol. VII, doc. 79, p. 96. As it happened, Feria did not escort Isabel; his place was taken by another grandee, the duke of In-

fantado (see Jean de Vandenesse, "Diario de los viajes de Felipe II," in J. García Mercadal, ed. and trans., *Viajes de extranjeros por España y Portugal* (Madrid, 1952), vol. I, p. 1098).

58. Challoner to Cecil, from Antwerp, 13 October 1559, *CalStP–F, 1559–1560,* doc. 78, p. 38.

59. Ibid.; Challoner to Queen Elizabeth, from Brussels or Antwerp(?), 9 November 1559, ibid., doc. 220, p. 92.

60. See Charles IX's certification that Mary Stuart had returned the Crown jewels given her upon the accession of Francis II, 6 December 1560, in Paris, *Négociations . . . de Sebastien de l'Aubespine,* p. 743.

61. Lagomarsino, "Court Factions," pp. 32–33. For a list of members of the expanded Council of State, see enclosure in Paolo Tiepolo to the Doge and Senate of Venice, from Toledo, 22 December 1559, *CalStP–V,* vol. VII, doc. 121, p. 140.

62. Paolo Tiepolo, "Relazione," in Eugenio Albèri, ed., *Le relazioni degli ambasciatori veneti al Senato durante il secolo decimosesto,* ser. I, vol. V (Florence, 1861), p. 68.

63. Enclosure, Paolo Tiepolo to the Doge and Senate of Venice, 22 December 1559, *CalStP–V,* vol. VII, doc. 121, p. 140 (see notation concerning the duke of Alba); same to same, from Toledo, 7 January 1560, ibid., doc. 125, p. 146.

64. Jean de Vandenesse, "Diario de los viajes de Felipe II," p. 1098.

65. Mariana, *Historia general de España,* vol. II, p. 685.

66. For Ruy Gómez's presence, see Salazar y Castro, *Casa de Silva,* vol. II, p. 483; for arrangements, Ruy Gómez de Silva to Don Francisco de Mendoza y Bobadilla, Cardinal-Archbishop of Burgos, from Valladolid, 15 August 1559, CODOIN, vol. III, pp. 420–421.

67. Tiepolo to the Doge and Senate of Venice, from Toledo, 16 February 1560, *CalStP–V,* vol. VII, doc. 129, pp. 150–151.

68. Ibid.

69. Lagomarsino, "Court Factions," p. 33; see Paolo Tiepolo, "Relazione," p. 65, for the dominance of these allies in the Council of Hacienda.

70. Jules Gounon-Loubens, *Essais sur l'administration de la Castille au XVIe siècle* (Paris, 1860), pp. 283–286.

71. For a royal appreciation of the fiscal situation, see the "Memorial de las finanças de España en los años 1560 y 1561," evidently drafted in Philip's own hand, in Charles Weiss, ed., *Papiers d'État du Cardinal de Granvelle,* vol. VI (Paris, 1846), pp. 156–165.

72. The *merced* was granted at Monzón, 15 September 1563. Salazar y Castro, *Casa de Silva,* vol. II, p. 487.

73. Paolo Tiepolo to the Doge and Senate of Venice, from Toledo, 11 September 1560, *CalStP–V,* vol. VII, doc. 198, p. 256.

74. Ibid., p. 257; "Memoir drafted by the Bishop of Limoges," pp. 560–561.

75. The origins and recurrence of this malady can be traced in Giovanni Michiel to the Doge and Senate of Venice, from Paris, 3 September 1558,

CalStP–V, vol. VI, pt. III, doc. 1262, pp. 1527–1528; the Spanish Peace Commissioners [Alba, Ruy Gómez de Silva, Orange, Arras, Viglius] to Philip II, from Cercamp, 15 October 1558, *CalStP–S*, vol. XIII, doc. 475, pp. 414–415; same to same, 15 October 1558, *CalStP–S*, vol. XIII, doc. 476, p. 415; Paolo Tiepolo to the Doge and Senate of Venice, from Toledo, 22 December 1559, *CalStP–V*, vol. VII, doc. 121, p. 140; same to same, 16 February 1560, *CalStP–V*, vol. VII, doc. 129, pp. 150–151; same to same, 7 April 1560, *CalStP–V*, vol. VII, doc. 148, pp. 186–187; same to same, 25 June 1560, *CalStP–V*, vol. VII, doc. 176, p. 229.

76. Paolo Tiepolo to the Doge and Senate of Venice, from Toledo, 16 February 1560, *CalStP–V*, vol. VII, doc. 129, pp. 150–151.

77. "Memoir drafted by the Bishop of Limoges," p. 559.

78. Ibid.

79. Ibid.

80. Ibid.

81. Paolo Tiepolo, "Relazione," p. 68.

82. S. de l'Aubespine to Catherine de' Medici, November 1560, in Paris, *Négociations . . . de Sebastien de l'Aubespine*, p. 711.

83. Paolo Tiepolo, "Relazione," p. 68.

84. Ibid., p. 69. The bishop of Limoges observed the same pattern of withdrawal from public affairs, compensated by the fact that Ruy Gómez still enjoyed "in the evenings—since he is *grand-sommelier de corps*—two or three hours of privy friendship" with Philip. "Memoir drafted by the Bishop of Limoges," p. 559.

85. Paolo Tiepolo, "Relazione," p. 69.

86. Count of Buendía to Ruy Gómez de Silva, from Madrid, 16 March 1561, AGS CJH, leg. 42, no. 161, and Ruy Gómez de Silva to Juan de Escobedo, no date, ibid. (this letter is filed with Buendía's and responds to its complaints).

87. Tiepolo, "Relazione," p. 69.

88. Elliott, *Imperial Spain*, p. 277.

89. Michiel Surian (Michele Suriano), quoted in Ranke, *The Ottoman and the Spanish Empires*, p. 42.

90. De l'Aubespine to Catherine de' Medici, from Madrid, 16 February 1562, in Gachard, *Bibliothèque Nationale à Paris*, vol. II, p. 134.

91. Lagomarsino, in "Court Factions," documents a number of shifts, often involving men who were the most prominent members of their previous faction. For one such major realignment, see pp. 225–236.

CHAPTER SIX

1. Paolo Tiepolo to the Doge and Senate of Venice, from Toledo, 16 February 1560, *Calendar of State Papers and Manuscripts, relating to English Affairs, Existing in the Archives and Collections of Venice, and in other Libraries of Northern Italy* (cited henceforth as *CalStP–V*), ed. by Rawdon Brown and G. Cavendish Bentinck (London, 1873–1890), vol. VII, doc. 129, pp. 150–151. See

also the similar report in same to same, 7 April 1560, ibid., doc. 148, pp. 186–187.

2. "Memoir drafted by the Bishop of Limoges and sent to the Cardinal of Lorraine," from Toledo, 26 September 1560, in Louis Paris, ed., *Négociations, lettres et pièces diverses relatives au regne de François II, tirées du portefeuille de Sébastien de l'Aubespine, évêque de Limoges* (Paris, 1841), p. 560.

3. Ibid., pp. 559–560.

4. Ibid.; De l'Aubespine and d'Ozances to Charles IX, from Madrid, 1 October 1561, in Louis-Prosper Gachard, ed., *La Bibliothèque Nationale à Paris* (Brussels, 1877), vol. II, p. 120.

5. De l'Aubespine to Charles IX, from Madrid, 12 August 1561, in Gachard, *Bibliothèque Nationale à Paris*, vol. II, pp. 116–117.

6. See De l'Aubespine to Catherine de' Medici, 13 February, 16 February, 25 February, 25 March, and 15 April 1562, ibid., pp. 132–140. The permanent appointment went to Juan Manrique de Lara, in August 1562 (William Maltby, *Alba: A Biography of Fernando Alvarez de Toledo, Third Duke of Alba, 1507–1582* [Berkeley, 1983], p. 124).

7. Saint-Sulpice to Catherine de' Medici, from Madrid, 27 August 1563, in Gachard, *Bibliothèque Nationale à Paris*, vol. II, p. 153.

8. Juan Vargas to Granvelle, from Madrid, 4 August 1564, in Charles Weiss, ed., *Papiers d'État du Cardinal de Granvelle*, vol. VIII (Paris, 1850), p. 206.

9. Maltby, *Alba*, pp. 123–124; Paul David Lagomarsino, "Court Factions and the Formulation of Spanish Policy Towards the Netherlands (1559–1567)," Ph.D. dissertation, University of Cambridge, 1973, pp. 70–74; for Eboli's activities in the eastern kingdoms in 1563–1564, see the dispatches of Saint-Sulpice from Monzón and Barcelona, between September 1563 and February 1564 in Edmond Cabié, ed., *Ambassade en Espagne de Jean Ebrard, Seigneur de Saint-Sulpice, de 1562 a 1565 et mission de ce diplomate dans le même pays en 1566* (Paris, 1903).

10. Saint-Sulpice to Catherine de' Medici and King Charles IX, 27 August 1563, in Cabié, *Ambassade en Espagne*, p. 152. See also Saint-Sulpice to Catherine de' Medici, from Barbastro, 11 October 1563, in Gachard, *Bibliothèque Nationale à Paris*, vol. II, p. 157, where Ruy Gómez is mentioned as "ung des plus privez des affaires du roy catholique."

11. Granvelle to Gonzalo Pérez, from Baudoncourt, 12 October 1564, in Weiss, *Cardinal de Granvelle*, vol. VIII, pp. 412–413.

12. Baldesar Castiglione, *The Book of the Courtier* (Garden City, 1959), p. 115.

13. Ibid., p. 36.

14. Federico Badoero, "Relazione delle persone, governo e stati di Carlo V e di Filippo II" (1557), in Eugenio Albèri, ed., *Le relazioni degli ambasciatori veneti al Senato durante il secolo decimosesto*, ser. I, vol. III (Florence, 1853), p. 241.

15. Badoero and Antonio Tiepolo, quoted in Gregorio Marañón, *Antonio Pérez* (Madrid, 1951), vol. I, pp. 29–30.

16. The best-known portrait is by an anonymous painter, its current location unknown. This image, likely depicting Ruy Gómez in his late thirties or early forties, is reproduced facing the title page above. Full-length depictions of Eboli may be seen in a painting cycle commemorating Pastrana's religious foundations, reproduced in Marañón, *Antonio Pérez*, vol. I, between pp. 176 and 177.

17. Castiglione, *Courtier*, p. 29.

18. Ibid., pp. 99–100.

19. See "Torneo celebrado en Valladolid con ocasión de la boda del Príncipe Don Felipe con la Infanta Doña María de Portugal," in Amalio Huarte, ed., *Relaciones de los reinados de Carlos V y Felipe II* (Madrid, 1941), pp. 87–88; Luis de Salazar y Castro, *Historia genealógica de la Casa de Silva* (Madrid, 1685), vol. II, pp. 460–462; Juan Cristóbal Calvete de Estrella, *El felicissimo viaje del muy alto y muy poderoso principe don Phelippe* (1552) (Madrid, 1930), vol. I, pp. 82–88, 142, 189–204, 306–311, and vol. II, pp. 13–15; *The Diary of Henry Machyn*, ed. by John Gough Nichols (London, 1848), p. 76; Gustav Ungerer, *A Spaniard in Elizabethan England: The Correspondence of Antonio Pérez's Exile* (London, 1974–1976), vol. I, p. 33; Don Pedro de Córdoba to Ferdinand, King of the Romans, 10 December 1554, *Calendar of Letters, Despatches and State Papers relating to the Negotiations between England and Spain, Preserved in the Archives at Vienna, Simancas, Besancon, Brussels, Madrid and Lille* (cited henceforth as *CalStP–S*), ed. by Royall Tyler, vol. XIII, *Philip and Mary, July 1554–November 1558* (London, 1954), doc. 127, p. 119; Paolo Tiepolo to the Doge and Senate of Venice, from Toledo, 11 September 1560, *CalStP–V*, vol. VII, doc. 198, pp. 257–258.

20. Badoero, "Relazione," p. 241.

21. Melchor de Herrera to Ruy Gómez de Silva, from Medina del Campo, 20 February 1563, Archivo General de Simancas (AGS), Consejo y Juntas de Hacienda (CJH), legajo 50, no. 155; Pedro de Vivero to Ruy Gómez de Silva, from Medina del Campo, 20 February 1563, ibid., no. 173; quotation from Ruy Gómez de Silva to Pedro de Vivero, from Madrid, 24 February 1563, ibid., *borrador* filed with no. 173.

22. Castiglione, *Courtier*, p. 38.

23. Information on Ruy Gómez's stable comes from Archivo Histórico Nacional, Madrid (AHN), Sección Osuna, leg. 1838, no. 25. This is an account of an auction conducted on 3 September 1573, after Eboli's death, by his stable master Millan de Barrionuebo Sota. The horse "Rribera" [*sic*] brought the substantial sum of 82 ducats, considerably more than any of the other animals sold. The leather-covered carriage is described as "El coche grande biejo"; presumably the heirs retained others of more recent manufacture. For news of his horses in 1557, see Juan de Escobedo to Ruy Gómez de Silva, from Valladolid, 16 October 1557, AGS CJH, leg. 32, no. 121.

24. Many passages in *The Book of the Courtier* touch on these themes; see in particular pp. 70 (source of the quoted passage) and 135.

25. See Antonio Ossorio, *Vida y hazañas de Don Fernando Alvarez de Toledo,*

Duque de Alba (Madrid, 1945), p. 311: "Juntos [Felipe II y Ruy Gómez de Silva] recibieron la misma educación." Cabrera de Córdoba wrote, more ambiguously, that Ruy Gómez "crióse con el Principe" (Luis Cabrera de Córdoba, *Historia de Felipe II, rey de España* [Madrid, 1876–1877], vol. I, libro IV, capítulo XIX, p. 216).

26. For a brief assessment of Siliceo's strengths and weaknesses as a tutor, see A. W. Lovett, *Early Habsburg Spain, 1517–1598* (Oxford, 1986), pp. 117–118.

27. Badoero, "Relazione," p. 241.

28. Ibid. His facility in Italian is suggested by the considerable correspondence addressed to him in that language; see, for instance, Negro de Negro to Ruy Gómez de Silva, from Turin, 6 August 1570, AGS, Secretaría de Estado (Estado), leg. 1229, no. 39, and Filippo d'Este to Ruy Gómez de Silva, from Turin, 7 August 1570, AGS Estado, leg. 1229, no. 46.

29. See Chapter 3.

30. Saint-Sulpice to Catherine de' Medici, from Barbastro, 11 October 1563, in Gachard, *Bibliothèque Nationale à Paris*, vol. II, p. 158; Ruy Gómez de Silva to Eraso(?), from Hampton Court, 15 April 1555, *CalStP–S*, vol. XIII, doc. 175, p. 163. As it turned out, he was not offered the position; other men were named to the commission while Ruy Gómez deliberated.

31. Ruy Gómez de Silva to Eraso(?), from Hampton Court, 15 April 1555, *CalStP–S*, vol. XIII, doc. 175, p. 163; there are similar instances of self-deprecation in Ruy Gómez de Silva to Eraso, from Hampton Court, 20 June 1555, ibid., doc. 215, p. 224, and in same to same, from Madrid, 25 November 1552, AGS Estado, leg. 89, no. 123; see Castiglione, *Courtier*, pp. 71, 135–141 for a discussion of courtly modesty.

32. Castiglione, *Courtier*, pp. 97–98 (quotation at p. 97).

33. Cabrera de Córdoba, *Felipe II*, vol. II, lib. X, cap. I, p. 141.

34. Antonio Pérez, *Aphorismos de las cartas españolas y latinas de Ant. Perez* (Paris, 1598[?]), fol. 30.

35. Dr. Juan Milio to Juan de Albornoz, from Madrid, 14 August 1573, in Duquesa de Berwick y de Alba, ed., *Documentos escogidos del archivo de la Casa de Alba* (Madrid, 1891), p. 460.

36. The quotation is from Atey's preface to his unpublished 1595 translation of the *Relaciones* of Antonio Pérez, reproduced in Ungerer, *A Spaniard in Elizabethan England*, vol. II, doc. no. 502, p. 259. Atey's description of the dramatis personae of Pérez's account bears repetition simply for its felicity: "And the Actors are no lesse than the kinge of Spayne that now is Philippe the seconde of Castile, Don John de Austria, brother to him and sonne of an Emperor; a princesse of Ebolye, widowe of Ruygomez de Sylva, prince of Ebolye, Duke of Francavilla, the most inwarde favourite that ever was with kinge; Diego de Chaves, the ks Confessor, a notable hypochryticall fryar;" etc.

37. Badoero, "Relazione," pp. 241–242. See also the comments and analysis of William H. Prescott, *History of the Reign of Philip the Second, King of Spain* (1858) (Philadelphia, 1904), vol. IV, pp. 352–353.

38. Lansac de Saint-Gelais to the Cardinal of Lorraine, June 1559, in Paris, *Négociations . . . de Sébastien de l'Aubespine,* p. 177.

39. Antonio Pérez, "A un gran Privado," *Cartas de Antonio Perez* (Paris, [1598?]), fol. 73 obv. An excellent modern edition of these writings has recently appeared: Antonio Pérez, *Relaciones y cartas,* ed. by Alfredo Alvar Ezquerra, 2 vols. (Madrid, 1986).

40. Jorge Manrique to Ruy Gómez de Silva, from Turin, 8 August 1570, AGS Estado, leg. 1229, no. 52.

41. Marañón, *Antonio Pérez,* vol. I, pp. 39, 47. Marañón's vision of Philip is well summarized and seconded by Peter Pierson, *Philip II of Spain* (London, 1975), pp. 40–41.

42. Cabrera de Córdoba, *Felipe II,* vol. II, lib. X, cap. I, pp. 140–141.

43. Sigismondo Cavalli, "Relazione," in Eugenio Albèri, ed., *Le relazioni degli ambasciatori veneti al Senato durante il secolo decimosesto,* ser. I, vol. V (Florence, 1861), pp. 180–181.

44. Giovanni della Casa, *Galateo* (1558) (Boston, 1914), pp. 14–15.

45. Marañón, *Antonio Pérez,* vol. I, p. 39.

46. Ibid., pp. 47–49; Pierson, *Philip II of Spain,* pp. 40, 43ff.

47. M. d'Ozances to Charles IX, from Madrid, 19 December 1561, in Gachard, *Bibliothèque Nationale à Paris,* vol. II, p. 126.

48. Philip's predilection for Portuguese advisors was noted soon after the king's death by Agustín Manuel de Vasconcelos in *El libro de la Sucession de Felipe II en la Corona de Portugal,* quoted by Salazar y Castro, *Casa de Silva,* vol. II, p. 518.

49. Castiglione, *Courtier,* p. 112.

50. Ibid., p. 289.

51. Sydney Anglo, "The Courtier: The Renaissance and Changing Ideals," in *The Courts of Europe: Politics, Patronage and Royalty, 1400–1800,* ed. by A. G. Dickens (1977) (New York, 1984), p. 51.

52. Archbishop Rossano to Cardinal Alessandrino, from Madrid, 7 January 1567, in Louis-Prosper Gachard, ed., *Les Bibliothèques de Madrid et de l'Escurial* (Brussels, 1875), p. 96.

53. Gutierre López de Padilla to Ruy Gómez de Silva, 1557 (no date specified), AGS CJH, leg. 32, no. 122.

54. Antonio Pérez certainly had opportunity as a young man to study at the feet of Eboli, the "courtier-Aristotle." Ruy Gómez de Silva was instrumental in bringing Antonio, the illegitimate son of the secretary Gonzalo Pérez, to Philip's attention and in securing him a position as secretary for Italian affairs in the mid-1560s. Their relationship may indeed have been more binding than that of patron and client. Marañón, who studied the extant evidence exhaustively, refused to rule out the possibility, much bruited at Philip's court, that Antonio Pérez was actually Ruy Gómez's bastard (Marañón, *Antonio Pérez,* vol. I, pp. 27–30). He cites evidence indicating that Eboli's children by Doña Ana regarded Antonio as their father's son and finds otherwise inexplicable Pérez's nickname at the court of "El Portugués" (ibid., pp. 28–29). Moreover, Pérez's letter to Philip II of 29 July 1573

expresses filial devotion to the just-deceased Ruy Gómez (quoted in ibid., p. 29). Cf. Gaspar Muro, *Vida de la Princesa de Eboli* (Mexico City, 1883), app. 161, pp. 22–23, n. 1: Muro dismisses the notion of Ruy Gómez's paternity as "completely inadmissible." Whatever the truth of this speculation, it is clear that Antonio Pérez, along with Juan de Escobedo (whose murder was eventually to disgrace Antonio), spent considerable time as young men in Eboli's household and were both boosted into secretarial careers in the 1560s by Ruy Gómez de Silva. Escobedo served first the house of Mélito and then Ruy Gómez as a personal secretary from the late 1550s until the mid-1560s, and it is possible that Antonio performed some analogous role. In addition to Marañón, see James A. Froude, "Antonio Pérez: An Unsolved Historical Riddle," in *The Spanish Story of the Armada and Other Essays* (London, 1904), p. 127. On Escobedo, see Cabrera de Córdoba, *Felipe II*, vol. II, lib. XII, cap. III, p. 449; and Geoffrey Parker, *Philip II* (Boston, 1978), p. 131. For Escobedo's service, see, for example, Juan de Escobedo to Ruy Gómez de Silva, from Valladolid, 26 September 1557, *Colección de documentos inéditos para la historia de España* (cited henceforth as CODOIN) (Madrid, 1842–1895), vol. XCVII, pp. 292–295; and Luis de Requesens to Ruy Gómez de Silva, from Rome, 6 April 1564, in *Pio IV y Felipe Segundo*, ed. by "F. del V." and "S. K." (Madrid, 1891), pp. 287–288. Considerable correspondence between Ruy Gómez and Escobedo is preserved in AGS CJH and has been utilized in this work; see the inventory published by Margarita Cuartas Rivero, "Correspondencia del Príncipe de Eboli (1554–1569)," *Cuadernos de investigación histórica* 2 (1978), pp. 201–214.

55. Pérez, "A un amigo," *Cartas*, fol. 143 rev.; "A un gran privado," ibid., fol. 73 obv.

56. Pérez, "A un amigo," ibid., fol. 143 rev.

57. Pérez, "A un gran privado," ibid., fol. 72 rev.

58. Ibid., fol. 73.

59. Ibid., fols. 73–74.

60. Pérez, *Aphorismos*, fol. 14 obv.

61. Lagomarsino, "Court Factions," pp. 102–103, 121; Saint-Sulpice, in Cabié, *Ambassade en Espagne*, p. 357.

62. Saint-Sulpice to Charles IX, from Madrid, 16 March 1565, in Gachard, *Bibliothèque Nationale à Paris*, vol. II, p. 183. Curiously, the historian Amezúa y Mayo resorted to a similar ethnic slight in explaining Philip's choice of Alba for the Bayonne mission; in his view, "Eboli was too Portuguese—suave, tractable and acquiescent in the extreme," and thus could not handle the wily Catherine de' Medici as well as Alba, who, possessed of "a firm, energetic, resolute will, was more dominant when the occasion demanded, like a good Castilian" (Agustín G. de Amezúa y Mayo, *Isabel de Valois, Reina de España (1546–1568)*, 3 vols. [Madrid, 1949], vol. II, p. 200).

63. See Geoffrey Parker, *The Dutch Revolt* (Ithaca, 1977), pp. 66–67.

64. Granvelle to Viglius, from Besançon, 26 December 1564, in Weiss, *Cardinal de Granvelle*, vol. VIII, p. 570.

65. The most thorough account of Eraso's fall is in Lagomarsino, "Court Factions," pp. 136–147, 161. See also Francisco de Eraso to Don García de

Toledo, from Madrid, 12 May 1566, CODOIN, vol. XXX, pp. 239–241; Don García de Toledo to Francisco de Eraso, from Messina, 28 June 1566, CODOIN, vol. XXX, pp. 311–313; Parker, *Philip II*, p. 29.

66. On Espinosa's meteoric rise and career, see Prescott, *Philip the Second*, vol. IV, pp. 356–357; Louis-Prosper Gachard, *Don Carlos et Philippe II* (Paris, 1867), pp. 211–212; A. W. Lovett, "A Cardinal's Papers: the Rise of Mateo Vázquez de Leca," *English Historical Review* 88:347 (1973), p. 243, n. 2; Parker, *Philip II*, pp. 29–30, 104. Chinchón is quoted in Parker, *Philip II*, p. 30.

67. Luciano Serrano, ed., *Correspondencia diplómatica entre España y la Santa Sede durante el pontificado de S. Pio V* (Madrid, 1914), vol. II, p. lxxxiv.

68. Ruy Gómez de Silva to Juan de Escobedo, from Bosque de Segovia, 17 July 1566, AGS CJH, leg. 74, no. 3; same to same, 2 August 1566, ibid., no. 5.

69. Ruy Gómez de Silva to Juan de Escobedo, from Pellejeros, 22 August 1566, AGS CJH, leg. 74, no. 9.

70. For Egmont's ties to Ruy Gómez de Silva, see Lagomarsino, "Court Factions," pp. 95–102; the letter sent by Montigny and Berghes is reproduced in Adela Repetto Alvarez, "Acerca de un posible Segundo Gobierno de Margarita de Parma y el Cardenal de Granvela en los Estados de Flandes" *Hispania* 32:121 (1972), doc. 75, p. 474. Further evidence of the sympathy between the Netherlandish lords and Ruy Gómez is plentiful; for examples, see Philip II to Margaret of Parma, from Madrid, 3 April 1565, précis in Louis-Prosper Gachard, ed., *Correspondance de Philippe II sur les affaires des Pays-Bas, 1558–1577*, vol. I (Brussels, 1848), p. 348, and Berghes and Montigny to Margaret of Parma, from Segovia, 31 August 1566, in H. A. Enno van Gelder, ed., *Correspondance française de Marguerite d'Autriche, duchesse de Parme, avec Philippe II* (Utrecht, 1941), vol. II, p. 363.

71. No minutes of this meeting have survived; the most contemporary accounts are those of Cabrera de Córdoba, *Felipe II*, vol. I, lib. VII, cap. VII, pp. 490–497, and of Ossorio, *Vida y hazañas*, pp. 336–343. Many historians have analyzed the options presented and the decision to send Alba, but none have provided an account as thorough as that of Lagomarsino, "Court Factions," pp. 254–264. Despite his opposition to this course, Ruy Gómez seems to have believed as late as August 1566 that Philip would go in person to the Low Countries (see Ruy Gómez de Silva to Juan de Escobedo, from Pellejeros, 11 August 1566, AGS CJH, leg. 74, no. 7).

72. Morillon to Granvelle, from Ruckelingen, 19 November 1566, in Edmond Poullet, ed., *Correspondance du Cardinal de Granvelle, 1565–1586*, vol. II (Brussels, 1880), p. 115.

73. Fourquevaulx to Charles IX, from Madrid, 9 December 1566, in Gachard, *Bibliothèque Nationale à Paris*, vol. II, p. 226.

74. Ossorio, *Vida y hazañas*, p. 341.

75. Morillon to Granvelle, from Brussels, 17 November 1566, in Poullet, *Correspondance du Cardinal de Granvelle*, vol. II, p. 107.

76. Fourquevaulx to Charles IX, c.4 January 1567, in Gachard, *Bibliothèque Nationale à Paris*, vol. II, p. 226.

77. Bave to Granvelle, from Brussels, 14 September 1564, in Weiss,

Cardinal de Granvelle, vol. VIII, p. 323; Saint-Sulpice to Charles IX or his ministers, from Madrid, 7 October 1564, in Cabié, *Ambassade en Espagne,* p. 305; Salazar y Castro, *Casa de Silva,* vol. II, p. 488. Ruy Gómez assumed this post on 11 August 1564 (L.-P. Gachard, *Don Carlos y Felipe II* (San Lorenzo de el Escorial, 1984), p. 128.

78. Saint-Sulpice, as reported in Muro, *Vida de la Princesa de Eboli,* ch. II, p. 138, n. 6.

79. Saint-Sulpice to Catherine de' Medici, from Madrid, 7 October 1564, in Gachard, *Bibliothèque Nationale à Paris,* vol. II, p. 177.

80. Gachard, *Don Carlos y Felipe II,* p. 128; Lagomarsino, "Court Factions," pp. 103–104.

81. Cabrera de Córdoba, *Felipe II,* vol. I, lib. VI, cap. XXVIII, p. 458; Salazar y Castro, *Casa de Silva,* vol. II, p. 489.

82. Fourquevaulx to Charles IX, c. 4 January 1567, in Gachard, *Bibliothèque Nationale à Paris,* vol. II, pp. 226–227.

83. Fourquevaulx to Catherine de' Medici, 24 August 1567, ibid., pp. 246–247; for the enemies list, Castagna to Cardinal Alessandrino, from Madrid, 30 March 1568, in Serrano, *Correspondencia diplómatica,* vol. II, p. 335.

84. See his comments to this effect reported by Fourquevaulx, "Avis secret au roy," 30 June 1567, in Gachard, *Bibliothèque Nationale à Paris,* vol. II, p. 243.

85. Fourquevaulx to Catherine de' Medici, 24 August 1567, ibid., pp. 246–247.

86. Quoted in Fourquevaulx to Catherine de' Medici, from Madrid, 29 November 1569, ibid., p. 294.

87. Gachard, *Don Carlos et Philippe II,* pp. 149–150.

88. Giovanni Soranzo, "Relazione," in Eugenio Albèri, ed., *Le relazioni degli ambasciatori veneti al Senato durante il secolo decimosesto,* ser. I, vol. V (Florence, 1861), p. 89.

89. Cavalli, "Relazione," p. 181.

90. Fourquevaulx to Catherine de' Medici, 21 August 1567, in Gachard, *Bibliothèque Nationale à Paris,* vol. II, p. 246; Same to same, 12 September 1567, ibid., p. 247; Rossano to Cardinal Alessandrino, from Madrid, 4 February 1568, in Gachard, *Bibliothèques de Madrid et de l'Escurial,* p. 108; Amezúa y Mayo, *Isabel de Valois,* vol. II, p. 417. For the house in Santa María, and the transaction that brought it to Ruy Gómez de Silva, see the latter's will (AHN Osuna, leg. 2024, no. 13¹), and Marañón, *Antonio Pérez,* vol. I, p. 54.

91. Philip II to Ruy Gómez de Silva, from the Escorial, 16 May 1567, in Gachard, *Correspondance de Philippe II,* vol. I, pp. 535–536.

92. Fourquevaulx to Charles IX, from Madrid, 21 May 1567, in Gachard, *Bibliothèque Nationale à Paris,* vol. II, p. 238; Antonio Pérez to Philip II, from Madrid, 17 May 1567, in Gachard, *Correspondance de Philippe II,* vol. I, pp. 536–537; Ruy Gómez de Silva to the Duchess of Parma, from Madrid, 21 May 1567, in Gachard, *Correspondance de Philippe II,* vol. I, p. 537; Antonio Pérez to Philip II, from Madrid, 21 May 1567, in Gachard, *Correspondance de Philippe II,* vol. I, pp. 537–538; Duchess of Parma to Ruy Gómez de Silva,

from Antwerp, 1 June 1567, in Gachard, *Correspondance de Philippe II*, vol. I, pp. 543–544; Gabriel de Çayas to Duke of Alburquerque, from Madrid, 23 May 1567, AGS Estado, leg. 1222, no. 123.

93. Morillon to Granvelle, from St.-Amand, 10 July 1567, in Poullet, *Correspondance du Cardinal de Granvelle*, vol. II, p. 522.

94. Ruy Gómez de Silva to the Duchess of Parma, from Madrid, 6 October 1567, Gachard, *Correspondance de Philippe II*, vol. I, p. 583.

95. Rossano to Cardinal Alessandrino, from Madrid, 17 April 1568, in Gachard, *Bibliothèques de Madrid et de l'Escurial*, pp. 109–110; Gachard, *Correspondance de Philippe II*, vol. I, p. lx; Serrano, *Correspondencia diplomática*, vol. II, pp. lxxiv–lxxv.

96. Serrano, *Correspondencia diplómatica*, vol. II, p. lxxvii.

97. See Castagna [the nuncio, Archbishop Rossano] to Cardinal Alessandrino, from Madrid, 22 March 1567, ibid., p. 86; Fourquevaulx, despatch of 24 March 1567, in Gachard, *Bibliothèque Nationale à Paris*, vol. II, p. 234.

98. Rossano to Cardinal Alessandrino, from Madrid, 1 May 1568, in Gachard, *Bibliothèques de Madrid et de l'Escurial*, p. 111; same to same, 11 July 1568, ibid., pp. 112–113; for the nephew's advancement, Gabriel de Çayas to Duke of Alburquerque, from Madrid, 11 January 1567(?), AGS Estado, leg. 1222, no. 115.

99. Fourquevaulx to Catherine de' Medici, from Madrid, 6 August 1569, in Gachard, *Bibliothèque Nationale à Paris*, vol. II, p. 290; same to same, 4 September 1570, ibid., p. 313. See also Fourquevaulx to Charles IX, from Madrid, 29 November 1569, ibid., p. 293. For more in the same vein, see Note 66.

100. Fourquevaulx to Charles IX, from Madrid, 7 September 1571, in Gachard, *Bibliothèque Nationale à Paris*, vol. II, p. 346.

101. Salazar y Castro, *Casa de Silva*, vol. II, pp. 528–539; Muro, *Vida de la Princesa de Eboli*, ch. II, pp. 122–123, n. 9.

102. The estimate, almost certainly too high, is from Soranzo, "Relazione," p. 89.

103. The accounts of the estate of Mélito for the period of Ruy Gómez's management are summarized in "Relacion del dinero que se ha cobrado del estado de Melito y la Mendolia desde principio del año 1557 que esta a cargo del s^r Mardones en adelante/. y razon de como se ha gastado," AHN Osuna, leg. 2078, no. 2. The receiver Mardones concluded that, after necessary expenses, "7760 ducats remain as the true [annual] value [of the estate], and in order for it to reach even this sum it is necessary that wheat be valued at eight *reales*, and in the year that it is not, this value will drop in proportion as the wheat falls. Also it must be borne in mind that year in and year out a *servicio extraordinario* of nearly 1000 ducats will be paid [further diminishing the yield of the estate]." The quotations concerning the condition of Mileto, the count's properties, and the lack of justice are from the report of Father Joan Hieronimo Domenes, AGS, Visitas de Italia, leg. 348, no. 14. More information on conditions on the estate along with initiatives to improve them may be found in AHN Osuna, leg. 2077, no. 25.

104. For the origins and dimensions of the family dispute, see CODOIN, vol. XCVII, pp. 285–356. The situation is summarized in Erika Spivakovsky, "La Princesa de Eboli," *Chronica Nova* 9 (1974), pp. 5–48. Some insights into the subsequent unfolding of the conflict are available from various letters of Juan de Escobedo to Ruy Gómez de Silva, from Valladolid, 26 September 1557, AGS CJH, leg. 32, no. 120, 16 October 1557, AGS CJH, leg. 32, no. 121 (the source for the quotation regarding the duchess's grumbling), and 5 November 1557, AGS CJH, leg. 32, no. 124; from AHN Osuna, leg. 2038, no. 7; from a letter of Don Luis de Requesens, in José M. March, "Una novia díscola comparada por Requesens a la Princesa de Eboli," *Razón y Fe* 145:650 (March 1952), pp. 289–290; from Marañón, *Antonio Pérez*, vol. I, pp. 171–176. See AGS Estado, leg. 515, no. 106, for Philip's summons to Francavila, 1557. For Francavila's support of Alba, see Alfonso Danvila y Burguero, *Don Cristóbal de Moura, primer Marqués de Castel-Rodrigo (1538–1613)* (Madrid, 1900), p. 197. Ruy Gómez's comments regarding his familial burden are in Ruy Gómez de Silva to Juan de Escobedo, from Aranjuez, 6 June 1563, AGS CJH, leg. 50, no. 272.

105. The claim against Doña Ana's inheritance was pressed by her first cousin Don Iñigo de Mendoza, subsequently marquis of Almenara. For the legal arguments and their basis, see AHN Osuna, leg. 2080, nos. 9^2 and 9^3. See also Marañón, *Antonio Pérez*, vol. I, p. 139. For some more general remarks on litigation over female inheritance, see J. P. Cooper, "Patterns of inheritance and settlement by great landowners from the fifteenth to the eighteenth centuries," in *Family and Inheritance: Rural Society in Western Europe, 1200–1800,* ed. by Jack Goody, Joan Thirsk and E. P. Thompson (Cambridge, 1976), pp. 251–252.

106. Castiglione, *Courtier*, p. 285.

107. Pérez, *Aphorismos*, fol. 10 rev.

108. Ibid., fol. 25 obv.

109. Pérez, *Cartas*, fols. 143–144.

110. Antonio de Guevara, *Libro primero de las epístolas familiares* (Madrid, 1950), vol. I, no. 32 (7 January 1535).

111. Diego de Hermosilla, *Diálogo de los pajes* (Madrid, 1901), p. 4.

112. Guevara, *Epístolas familiares*, vol. I, no. 32.

113. Pérez, *Cartas*, fol. 145 obv.

114. Chantonnay to Granvelle, from Vienna, 12 May 1565, in Weiss, *Cardinal de Granvelle*, vol. IX (Paris, 1852), p. 186.

115. Same to same, 2 June 1565, ibid., pp. 187–188.

116. See Ulloa, *La hacienda real*, pp. 163–169. For more information on the alienation of Crown and military-order lands in the sixteenth century, see Helen Nader, *Liberty in Absolutist Spain: The Habsburg Sale of Towns, 1516–1700* (Baltimore, 1990), esp. ch. 4; Joan Reglà Campistol, "La época de los tres primeros Austrias," in *Historia social y económica de España y América*, ed. by Jaime Vicens Vives (Barcelona, 1972), vol. III, p. 55; Fernand Braudel, *The Mediterranean and the Mediterranean World in the Age of Philip II* (New York, 1976), vol. II, p. 711.

117. AHN Osuna, leg. 2015, nos. 1, 2[1].

118. Ruy Gómez de Silva to Juan de Escobedo, from Estremera, March 1561, AGS CJH, leg. 42, no. 161; Ruiz de Velasco to Juan de Escobedo, March 1561, ibid.

119. AHN Osuna, leg. 2224, no. 2[1-17]; AHN Osuna, leg. 2031, nos. 2–3; Ruy Gómez de Silva to Juan de Escobedo, from Madrid, 8 October 1562, AGS CJH, leg. 46, no. 85; Salazar y Castro, *Casa de Silva,* vol. II, pp. 495–497; and Mariano Pérez y Cuenca, *Historia de Pastrana y sucinta noticia de los pueblos de su partido* (Madrid, 1858), pp. 30–32. There is a vast amount of documentation for Ruy Gómez's purchases of property and jurisdictions in the 1560s. A full inventory of the estate appears in the *mayorazgo* of Pastrana (many copies exist; I have worked from AHN Osuna, leg. 2326, no. 9[1]).

120. The contract of sale is in AHN Osuna, leg. 2502, no. 1. For information on Francisco de Mendoza's prior purchase of these properties upon their "dismemberment" from the Order of Santiago in 1559, see Ulloa, *La hacienda real,* p. 168. On Mendoza himself, see Diego Gutiérrez Coronel, *Historia genealógica de la casa de Mendoza* (1772) (Madrid, 1946), p. 338; Cabrera de Córdoba, *Felipe II,* vol. I, lib. VI, cap. XV, p. 395, and vol. III, lib. IV, cap. III, pp. 354–356.

121. AHN Osuna, leg. 2015, no. 8[4]; AHN, Sección Consejos Suprimidos 36,253, P. 13; AHN Osuna, leg. 2708, "Alcav[s] Cajon 13"; AHN Osuna, leg. 2032, no. 5[1-2]; AHN Osuna, leg. 2326, no. 9[1]; Salazar y Castro, *Casa de Silva,* vol. II, pp. 490–491.

122. Ruy Gómez de Silva to Juan de Escobedo, from Aranjuez, 6 June 1563, AGS CJH, leg. 50, no. 272.

123. Salazar y Castro, *Casa de Silva,* vol. II, pp. 509–511; AHN Consejos, leg. 36,253, P. 13; Silverio de Santa Teresa, *Obras de Santa Teresa de Jesús,* vol. VI (Burgos, 1919), pp. 136–137; Marañón, *Antonio Pérez,* vol. I, pp. 172–173; Gerald Brenan, *San Juan de la Cruz* (Barcelona, 1974), pp. 26–29.

124. Ruy Gómez de Silva to Juan de Escobedo, from Pellejeros, 12 July 1566, AGS CJH, leg. 74, no. 1; same to same, 2 August 1566, ibid., no. 5; same to same, from Pellejeros, 11 August 1566, ibid., no. 7; same to same, from Pellejeros, 22 August 1566, ibid., no. 9; same to same, from Albalate, 22 November 1566, ibid., no. 14.

125. Ruy Gómez de Silva to Juan de Escobedo, 1568 (no day or month specified), AGS CJH, leg. 90, no. 28.

126. Purchase prices and Grimaldo's involvement in the Estremera–Valdaracete transaction are from contracts cited above. Debts to Herrera and the Fuggers are listed and itemized in AHN Consejos 36,253, P. 13. Part of Herrera's involvement appears to have been in refinancing Eboli's debt to the Fuggers on more favorable terms with other financiers; see Melchor de Herrera to Ruy Gómez de Silva, from Seville, 29 November 1566, AGS CJH, leg. 82, no. 314. For the sale of Eboli and Grimaldo's ducal title, see AHN Osuna, leg. 2708, "Razon de los papeles . . . tocantes a quentas con Nicolao de Grimaldo," AHN, Sección Ordenes Militares, Pruebas de Caballeros de Alcántara, expediente 660, and Salazar y Castro, *Casa de Silva,*

vol. II, pp. 481–482. For the related sale of Rapolla, see Lope de Mardones to Ruy Gómez de Silva, from Naples, 7 January 1566, AGS CJH, leg. 82, no. 307; Duke of Francavila to Ruy Gómez de Silva, from Barcelona, 7 March 1568, AGS CJH, leg. 90, no. 8; Ruy Gómez de Silva to Duke of Francavila(?), 1568(?), AGS CJH, leg. 90, no. 29. Grimaldo had been involved as a receiver and guarantor in an earlier effort to sell Eboli and related properties to Tomás de Marín, and it is possible that his eventual acquisition of these estates resulted from foreclosing on Marín or his heirs; this confusing transaction can be followed, up to a point, in letters of 1562–1563 from Ruy Gómez to Escobedo in Naples, AGS CJH, leg. 46, nos. 86–90, and leg. 50, no. 269.

127. "Razon de los papeles . . . ," AHN Osuna, leg. 2708.

128. Saint-Sulpice to Charles IX and Catherine de' Medici, 21 November 1564, in Cabié, *Ambassade en Espagne*, p. 317; De l'Aubespine to Saint-Sulpice, from Montpellier, 26 December 1564, ibid., p. 327; Saint-Sulpice to Vicomte d'Orthe, 6 February 1565, ibid., p. 346. For earlier instances of Grimaldo's interest in obtaining *licencias de saca* to remove bullion from Spain, see "El assiento que se tomo en España con nicolo de grimaldo de un millon de escudos," AGS Estado, leg. 129, no. 233, and Braudel, *The Mediterranean*, vol. I, p. 481.

129. For the important roles played by Herrera and Grimaldo in the crown finances, and for allegations of corruption against them, see Ulloa, *La hacienda real, passim*; A. W. Lovett, *Philip II and Mateo Vázquez de Leca: The Government of Spain (1572–1592)* (Geneva, 1977), pp. 60–61, 101; Cabrera de Córdoba, *Felipe II*, vol. III, lib. IV, cap. XIII, p. 447; David Ebron to Philip II, from Costantina, 9 December 1597, in Berwick y de Alba, *Documentos escogidos . . . de la casa de Alba*, p. 233; Marañón, *Antonio Pérez*, vol. I, pp. 82–83; Henri Lapeyre, *Simon Ruiz et les 'asientos' de Philippe II* (Paris, 1953), p. 43.

130. Cavalli, "Relazione," p. 181.

131. Saint-Sulpice to Charles IX, from Madrid, 16 March 1565, in Gachard, *Bibliothèque Nationale à Paris*, vol. II, p. 182. The sale had been concluded on 10 March 1565 (AHN Osuna, leg. 2502, no. 1).

132. Ruy Gómez de Silva to Juan de Escobedo, from Madrid, 14 April 1562, AGS CJH, leg. 46, no. 94.

133. Ruy Gómez de Silva to Juan de Escobedo, from Barcelona, 6 March 1564, AGS CJH, leg. 50, no. 260.

134. AGS Escribanía Mayor de Rentas, Quitaciones de Corte, leg. 39, fol. 687.

135. AGS Contaduría de Mercedes, leg. 486, no. 8.

136. See, for instance, ibid., nos. 9–10.

137. Donato, "Relación," in Cabrera de Córdoba, *Felipe II*, vol. IV, p. 418.

138. Milio to Juan de Albornoz, from Madrid, 14 August 1573, in Berwick y de Alba, *Documentos escogidos . . . de la Casa de Alba*, p. 459.

139. AGS Contaduría de Mercedes, leg. 363, no. 24.

140. Antonio Tiepolo, "Relazione di Antonio Tiepolo tornato ambasciatore straordinario dalle corti di Spagna e di Portogallo nel 1572," in Eugenio

Albèri, ed., *Le relazioni degli ambasciatori veneti al Senato durante il secolo decimosesto*, ser. I, vol. V (Florence, 1861), p. 220.

141. For use of this "title," see for example AHN Osuna, leg. 1731, no.
16⁸, AGS Contaduría de Mercedes, leg. 486, no. 8, and AGS Estado, leg.
1229, no. 79; see also Salazar y Castro, *Casa de Silva*, vol. II, pp. 492–493.
Doubtless more accurate is the title granted Ruy Gómez in a royal *carta de
venta* of 1567: "señor de las villas de estremera y baldarazete" (AHN Osuna,
leg. 2015, no. 8⁴).

142. The marriage capitulations of 3 June 1566 and the duke's subsequent ratification may be found in AHN Osuna, leg. 2029, no. 22 and leg.
2030, no. 2. The betrothal by proxies is recorded in AHN Osuna, leg. 2030,
no. 1. For the payment of the dowry, see AHN Osuna, leg. 2030, nos. 10–11,
and for the expenses—6,000 ducats—incurred by the bride's family in connection with the 1574 wedding, AHN Consejos, leg. 36,253, P. 13. A fine
modern account of this marriage is provided in Peter Pierson, *Commander
of the Armada: The Seventh Duke of Medina Sidonia* (New Haven, 1989), pp.
13–18. See also Muro, *Vida de la Princesa de Eboli*, ch. II, pp. 116–117, n. 19;
David Howarth, *The Voyage of the Armada: The Spanish Story* (Harmondsworth, 1982), pp. 21–22.

143. For Medina Sidonia motives, see Pierson, *Commander of the Armada*,
pp. 13–17.

144. Ruy Gómez de Silva to Juan de Escobedo, from Pellejeros, 24 September 1566, AGS CJH, leg. 50, no. 259.

145. For the basic outlines, see Salazar y Castro, *Casa de Silva*, vol. II, pp.
696–697. According to a summary in the second contract (Colmenar de Oreja, 27 December 1571, AHN Osuna, leg. 2029, no. 17), the first contract had
been signed at Madrid on 9 February 1567. Ruy Gómez de Silva to Duke
of Alburquerque, from Madrid, October(?) 1570, AGS Estado, leg. 1227, no.
196, reports the first match, involving Don Rodrigo. By *cédula* (Aranjuez, 29
April 1572, AHN Osuna, leg. 1859, no. 2), Philip II granted Eboli and Doña
Ana leave to form the *mayorazgo* for Don Ruy Gómez that was stipulated
in the 1571 contract. (Incidentally, Don Ruy Gómez was the couple's third
surviving son when he was engaged to Doña Luisa de Cárdenas, his next
older brother, Don Pedro González de Mendoza, having died in December
1571.) For the demise of Cárdenas, see Cabrera de Córdoba, *Felipe II*, vol. II,
lib. IX, cap. XXV, p. 114. For the problematic match between Don Diego and
Doña Luisa, see AHN Osuna, leg. 1838, no. 14; AHN Consejos, leg. 4409
(año 1584), no. 84; AHN Consejos, leg. 36,253 for records of some of the
subsequent litigation. See also Cabrera de Córdoba, *Felipe II*, vol. III, lib. V,
cap. VII, p. 504.

146. Salazar y Castro, *Casa de Silva*, vol. II, pp. 529–539. For Savoy's offer
and Eboli's response, see Jorge Manrique to Ruy Gómez de Silva, from Turin, 8 August 1570, AGS Estado, leg. 1229, no. 50, and Ruy Gómez de Silva
to Duke of Savoy, from Madrid, 4 October 1570, AGS Estado, leg. 1227, no.
124. In AHN Osuna, leg. 2024, no. 15 (17 December 1571), the Franciscan
house "outside the walls" of Pastrana certifies the interment of Don Pedro

González. See also Manuel Santaolalla Llanas, *Pastrana: Apuntes de su historia, arte y tradiciones* (Pastrana, 1979), p. 12.

147. AHN Osuna, leg. 2326, no. 9[1]. The *juros* included in the entail amount to a nominal yearly income of 22,099 ducats, plus a considerable quantity of grain.

148. AHN Osuna, leg. 1731, no. 15[12]; Gutiérrez Coronel, *Casa de Mendoza*, p. 569, erroneously places this event on 20 December 1571.

149. A Castilian ducal title carried with it an automatic grandeeship. See Antonio Domínguez Ortiz, *La sociedad española en el siglo XVII*, vol. I (Madrid, 1964), pp. 214–215.

150. Salazar y Castro, *Casa de Silva*, vol. II, p. 499.

151. Cardinal F. Pacheco de Toledo to Juan de Albornoz, from Rome, 13 January 1571 (1572 N.S.), in Berwick y de Alba, *Documentos escogidos . . . de la casa de Alba*, pp. 454–455.

152. See, among others, St.-Gouard to Charles IX, from Madrid, 31 May 1572, in Gachard, *Bibliothèque Nationale à Paris*, vol. II, p. 370, for early signs of Espinosa's loss of favor. In *Philip II of Spain* (New York, 1969), p. 193, Martin A. S. Hume presents the traditional version of Espinosa's fall from grace and subsequent death, but Luciano Serrano, while not disputing the king's growing coolness, attributes the cardinal's death to ill health and overwork (*Correspondencia diplomática*, vol. II, p. lxxxiii).

153. Antonio Domínguez Ortiz, *Notas para una periodización del reinado de Felipe II* (Valladolid, 1984), pp. 42–43, quotations from p. 43.

154. Zayas to Albornoz, from Madrid, 5 July 1571, in Gachard, *Correspondance de Philippe II*, vol. II, p. 179. Ruy Gómez had accompanied the king to Andalusia in 1570 and spoke in oblique opposition to Espinosa in the conciliar meetings held at Córdoba. See "Lo q parescio en c° destado con el Car[al] sobrelos neg[os] q ha traydo don Jorge Manrrique, en cordova a xvi de abril 1570," AGS Estado, leg. 1229, no. 26.

155. Leonardo Donà and Lorenzo Priuli to the Senate, from Madrid, 5 December 1572, in Mario Brunetti and Eligio Vitale, eds., *La Corrispondenza da Madrid dell'ambasciatore Leonardo Donà (1570–1573)* (Venice, 1963), vol. II, pp. 608–609.

156. See Note 36.

157. For reports of Ruy Gómez's repeated sojourns in Pastrana, see Ruy Gómez de Silva to Jorge Manrique, from Pastrana, 4 January 1571, AGS Estado, leg. 1229, no. 125; Leonardo Donà to the Senate, from Madrid, 2 April 1571, in Brunetti and Vitale, *La Corrispondenza*, vol. I, p. 254; same to same, 22 May 1571, in Brunetti and Vitale, *La Corrispondenza*, vol. I, p. 282; Donà and Lorenzo Priuli to the Senate, from Madrid, 18 March 1573, in Brunetti and Vitale, *La Corrispondenza*, vol. II, p. 666; same to same, 1 May 1573, in Brunetti and Vitale, *La Corrispondenza*, vol. II, p. 699.

158. For some notion of his visits to Albalate and Estremera in 1567–1568, see AGS CJH, leg. 82, nos. 341–343, and AGS CJH, leg. 90, nos. 25–27. Ruy Gómez de Silva to Juan de Escobedo, from Albalate, 2 September 1568, AGS CJH, leg. 90, no. 27, reports preparations for a brief visit to Madrid.

159. Melchor de Herrera to Ruy Gómez de Silva, from Medina del Campo, 4 October 1568, AGS CJH, leg. 90, no. 13; Jorge Manrique to Ruy Gómez de Silva, from Milan, 12 August 1570, AGS Estado, leg. 1229, no. 55; same to same, from Milan, 17 August 1570, AGS Estado, leg. 1229, no. 58; same to same, from Turin, 25 August 1570, AGS Estado, leg. 1229, no. 68.

160. Juan de Mariana, *Historia general de España* (Valencia, 1794), vol. II, p. 709.

CONCLUSION

Source for epigraph: Antonio Pérez, *Aphorismos de las cartas españolas y latinas de Ant. Perez* (Paris, [1598?]), fol. 8 rev.

1. Guy Chaussinand-Nogaret, *The French Nobility in the Eighteenth Century* (Cambridge, 1985), p. 7.

2. See Charles V to Philip, "Carta autógrafa e instrucción secreta de 6 de mayo de 1543," in José M. March, ed., *Niñez y juventud de Felipe II* (Madrid, 1941–1942), vol. II, p. 27.

3. Antonio Pérez, *Aphorismos*, fol. 6 obv.

4. Bartolomé Bennassar, *La España del siglo de oro* (Barcelona, 1983), pp. 49–50.

5. Garrett Mattingly, *Renaissance Diplomacy* (Boston, 1971), pp. 228–229.

6. The term of derision "partos de la pluma" was coined by Matías de Novoa, a seventeenth-century partisan of the duke of Lerma. Quoted by Modesto Ulloa, *Las rentas de algunos señores y señoríos castellanos bajo los primeros Austria* (Montevideo, 1971), p. 12.

7. Antonio Pérez, *Aphorismos*, fol. 6 rev.

8. Antonio Pérez, "A un gran privado," *Cartas de Antonio Perez* (Paris, [1598?]), fol. 73 obv.

9. Antonio Tiepolo, "Relazione di Antonio Tiepolo tornato ambasciatore straordinario dalle corti di Spagna e di Portogallo nel 1572," in Eugenio Albèri, ed., *Le relazione degli ambasciatori veneti al Senato durante il secolo decimosesto,* ser. I, vol. V (Florence, 1861), p. 220.

10. Quoted by Geoffrey Parker, *Philip II* (Boston, 1978), p. 30.

11. Quoted by Ciríaco Pérez Bustamante, *Felipe III. Semblanza de un monarca y perfiles de una privanza* (Madrid, 1950), p. 41.

12. Baltasar Porreño, *Dichos y hechos del rey D. Felipe II* (1628) (Madrid, 1942), pp. 6–7.

Glossary

alcabala: tax on commercial transactions, forming one of the basic revenues of the Castilian Crown and, when alienated, a principal source of noble income.

alcalde: magistrate.

alcázar: royal fortress and/or palace.

alfoz: municipal territory; town or village administratively dependent on another.

apellido: surname.

arras: jointure; endowment of the bride by the groom as a precondition of marriage.

ayuda de costa: subsidy or gratuity granted by the Crown to defray expenses incurred in royal service.

bando: faction, party.

caballerizo mayor: master of the horse in the royal household.

caballero: knight; member of one of the Spanish military orders.

clavero: literally, keeper of the keys; holder of one of the highest posts (the *clavería*) in the military order of Calatrava.

comendador: knight-commander; holder of an *encomienda* in one of the Spanish military orders.

comuneros: adherents of the urban-centered Castilian revolt against Charles V, 1520–1521.

contador mayor de Castilla: literally, chief accountant or auditor; under Philip II, a leading position in the fiscal bureaucracy, carrying with it a seat on the Council of Finance (Hacienda).

cortes: parliamentary institutions of the Spanish kingdoms (*corts* in Catalonia and Valencia).

criado: servant, client, creature.

cruzada: indulgence revenues granted to the Crown by the papacy, in theory to defray the expenses of crusading.

donativo: donation offered by the privileged orders to the Crown, usually in the form of a forced loan.

dote: dowry, marriage portion.

ducat (*ducado*): Castilian unit of account (prior to 1537, a gold coin), worth 375 *maravedís* or eleven silver *reales*, one *maravedí*.

encomienda: estates and revenues assigned to a *comendador* of the military orders.

escudo: heraldic shield, coat-of-arms; also, a Castilian gold coin, worth 350 (from 1566, 400) *maravedís.*

grandees (*grandes de España*): the elite among the titled aristocracy of Spain; initially, twenty-five titles were granted the status of *grandeza* (grandeeship) by Charles V.

hábito: distinctive vestment worn by knights of the military orders; "taking the *hábito*" was shorthand for initiation into the order.

hidalgo (Portug. *fidalgo*): person of noble blood.

infante: legitimate son of a king or prince; not used of the current heir to the throne (*príncipe*).

juro: perpetual or term annuity, secured on the Crown revenues of Castile; sometimes granted to individuals as reward for services; more often Crown creditors received *juros* in return for lump-sum loans. (In deference to usury prohibitions, such loans were thinly disguised as annuity purchases; in perhaps the most usual case, the purchaser would receive an annuity equivalent to $\frac{1}{14}$ of the original loan—or a return of 7.14 percent per year—until the Crown redeemed the *juro* by repayment of the original principal.)

maravedí: Castilian unit of account (0.00266 ducat).

mayorazgo: entail, heritable trust; establishment of a *mayorazgo* created a perpetual impartible estate for the lineage designated by its founders.

mayordomo mayor: chief steward of the household of a royal personage; most exalted of the household posts in the service of Philip II.

merced (pl. *mercedes*): royal gift to a subject or servant.

padrinos: godparents, sponsors.

privado: king's favorite and intimate counselor, enjoying influence in the state by virtue of this position (of *privanza*).

procuradores: voting delegates in the Castilian *cortes.*

reguengos: royal revenues (Portug.)

ricos-hombres: literally, rich men; medieval designation of elite aristocrats in peninsular kingdoms.

segundón: younger son of a noble house.

subsidio: tax on clerical income granted to the Crown by the papacy.

sumiller de corps: first gentleman of the king's bedchamber in the Castilian royal household.

tercias or *tercias reales:* two-ninths of ecclesiastical tithe income, belonging to the Crown under terms of a papal grant.

trinchante: literally, a carver; position in royal household, entailing service at table.

valido: king's favorite or *privado;* in the seventeenth century, *valido* status (*valimiento*) included more or less explicit royal grant of ministerial powers.

Bibliography

MANUSCRIPT COLLECTIONS (with abbreviations used in notes)

Archivo General de Simancas (AGS)
  Consejo y Juntas de Hacienda (CJH)
  Contaduría de Mercedes
  Escribanía Mayor de Rentas, Quitaciones de Corte (EMR–QC)
  Guerra y Marina
  Patronato Real
  Secretaría de Estado (Estado)
  Visitas de Italia
Archivo Histórico Nacional, Madrid (AHN)
  Sección Consejos Suprimidos
  Sección Ordenes Militares
  Sección Osuna
Biblioteca Nacional, Madrid (BN)
  Manuscritos

PRINTED DOCUMENTS AND CONTEMPORARY WORKS

Alba, Duque de, ed. *Epistolario del III Duque de Alba, Don Fernando Alvarez de Toledo.* 3 vols. Madrid: La Casa de Alba, 1952.

Albèri, Eugenio, ed. *Le relazioni degli ambasciatori veneti al Senato durante il secolo decimosesto.* Series I. Vol. III. Florence: Società Editrice Fiorentina, 1853. Vol. V. Florence: A spese dell'editore, 1861. Vol. VI. Florence: A spese dell'editore, 1862.

Archivo documental español. Vol. I. *Negociaciones con Francia (1559–1560).*

Beer, Barrett L., and Sybil M. Jack, eds. "The Letters of William, Lord Paget of Beaudesert, 1547–1563." In *Camden Miscellany,* vol. XXV. Camden Fourth Series, vol. XIII. London: Royal Historical Society, 1974. Pp. 1–141.

Berwick y de Alba, Duquesa de, ed. *Documentos escogidos del archivo de la Casa de Alba* (DECA). Madrid, 1891.

Boethius. *The Consolation of Philosophy.* Edited and translated by Richard Green. New York: Macmillan Library of Liberal Arts, 1962.

Brantôme, Pierre de Bourdeille, Seigneur de. *Oeuvres Complètes.* Edited by Ludovic Lalanne. Vols. I, II, and VII. Paris: Renouard, 1864–1873.

Brunetti, Mario, and Eligio Vitale, eds. *La Corrispondenza da Madrid dell'am-*

basciatore Leonardo Donà (1570–1573). Foreword by Fernand Braudel. 2 vols. Venice and Rome: Istituto per la Collaborazione Culturale, 1963.

Cabié, Edmond, ed. *Ambassade en Espagne de Jean Ebrard, Seigneur de Saint-Sulpice, de 1562 a 1565 et mission de ce diplomate dans le même pays en 1566.* Paris: Librairie Alph. Picard et Fils, 1903.

Cabrera de Córdoba, Luis. *Historia de Felipe II, rey de España.* 4 vols. Madrid: Imprenta, Estereotipia y Galvanoplastia de Aribau y Cᵃ (sucesores de Rivadeneyra), Impresores de Cámara de S. M., 1876–1877.

Calendar of Letters and State Papers relating to English Affairs, Preserved Principally in the Archives of Simancas. Edited by Martin A. S. Hume. Vol. I. London: Eyre and Spottiswood for H.M.S.O., 1892.

Calendar of Letters, Despatches and State Papers relating to the Negotiations between England and Spain, Preserved in the Archives at Vienna, Simancas, Besancon, Brussels, Madrid and Lille. Edited by Royall Tyler. Vols. XI–XIII. London: H.M.S.O., 1916–1954.

Calendar of State Papers and Manuscripts, relating to English Affairs, Existing in the Archives and Collections of Venice, and in other Libraries of Northern Italy. Edited by Rawdon Brown and G. Cavendish Bentinck. Vols. VI–VII. London: H.M.S.O., 1873–1890.

Calendar of State Papers, Foreign Series, of the Reign of Elizabeth, 1558–1559. Edited by Joseph Stevenson. London: H.M.S.O., 1863.

Calendar of State Papers, Foreign Series, of the Reign of Elizabeth, 1559–1560. Edited by Joseph Stevenson. London: H.M.S.O., 1865.

Calvete de Estrella, Juan Cristóbal. *El felicissimo viaje del muy alto y muy poderoso principe don Phelippe, hijo del Emperador don Carlos Quinto Maximo desde España a sus tierras dela baxa Alemaña: con la descripcion de todos los Estados de Brabante y Flandes, escrito en quatro libros.* Edited by Miguel Artigas y Ferrando. 2 vols. Madrid: Sociedad de Bibliófilos Españoles, 1930 (first ed., Antwerp, 1552).

Castiglione, Baldesar. *The Book of the Courtier.* Translated by Charles S. Singleton. Garden City, N.Y.: Doubleday Anchor Books, 1959.

Colección de documentos inéditos para la historia de España (CODOIN). 112 vols. Madrid, 1842–1895.

Cornide, José. *Estado de Portugal en el año de 1800.* In *Memorial histórico español,* vol. XXVII. Madrid: Imprenta y fundición de M. Tello, 1894.

Della Casa, Giovanni. *Galateo: Of Manners and Behaviors* (1558). Introduced by J. E. Spingarn. Reproduces the first English translation of 1576. Boston: Merrymount Press, 1914.

Donato, Leonardo. "Relación de las cosas de España, leída al senado veneciano por Leonardo Donato, embajador de aquella república." In *Historia de Felipe II.* By Luis Cabrera de Córdoba. Vol. IV. Madrid: Aribau, 1877. Pp. 403–480.

Douais, E., ed. *Dépêches de M. de Fourquevaux, Ambassadeur du roi Charles IX en Espagne, 1565–1572.* 3 vols. Paris: E. Leroux, 1896; Librairie Plon, 1900–1904.

Enno van Gelder, H. A., ed. *Correspondance française de Marguerite d'Autriche, duchesse de Parme, avec Philippe II.* Vol. II. Utrecht: Kemink et Fils, 1941.

Fiore, Giovanni. *Della Calabria illustrata. Opera varia istorica.* 2 vols. Naples, 1691–1743 (facsimile reprint ed., Bologna: Arnaldo Forni, 1974).

Firpo, Luigi, ed. *Relazioni di ambasciatori veneti al senato.* Vol. VIII, *Spagna, 1497–1598.* Turin: Bottega d'Erasmo, 1981.

Foulché-Delbosc, R., ed. "Cartas de Don Diego Hurtado de Mendoza." *Archivo de investigaciones históricas* (Madrid) II (1911): 155–195, 270–275, 463–475, 537–600.

Gachard, Louis-Prosper, ed. *La Bibliothèque Nationale à Paris. Notices et extraits des manuscrits qui concernent l'histoire de Belgique.* Vol. II. Brussels: M. Hayez, Imprimeur de la Commission Royale d'Histoire, 1877.

———, ed. *Les Bibliothèques de Madrid et de l'Escurial. Notices et extraits des manuscrits qui concernent l'histoire de Belgique.* Brussels: F. Hayez, 1875.

———, ed. *Correspondance de Philippe II sur les affaires des Pays-Bas, 1558–1577.* Vol. I. Brussels: Librairie ancienne et moderne, 1848. Vols. II–III. Brussels-Ghent-Leipzig: C. Muquardt, 1851–1858.

———, ed. *Relations des ambassadeurs vénitiens sur Charles-Quint et Philippe II.* Brussels: M. Hayez, Imprimeur de la Commission Royale d'Histoire, 1855.

———, ed. *Retraite et mort de Charles-Quint au Monastère de Yuste. Lettres inédites pub. d'après les originaux conservés dans les archives royales de Simancas.* 3 vols. Brussels: M. Hayez, 1854–1855.

García Mercadal, J., ed. and trans. *Viajes de extranjeros por España y Portugal.* Vol. I. Madrid: Aguilar, 1952.

Gayangos, Pascual de, ed. *Viaje de Felipe Segundo á Inglaterra, por Andrés Muñoz (impreso en Zaragoza en 1554), y relaciones varias relativas al mismo suceso.* Madrid: Sociedad de Bibliófilos Españoles / Aribau (sucesores de Rivadeneyra), 1877.

Guevara, Antonio de. *The Diall of Princes.* Translated by Thomas North and edited by K. N. Colville. London: Philip Allan, 1919.

———. *Libro primero de las epístolas familiares.* Edited by José María de Cossío. 2 vols. Madrid: Aldus, 1950.

Gutiérrez Coronel, Diego. *Historia genealógica de la casa de Mendoza* (1772). Edited by Angel González Palencia. In *Biblioteca Conquense*, vols. III–IV. Madrid: C.S.I.C. and el Ayuntamiento de Cuenca, 1946.

Hermosilla, Diego de. *Diálogo de los pajes en que se trata de la vida que á mediados del siglo XVI llevaban en los palacios de los Señores, del galardón de sus servicios, y del modo como los Grandes se gobernaban y debieran gobernarse. (1573).* Edited by A. Rodríguez Villa. Madrid: Imprenta de la Revista Española, 1901.

Huarte, Amalio, ed. *Relaciones de los reinados de Carlos V y Felipe II.* Madrid: Sociedad de Bibliófilos Españoles, 1941.

Kervyn de Lettenhove, Baron, ed. *Relations politiques des Pays-Bas et de l'Angleterre, sous le règne de Philippe II.* Vol. I. Brussels: F. Hayez, 1882.

Laiglesia y Auset, Francisco de. *Estudios históricos (1515–1555).* 3 vols. Madrid: Asilo de Huérfanos del S. C. de Jesús, 1918.

López de Gómara, Francisco. *Annals of the Emperor Charles V. Spanish Text and English Translation.* Edited and translated by R. B. Merriman. Oxford: Clarendon Press, 1912.

Machiavelli, Niccolò. *The Prince and the Discourses.* Translated by Luigi Ricci and Christian Detmold. New York: Modern Library College Editions, 1950.

Machyn, Henry. *The Diary of Henry Machyn, Citizen and Merchant-Taylor of London, from A.D. 1550 to A.D. 1563.* Edited by John Gough Nichols. London: Printed for the Camden Society by J. B. Nichols and Son, 1848.

March, José M., ed. *Niñez y juventud de Felipe II: Documentos inéditos sobre su educación civil, literaria y religiosa y su iniciación al gobierno (1527–1547).* 2 vols. Madrid: Ministerio de Asuntos Exteriores (Relaciones Culturales), 1941–1942.

Mariana, Juan de. *Historia general de España, compuesta, emendada y añadida por el padre Juan de Mariana de la compañia de Jesus, con el sumario y tablas.* Vol. II. 16th printing. Valencia: D. Benito Monfort, 1794.

Martínez Ferrando, Jesús Ernesto, ed. *Privilegios otorgados por el Emperador Carlos V en el Reino de Nápoles. (Sicilia aquende el Faro.) Serie conservada en el Archivo de la Corona de Aragón.* Barcelona: C.S.I.C., 1943.

Morel-Fatio, Alfred, ed. *L'Espagne au XVIe et au XVIIe siècle: Documents historiques et littéraires.* Heilbronn: Henninger Frères, 1878.

Nichols, John G., ed. *The Chronicle of Queen Jane, and of Two Years of Queen Mary, and especially of the Rebellion of Sir Thomas Wyat, written by a Resident in the Tower of London.* London: For the Camden Society, 1850.

Nuñez de Salcedo, Pero. "Relación de los títulos que hay en España, sus rentas, solares, linajes, etc." Edited by Vicente Castañeda. *Boletín de la Real Academia de la Historia* 73:5 (November 1918): 468–491.

Ossorio, Antonio. *Vida y hazañas de Don Fernando Alvarez de Toledo, Duque de Alba* (1669). Translated by José López de Toro. Madrid: Blass, 1945.

Pacichelli, Giovanni Battista. *Il Regno di Napoli in prospettiva.* 3 vols. Naples: Parrino, 1702–1703 (facsimile reprint ed., Bologna: Arnaldo Forni, 1975).

Paris, Louis, ed. *Négociations, lettres et pièces diverses relatives au regne de François II, tirées du portefeuille de Sébastien de l'Aubespine, évêque de Limoges.* Paris: Imprimerie Royale, 1841.

Paz, Julián. *Documentos relativos a España existentes en los Archivos nacionales de París: Catálogo y extractos de más de 2.000 documentos de los años 1276 a 1844.* Madrid: Instituto de Valencia de Don Juan, 1934.

Pérez, Antonio. *Aphorismos de las cartas españolas y latinas de Ant. Perez.* Paris: no publisher, no date [1598?]. Bound together with Pérez's *Cartas.*

———. *Cartas de Antonio Perez, Secretario de Estado que fue del Rey Catholico Don Phelippe II. de este nombre. Para diversas personas despues de su salida de España.* Paris: no publisher, no date [1598?]. Bound together with Pérez's *Aphorismos.*

———. *Norte de príncipes, virreyes, presidentes, consejeros y gobernadores, y advertencias políticas sobre lo público y particular de una monarquía.* With a preliminary study by Francisco Ayala. Buenos Aires: Ed. Americalee, 1943.

————. *Relaciones y cartas.* Edited by Alfredo Alvar Ezquerra. 2 vols. Madrid: Ediciones Turner, 1986.

Pio IV y Felipe Segundo. Primeros diez meses de la embajada de Don Luis de Requesens en Roma, 1563–1564. Edited by "F. del V." and "S. K." Colección de libros españoles raros ó curiosos, vol. XX. Madrid: Imprenta de Rafael Marco, 1891. ("F. del V." may well have been the marqués de la Fuensanta del Valle, who edited vol. XCVII of CODOIN for the same publisher in 1890.)

Piot, Charles, ed. *Correspondance du Cardinal de Granvelle, 1565–1583.* Vol. IV. Brussels: F. Hayez, 1884.

Porreño, Baltasar. *Dichos y hechos del rey D. Felipe II.* Edited by Angel González Palencia. Madrid: Ed. Saeta, 1942 (first ed., Cuenca, 1628).

Poullet, Edmond, ed. *Correspondance du Cardinal de Granvelle, 1565–1586.* Vols. II–III. Brussels: F. Hayez, 1880–1881.

Relaciones histórico-geográfico-estadísticas de los pueblos de España hechas por iniciativa de Felipe II. Provincia de Madrid. Edited by Carmelo Viñas y Mey and Ramón Paz. Madrid: C.S.I.C., 1949.

Relaciones topográficas de España: Relaciones de pueblos que pertenecen hoy á la provincia de Guadalajara, con notas y aumentos de D. Juan Catalina García, Académico de número. Edited by Juan Catalina García et al. In *Memorial histórico español,* vols. XLI–XLVII. Madrid: Real Academia de la Historia, 1901–1915.

Salazar y Castro, Luis de. *Historia genealógica de la Casa de Lara, justificada con instrumentos, y escritores de inviolable fe. Dividida en XX libros.* 2 vols. Madrid: En la Imprenta Real, por Mateo de Llanos y Guzman, 1696.

————. *Historia genealógica de la Casa de Silva.* 2 vols. Madrid: Melchor Alvarez y Mateo de Llanos, 1685.

Sandoval, Prudencio de. *Historia de la vida y hechos del Emperador Carlos V.* Edited by Carlos Seco Serrano. Vol. III. Biblioteca de Autores Españoles, vol. LXXXII. Madrid: Atlas, 1956.

Santa Teresa, Silverio de, ed. *Obras de Santa Teresa de Jesús.* Vols. V–VI. Burgos: Tipografía de "El Monte Carmelo," 1918–1919.

Serrano, Luciano, ed. *Correspondencia diplómatica entre España y la Santa Sede durante el pontificado de S. Pio V.* 4 vols. Madrid: Junta para ampliación de estudios é investigaciones científicas, 1914.

"Torneo celebrado en Valladolid con ocasión de la boda del Principe Don Felipe con la Infanta Doña Maria de Portugal (1544)." In *Relaciones de los reinados de Carlos V y Felipe II.* Edited by Amalio Huarte. Madrid: Sociedad de Bibliófilos Españoles, 1941. Pp. 71–94.

Weiss, Charles, ed. *Papiers d'État du Cardinal de Granvelle d'après les manuscrits de la Bibliothèque de Besançon.* Vol. VI. Paris: Imprimerie Royale, 1846. Vols. VII–IX. Paris: Imprimerie Nationale, 1849–1852.

William, Prince of Orange. *The Apologie of Prince William of Orange against the*

Proclamation of the King of Spaine. Edited, after the English ed. of 1581, by H. Wansink. Leiden: E. J. Brill, 1969.

Williams, Roger. *The Actions of the Low Countries* (1618). Edited by D. W. Davies. Ithaca, N.Y.: Cornell University Press for the Folger Shakespeare Library, 1964.

SECONDARY WORKS

Aguado Bleye, Pedro. "Príncipe de Eboli." In *Diccionario de historia de España,* 2d ed. Edited by Germán Bleiberg. Madrid: Alianza Editorial, 1981. Vol. I, pp. 1181–1183.

Alba, Duque de. "La Hacienda Real de España en el siglo XVI." *Boletín de la Real Academia de la Historia* LXXX:II (February 1922): 146–185.

Altamira y Crevea, Rafael. *Ensayo sobre Felipe II hombre de estado: su psicología general y su individualidad humana.* Mexico City: Editorial Jus, 1950.

Alvar Ezquerra, Alfredo. *Felipe II, la corte y Madrid en 1561.* Madrid: C.S.I.C., 1985.

Amezúa y Mayo, Agustín G. de. *Isabel de Valois, Reina de España (1546–1568): Estudio biográfico.* 3 vols. Madrid: La Dirección General de Relaciones Culturales del Ministerio de Asuntos Exteriores / Gráficas Ultra, 1949.

Anglo, Sydney. "The Courtier: The Renaissance and Changing Ideals." In *The Courts of Europe: Politics, Patronage and Royalty, 1400–1800.* Edited by A. G. Dickens. London: Thames and Hudson, 1977 (reprint ed., New York: Greenwich House, 1984). Pp. 33–53.

Arteaga y Falguera, Cristina de. *La Casa del Infantado, cabeza de los Mendozas.* Madrid: Casa del Infantado, 1940.

Asch, Ronald G., and Adolf M. Birke, eds. *Princes, Patronage, and the Nobility: The Court at the Beginning of the Modern Age, c.1450–1650.* Oxford: The German Historical Institute London / Oxford University Press, 1991.

Atienza, Julio de. *Nobiliario español: Diccionario heráldico de apellidos españoles y de títulos nobiliarios.* 2d ed. Madrid: Aguilar, 1954.

Ballesteros y Beretta, Antonio. *Historia de España y su influencia en la historia universal.* Vol. IV. Barcelona: Casa editorial P. Salvat, 1927.

Barriobero y Armas, Juan. "Los Consejos de Estado del pasado al presente." *Boletín de la Real Academia de la Historia* XC:I (January-March 1927): 66–91.

Beneyto Pérez, Juan. *Historia de la administración española e hispanoamericana.* Madrid: Aguilar, 1958.

Bennassar, Bartolomé. *La España del siglo de oro.* Translated by Pablo Bordonava. Barcelona: Ed. Crítica, 1983.

Bertrand, Louis. *Philippe II: une ténébreuse affaire.* Paris: Bernard Grasset, 1929.

Bratli, Carl. *Felipe II, rey de España: Estudio sobre su vida y su carácter.* Translated by P. Angel C. Vega from the French ed. of 1912. Madrid: Bruno del Amo, c.1927 (first published, Copenhagen, 1909).

Braudel, Fernand. *The Mediterranean and the Mediterranean World in the Age of Philip II.* Translated by Siân Reynolds. 2 vols. New York: Harper Torchbooks, 1976.

Brenan, Gerald. *San Juan de la Cruz.* Translated by Jaume Reig. Barcelona: Ed. Laia, 1974.

Carande, Ramón. *Carlos V y sus banqueros.* 2ª ed. abreviada. 2 vols. Barcelona: Ed. Crítica, 1983.

————. "El destino de los tesoros ultramarinos en la hacienda del emperador (1520–1556)." *Moneda y Crédito* 101 (June 1967): 3–13.

Cárdenas, Francisco de. *Ensayo sobre la historia de la propiedad territorial en España.* 2 vols. Madrid: Imprenta de J. Noguera, 1873–1874.

Cárdenas Piera, Emilio de. *Catálogo de títulos nobiliarios sacados de los legajos de estado en el Archivo Histórico Nacional.* Madrid: Hidalguía / Instituto Salazar y Castro, 1982.

Carlos Morales, Carlos Javier de. "Grupos de poder en el Consejo de Hacienda en Castilla: 1551–1566." In *Instituciones y élites de poder en la Monarquía Hispana durante el siglo XVI.* Edited by José Martínez Millán. Madrid: Ediciones de la Universidad Autónoma de Madrid, 1992. Pp. 107–136.

Castillo Pintado, Alvaro. "Los juros de Castilla. Apogeo y fin de un instrumento de crédito." *Hispania* 23 (1963): 45–70.

Cela, Camilo José. *Journey to the Alcarria.* Translated by Frances M. López-Morillas. Madison: University of Wisconsin Press, 1964.

Cernigliaro, Aurelio. *Sovranità e feudo nel regno di Napoli, 1505–1557.* 2 vols. Naples: Jovene Editore, 1983.

Chauchadis, Claude. *Honneur, morale et societé dans l'Espagne de Philippe II.* Paris: Editions du C.N.R.S., 1984.

Chaussinand-Nogaret, Guy. *The French Nobility in the Eighteenth Century: From Feudalism to Enlightenment.* Translated by William Doyle. Cambridge, Eng.: Cambridge University Press, 1985.

Cioffari, Vincenzo. "The Function of Fortune in Dante, Boccaccio, and Machiavelli." *Italica* 24 (1947): 1–13.

Cooper, J. P. "Patterns of Inheritance and Settlement by Great Landowners from the Fifteenth to the Eighteenth Centuries." In *Family and Inheritance: Rural Society in Western Europe, 1200–1800.* Edited by Jack Goody, Joan Thirsk and E. P. Thompson. Cambridge, Eng.: Cambridge University Press, 1976. Pp. 192–327.

Croce, Benedetto. *History of the Kingdom of Naples.* Translated by Frances Frenaye. Chicago and London: University of Chicago Press, 1970.

Cuartas Rivero, Margarita. "Correspondencia del Príncipe de Eboli (1554–1569)." *Cuadernos de investigación histórica* 2 (1978): 201–214.

Cuartero y Huerta, Baltasar, and Antonio de Vargas-Zúñiga y Montero de Espinosa, eds. *Indice de la Colección de Don Luis de Salazar y Castro.* Vol. V. Madrid: Real Academia de la Historia, 1951.

Danvila, Manuel. "Origen, naturaleza y extensión de los derechos de la Mesa Maestral de la Orden de Calatrava." *Boletín de la Real Academia de la Historia* XII:II (February 1888): 116–163.

Danvila y Burguero, Alfonso. *Don Cristóbal de Moura, primer Marqués de Castel Rodrigo (1538–1613).* Madrid: Est. tip. de Fontanet, 1900.

De Ruble, Alphonse. *Le Traité de Câteau-Cambrésis (2 et 3 avril 1559).* Paris: Labitte, 1889.

Dillard, Heath. *Daughters of the Reconquest: Women in Castilian Town Society, 1100–1300.* Cambridge, Eng.: Cambridge University Press, 1984 (paperback, 1989).

Dizionario biografico degli italiani. Vol. XIV. Rome: Istituto della Enciclopedia Italiana, 1972.

Domínguez Ortiz, Antonio. *El antiguo régimen: los Reyes Católicos y los Austrias.* Madrid: Alianza Editorial Alfaguara, 1973.

————. *Las clases privilegiadas en la España del antiguo régimen.* Madrid: Ed. ISTMO, 1973.

————. *The Golden Age of Spain, 1516–1659.* Translated by James Casey. New York: Basic Books, 1971.

————. *Instituciones y sociedad en la España de los Austrias.* Barcelona: Ed. Ariel, 1985.

————. *Notas para una periodización del reinado de Felipe II.* Valladolid: Colección "Sintesis," Universidad de Valladolid, 1984.

————. *La sociedad española en el siglo XVII.* Vol. I. Madrid: C.S.I.C., 1964.

Durand, Georges. "What Is Absolutism?" In *Louis XIV and Absolutism.* Edited by Ragnhild Hatton. Columbus: Ohio State University Press, 1976. Pp. 18–36.

Durme, Maurice van. *El Cardenal Granvela (1517–1586): Imperio y revolución bajo Carlos V y Felipe II.* Translated by E. Borrás Cubells and J. Pérez Ballestar, with an introduction by J. Reglà Campistol. Barcelona: Ed. Teide, 1957.

Elenco de grandezas y títulos nobiliarios españoles. Madrid: Ed. de la Revista Hidalguía, 1970.

Elliott, John H. *Imperial Spain, 1469–1716.* New York: St. Martin's, 1964. Also, Harmondsworth: Penguin Books, 1970.

Elton, G. R. "Constitutional Development and Political Thought in Western Europe." In *The New Cambridge Modern History,* vol. II, *The Reformation, 1520–1559.* Edited by G. R. Elton. Cambridge, Eng.: Cambridge University Press (paperback), 1976. Pp. 438–463.

Escudero, José Antonio. *Los secretarios de estado y del despacho (1474–1724).* 4 vols. Madrid: Instituto de Estudios Administrativos, 1969.

Espejo, Cristóbal. "Sobre organización de la hacienda en el siglo XVI." *Cultura Española* (Zaragoza) (1907): 403–428, 687–704.

Febvre, Lucien. *Philippe II et la Franche-Comté: Étude d'histoire politique, religieuse et sociale.* Paris, 1912 (reissue, Paris: Flammarion, 1970).

Fernández Alvarez, Manuel. *Charles V, Elected Emperor and Hereditary Ruler.* Translated by J. A. Lalaguna. London: Thames and Hudson, 1975.

————. *La sociedad española en el siglo de oro.* Madrid: Editora Nacional, 1983.

Forneron, Henri. *Histoire de Philippe II.* 3d ed. 2 vols. Paris: Librairie Plon, 1887.

Froude, James A. "Antonio Pérez: An Unsolved Historical Riddle." In *The Spanish Story of the Armada and Other Essays*. London: Longmans, Green and Co., 1904. Pp. 103–177.

Gachard, Louis-Prosper. *Don Carlos et Philippe II*. 2d ed. Paris: M. Lévy Frères, 1867.

———. *Don Carlos y Felipe II*. Translated by A. Escarpizo. San Lorenzo de el Escorial: Swan, Avantos y Hakeldama, 1984.

Galasso, Giuseppe. *Economia e società nella Calabria del cinquecento*. Naples: Arte Tipografica, 1967.

García Marín, José. *La burocracia castellana bajo los Austrias*. Seville: Ediciones del Instituto García Oviedo, Universidad de Sevilla, 1976.

García Mercadal, J. *La Princesa de Eboli*. Edición ilustrada. Barcelona: Iberia-Joaquín Gil, 1944.

González-Amao, Mariano. "La boda inglesa de Felipe II." *Historia 16* IX:97 (May 1984): 34–42.

González Palencia, Angel. *Gonzalo Pérez, secretario de Felipe II*. 2 vols. Madrid: C.S.I.C., 1946.

———, and Eugenio Mele. *Vida y obras de Don Diego Hurtado de Mendoza*. Vol. II. Madrid: Instituto de Valencia de Don Juan, 1942.

Gounon-Loubens, Jules. *Essais sur l'administration de la Castille au XVIe siècle*. Paris: Librairie de Guillaumin et Cie, 1860.

Headley, John M. *The Emperor and His Chancellor: A Study of the Imperial Chancellery under Gattinara*. Cambridge, Eng.: Cambridge University Press, 1983.

Hernández Peñalosa, Guillermo. *El derecho en Indias y en su metrópoli*. Bogotá: Ed. Temis, 1969.

Herrera Oria, E. "Felipe II, gobernante." *Razón y Fe* LXXVIII (1927): 97–109.

Highfield, J. R. L. "The Catholic Kings and the Titled Nobility of Castile." In *Europe in the Late Middle Ages*. Edited by John R. Hale, J. R. L. Highfield and B. Smalley. Evanston, Ill.: Northwestern University Press, 1965. Pp. 358–385.

Howarth, David. *The Voyage of the Armada: The Spanish Story*. Harmondsworth, Eng.: Penguin Books, 1982.

Hume, Martin A. S. *Philip II of Spain*. London: Macmillan, 1906. Also, New York: Haskell House, 1969 (reprint of 1897 ed.).

———. "The Visit of Philip II." *English Historical Review* VII (1892): 253–280.

Hunt, David. *Parents and Children in History: The Psychology of Family Life in Early Modern France*. New York: Harper Torchbooks, 1972.

Jones, Joseph R. *Antonio de Guevara*. Boston: Twayne, 1975.

Kamen, Henry. *Vocabulario básico de la historia moderna: España y América 1450–1750*. Translated by Montserrat Iniesta. Barcelona: Ed. Crítica, 1986.

Kellenbenz, Hermann. "El valor de las rentas de las encomiendas de la Orden de Calatrava en 1523 y en 1573." *Anuario de Historia Económica y Social* 1 (1968): 584–598.

Keniston, Hayward. *Francisco de los Cobos, Secretary of the Emperor Charles V*. Pittsburgh, Pa.: University of Pittsburgh Press, 1960.

Kenny, Michael. "Patterns of Patronage in Spain." *Anthropological Quarterly* 33:1 (1960): 14–23.

Koenigsberger, Helmut Georg. *The Practice of Empire. (The Government of Sicily under Philip II of Spain.).* Emended (2d) ed. Ithaca, N.Y.: Cornell University Press, 1969.

Lagomarsino, Paul David. "Court Factions and the Formulation of Spanish Policy Towards the Netherlands (1559–1567)." Ph.D. dissertation, University of Cambridge, 1973.

Laiglesia y Auset, Francisco de. *Estudios históricos (1515–1555).* 3 vols. Madrid: Asilo de Huérfanos del S. C. de Jesús, 1918.

Lapeyre, Henri. *Simon Ruiz et les 'asientos' de Philippe II.* Paris: Armand Colin, 1953.

Llorente, A. "La primera crísis de hacienda en tiempo de Felipe II." *Revista de España* (Madrid) I (1868): 317–361.

Loades, D. M. "Philip II and the Government of England." In *Law and Government under the Tudors.* Edited by Claire Cross, David Loades and J. J. Scarisbrick. Cambridge, Eng.: Cambridge University Press, 1988. Pp. 177–194.

———. *The Reign of Mary Tudor: Politics, Government, and Religion in England, 1553–1558.* London: Ernest Benn, 1979.

Lovett, A. W. "A Cardinal's Papers: The Rise of Mateo Vázquez de Leca." *English Historical Review* 88:347 (April 1973): 241–261.

———. *Early Habsburg Spain, 1517–1598.* Oxford and New York: Oxford University Press, 1986.

———. *Philip II and Mateo Vázquez de Leca: The Government of Spain, 1572–1592.* Geneva: E. Droz, 1977.

Lynch, John. *Spain under the Habsburgs.* 2d ed. paperback. 2 vols. New York: New York University Press, 1984.

Madoz, Pascual. *Diccionario geográfico-estadístico-histórico de España y sus posesiones de Ultramar.* Vol. XII. Madrid: Imprenta de D. Pascual Madoz, 1849.

Maltby, William. *Alba: A Biography of Fernando Alvarez de Toledo, Third Duke of Alba, 1507–1582.* Berkeley and Los Angeles: University of California Press, 1983.

Marañón, Gregorio. *Antonio Pérez (el hombre, el drama, la época).* 3d ed. 2 vols. Madrid: Espasa-Calpe, 1951.

———. *El Conde Duque de Olivares (La pasión de mandar).* Madrid: Espasa-Calpe, 1936.

———. *El Conde-Duque de Olivares.* Abridged 15th ed. Madrid: Espasa-Calpe Colección Austral, 1980.

Maravall, José Antonio. *Poder, honor y élites en el siglo XVII.* Madrid: Siglo XXI, 1984.

March, José M. "Una novia díscola comparada por Requesens a la Princesa de Eboli." *Razón y Fe* 145:650 (March 1952): 285–292.

———. "Otra reyerta de la Princesa de Eboli." *Razón y Fe* 129 (1944): 292–297.

————. "Sobre la Princesa de Eboli: Insistiendo." *Razón y Fe* 143:640 (May 1951): 495–504.

Martínez Millán, José. "Elites de poder en tiempos de Felipe II (1539–1572)." *Hispania* 49:171 (1989): 111–149.

Mattingly, Garrett. *Renaissance Diplomacy.* Boston: Houghton Mifflin Sentry Edition, 1971.

Meissner, William W. *Ignatius of Loyola: The Psychology of a Saint.* New Haven, Conn.: Yale University Press, 1992.

Merriman, Roger Bigelow. *The Rise of the Spanish Empire in the Old World and in the New.* 4 vols. New York: Macmillan, 1918.

Molas Ribalta, Pedro. *Consejos y audiencias durante el reinado de Felipe II.* Valladolid: Universidad de Valladolid, 1984.

Moxó, Salvador de. "La incorporación de señoríos eclesiásticos." *Hispania* XXIII (1963): 219–254.

Muro, Gaspar. *Vida de la Princesa de Eboli.* With a prologue by Antonio Cánovas del Castillo. Mexico City: Imprenta de la "Biblioteca Religiosa, Histórica, Científica y Literaria," 1883.

Nader, Helen. "Habsburg Ceremony in Spain: The Reality of the Myth." *Historical Reflections/Réflexions Historiques* 15:1 (1988): 293–309.

————. *Liberty in Absolutist Spain: The Habsburg Sale of Towns, 1516–1700.* Baltimore, Md., and London: Johns Hopkins University Press, 1990.

————. *The Mendoza Family in the Spanish Renaissance, 1350 to 1550.* New Brunswick, N.J.: Rutgers University Press, 1979.

Oliveira Marques, A. H. de. *History of Portugal.* 2d ed. paperback. 2 vols. in one. New York: Columbia University Press, 1976.

Ortega y Gasset, José. *La rebelión de las masas.* 20th ed. Mexico City: Espasa-Calpe, 1976.

Owens, John B. "Despotism, Absolutism, and the Law in Renaissance Spain: Toledo versus the Counts of Belalcázar (1445–1574)." Ph.D. dissertation, University of Wisconsin, 1972.

Parker, Geoffrey. *The Dutch Revolt.* Ithaca, N.Y.: Cornell University Press, 1977.

————. *Philip II.* Boston: Little, Brown and Co., 1978.

Partner, Peter. *Renaissance Rome, 1500–1559: A Portrait of a Society.* Berkeley and Los Angeles: University of California Press, 1976.

Pastor, Ludwig von. *The History of the Popes, from the Close of the Middle Ages.* Edited by Ralph Francis Kerr. Vol. XIV. London: Kegan Paul, Trench, Trubner & Co., 1924.

Patch, Howard R. *The Goddess Fortuna in Medieval Literature.* Cambridge, Mass.: Harvard University Press, 1927 (reprint ed., New York: Octagon, 1974).

Paz, Julián. *Catálogo de la colección de documentos inéditos para la historia de España.* 2 vols. Madrid: Instituto de Valencia de Don Juan, 1930–1931.

Pérez Bustamante, Ciríaco. *Felipe III. Semblanza de un monarca y perfiles de una privanza.* Madrid: Evaristo San Miguel, 1950.

Pérez y Cuenca, Mariano. *Historia de Pastrana y sucinta noticia de los pueblos de su partido.* Madrid: P. Montero, 1858.

Picatoste, Felipe. *Estudios sobre la grandeza y decadencia de España.* 3 vols. in one. Madrid: Sucesores de Hernando, 1887.

Pierson, Peter. *Commander of the Armada: The Seventh Duke of Medina Sidonia.* New Haven, Conn.: Yale University Press, 1989.

———. *Philip II of Spain.* London: Thames and Hudson, 1975.

Powis, Jonathan. *Aristocracy.* Oxford and New York: Basil Blackwell, 1984.

Prescott, William H. *History of the Reign of Philip the Second, King of Spain.* 1st ed. 3 vols. Boston: Phillips, Sampson and Co., 1855–1858. Also in 4 vols., Philadelphia and London: Lippincott, 1904.

Ranke, Leopold von. *The Ottoman and the Spanish Empires in the Sixteenth and Seventeenth Centuries.* Translated by Walter K. Kelly. London: Whittaker, 1843 (reprint ed., New York: AMS, 1975).

Reglà Campistol, Joan. "La época de los tres primeros Austrias." In *Historia social y económica de España y América,* vol. III. Edited by Jaime Vicens Vives. 2d ed. paperback. Barcelona: Ed. Vicens-Vives, 1972. Pp. 1–202.

———. *Felip II i Catalunya.* Barcelona, 1956.

———. "Presentación." Introduction to *El Cardenal Granvela (1517–1586): Imperio y revolución bajo Carlos V y Felipe II.* By Maurice van Durme. Barcelona: Ed. Teide, 1957. ix–xv.

———. *Els virreis de Catalunya. Els segles XVI i XVII.* 2d printing. Barcelona: Ed. Vicens-Vives, 1961.

Repetto Alvarez, Adela. "Acerca de un posible Segundo Gobierno de Margarita de Parma y el Cardenal de Granvela en los Estados de Flandes." *Hispania* 32:121 (1972): 379–475.

Rivero Rodríguez, Manuel. "La fundación del Consejo de Italia: Corte, grupos de poder y periferia (1536–1559)." In *Instituciones y élites de poder en la Monarquía Hispana durante el siglo XVI.* Edited by José Martínez Millán. Madrid: Ediciones de la Universidad Autónoma de Madrid, 1992. Pp. 199–221.

Rodríguez-Salgado, M. J. *The Changing Face of Empire: Charles V, Philip II and Habsburg Authority, 1551–1559.* Cambridge, Eng.: Cambridge University Press, 1988.

———. "The Court of Philip II of Spain." In *Princes, Patronage, and the Nobility: The Court at the Beginning of the Modern Age, c.1450–1650.* Edited by Ronald G. Asch and Adolf M. Birke. Oxford: The German Historical Institute London / Oxford University Press, 1991. Pp. 205–244.

Rodríguez Villa, Antonio. *Etiquetas de la Casa de Austria.* Madrid: Imprenta de Medina y Navarro, 1913?

Romano, Ruggiero. "Banchieri genovesi alla corte di Filippo II." *Rivista Storica Italiana* 61 (1949): 241–247.

Ruiz Martín, Felipe. "Los hombres de negocios genoveses de España durante el siglo XVI." In *Fremde Kaufleute auf der Iberischen Halbinsch.* Edited by Hermann Kellenbenz. Cologne: Böhlan, 1970. Pp. 84–99.

Russell, Joycelyne G. *Peacemaking in the Renaissance*. London: Duckworth, 1986.

Santaolalla Llanas, Manuel. *Pastrana: Apuntes de su historia, arte y tradiciones*. Pastrana: Published by the author, 1979.

Spivakovsky, Erika. "La Princesa de Eboli." *Chronica Nova* (Granada) 9 (1974; actually appeared c.1977): 5–48.

Stradling, R. A. *Philip IV and the Government of Spain, 1621–1665*. Cambridge, Eng.: Cambridge University Press, 1988.

Suárez Inclán, Julián. "Don Cristóbal de Moura, primer Marqués de Castel Rodrigo (1538–1613)." *Boletín de la Real Academia de la Historia* XXXIX:VI (December 1901): 513–523.

Tomás y Valiente, Francisco. *Los validos en la monarquía española del siglo XVII. Estudio institucional*. Madrid: Siglo XXI, 1982.

Tubino, Francisco M. "Felipe II y la Princesa de Eboli." *Revista Hispanoamericana* (Madrid) VII (1882): 46–58, 560–574.

Tyler, Royall. *The Emperor Charles the Fifth*. London: George Allen and Unwin, 1956.

Ulloa, Modesto. *La hacienda real de Castilla en el reinado de Felipe II*. 3d ed. rev. Madrid: Fundación Universitaria Española, 1986.

———. *Las rentas de algunos señores y señoríos castellanos bajo los primeros Austria*. Montevideo, 1971.

Ungerer, Gustav. *A Spaniard in Elizabethan England: The Correspondence of Antonio Pérez's Exile*. 2 vols. London: Támesis Books, 1974–1976.

Valente, Gustavo. *Dizionario dei luoghi della Calabria*. 2 vols. Chiaravalle: Edizione Framas, 1973.

Vicens Vives, Jaime. "The Administrative Structure of the State in the Sixteenth and Seventeenth Centuries." In *Government in Reformation Europe, 1520–1560*. Edited by Henry J. Cohn. London: Macmillan, 1971. Pp. 58–87.

Watson, Robert. *The History of the Reign of Philip the Second, King of Spain*. New York: Eastburn, 1818.

Index

RG = Ruy Gómez de Silva

Compositor: Graphic Composition, Inc.
Text: 10/13 Palatino
Display: Palatino
Printer: BookCrafters, Inc.
Binder: BookCrafters, Inc.